English A: Language and Literature

FOR THE IB DIPLOMA

Rob Allison

Brian Chanen

OXFORD

UNIVERSITY PRESS

OXFORD
UNIVERSITY PRESS

Great Clarendon Street, Oxford OX2 6DP

Oxford University Press is a department of the University of Oxford.
It furthers the University's objective of excellence in research,
scholarship, and education by publishing worldwide in

Oxford   New York

Auckland   Cape Town   Dar es Salaam   Hong Kong   Karachi
Kuala Lumpur   Madrid   Melbourne   Mexico City   Nairobi
New Delhi   Shanghai   Taipei   Toronto

With offices in

Argentina   Austria   Brazil   Chile   Czech Republic   France   Greece
Guatemala   Hungary   Italy   Japan   Poland   Portugal   Singapore
South Korea   Switzerland   Thailand   Turkey   Ukraine   Vietnam

Oxford is a registered trade mark of Oxford University Press
in the UK and in certain other countries

British Library Cataloguing in Publication Data

Data available

ISBN: 978-0-19-912971-3
10 9 8 7 6 5 4 3 2 1

Printed in Great Britain by Bell & Bain Ltd, Glasgow

Paper used in the production of this book is a natural, recyclable product made
from wood grown in sustainable forests. The manufacturing process conforms
to the environmental regulations of the country of origin

MIX
Paper from
responsible sources
FSC FSC® C007785
www.fsc.org

Acknowledgments

The authors and publisher are grateful for permission to reprint from the following copyright material:

Andre Agassi: extract from *Open: An autobiography* (HarperCollins, 2010), copy-
right © 2009 by AKA Publishing LLC, reprinted by permission of the publishers,
HarperCollins Publishers Ltd and Alfred A Knopf, a division of Random House,
Inc.

Raymond Carver: extract from 'Preservation', in *Cathedral: Stories* (Vintage,
2003), reprinted by permission of the publishers, The Random House Group Ltd
and Random House, Inc.

Caryl Churchill: extract from 'Top Girls' (1982) in *Plays 2* (Methuen Drama,
1990), copyright © Caryl Churchill 1982, reprinted by permission of Methuen
Drama, an imprint of Bloomsbury Publishing plc.

Nevill Coghill: Extract from his translation of 'The Prologue', *The Canterbury
Tales* by Geoffrey Chaucer (Penguin Classics, 2003), copyright © 1951 by Nevill
Coghill, copyright © The Estate of Nevill Coghill 1958, 1960, 1975, 1977, re-
printed by permission of Penguin Books Ltd

Lt Col Daniel L Davis: extract from 'Truth, Lies and Afghanistan' published in
the *Armed Forces Journal*, February 2012, reprinted by permission of the author.

Emily Dickinson: XVIII 'Two butterflies went out at noon' from *The Poems
of Emily Dickinson* edited by Thomas H Johnson (The Belknap Press of Harvard
University Press, Cambridge, Mass.), copyright © 1951, 1955, 1979, 1983 by the
President and Fellows of Harvard College, reprinted by permission of the publishers and the Trustees of Amherst College.

Dave Eggars: 'The Fighters', first published as 'Accident' in *The Guardian*, April
2005, copyright © Dave Eggars 2012, reprinted by permission of The Wylie
Agency (UK) Ltd.

Gotye: 'Somebody That I Used to Know', lyrics by Walter de Backer, copyright
© 2011, published by Op Shop Songs Pty Ltd , administered by Kobalt Music
Publishing Ltd and Hal Leonard Australia Pty Ltd, and reprinted with their
permission.

Claude McKay: 'Quashie to Buccra' (1912) from *Complete Poems* (University of Illinois Press, 2004), reprinted by permission and courtesy of the Literary Representative for the Works of Claude McKay, Schomberg Center for Research in Black
Culture, The New York Public Library, Astor, Lenox and Tilden Foundations.

Edna St Vincent Millay: 'Recuerdo' from *A Few Figs from Thistles: Poems and Son-
nets* (Harper & Bros, 1922), reprinted by permission of The Millay Society via The
Permissions Company, Inc.

Lorrie Moore: extract from 'How to Become a Writer', copyright © 1985 by
M L Moore, from *Self-Help* (Vintage Contemporaries, Knopf, 1985), reprinted by
permission of the publishers, Alfred A Knopf, a division of Random House, Inc,
and Faber & Faber Ltd.

Marianne Moore: 'The Fish' from *The Collected Poems of Marianne Moore* edited by
Grace Schulman (Viking Penguin, 2003), copyright © Marianne Moore 1935, ©
renewed 1963 by Marianne Moore and T S Eliot, reprinted by permission of the
publishers, Scribner, a division of Simon & Schuster, Inc, and Faber & Faber, and
of David M Moore Esq, Administrator of the Literary Estate of Marianne C Moore.
All rights reserved.

Amber Mortensen: 'Check Me Out: One Lucky Girl', 28 February 2012 from

www.painfullyhip.com, reprinted by permission of the author.

Flannery O'Connor: extract from 'The Displaced Person' in *A Good Man is Hard
to Find* (Harcourt Brace Jovanovich, 1977), reprinted by permission of Peters Fra-
ser & Dunlop (www.petersfraserdunlop.com) on behalf of the Estate of Flannery
O'Connor.

George Orwell: extract from 'How the Poor Die' first published in *Now* (1946),
copyright © George Orwell 1946, © Sonia Brownell Orwell 1950, © renewed
1978 by Sonia Pitt-Rivers, from *Shooting Elephants and Other Essays* (Penguin, 1968);
extract from 'Why I write' first published in *Such, Such Were the Joys* (Harcourt,
Brace & Co, 1953), copyright © Sonia Brownell Orwell 1953, © renewed 1981 by
Mrs George K Perultz, Mrs Miriam Gross, and Dr Michael Dickson, Executors of
the Estate of Sonia Brownell Orwell, from *Shooting Elephants and Other Essays* (Penguin, 1968); and extract from *Animal Farm* (Secker & Warburg, 1945), copyright
© George Orwell 1945, © renewed 1974 by Sonia Brownell Orwell; all reprinted
by permission of Bill Hamilton as the Literary Executor of the Estate of Sonia
Brownell Orwell, c/o A M Heath & Co Ltd, and of Houghton Mifflin Harcourt
Publishing Company. All Rights Reserved.

Carl Sandburg: 'All Day Long' from *Chicago Poems* (Henry Holt, 1916), copyright
© 1916 by Holt, Rinehart and Winston, © renewed 1944 by Carl Sandburg,
reprinted by permission of Houghton Mifflin Harcourt Publishing Company. All
Rights Reserved.

A O Scott and Manohla Dargis: extract from a discussion on *The Hunger Games*,
'A Radical Female Hero from Dystopia', *New York Times*, 8.4.2012, copyright ©
2012 The New York Times. All rights reserved. Reprinted by permission via PARS
International Corp, and protected by the Copyright Laws of the United States.
The printing, copying, redistribution, or retransmission of this content without
written permission is prohibited.

Graeme Smith: 'Men in Battle: When a brotherly bond turns deadly', Toronto
Globe & Mail, 20.1.2012, copyright © The Globe and Mail Inc, reprinted by permission of The Globe and Mail. All rights reserved.

Zadie Smith: extract from *White Teeth* (Hamish Hamilton, 2000), copyright ©
Zadie Smith 2000, reprinted by permission of Penguin Books Ltd and Random
House Inc.

Gertrude Stein: extract from *The Making of Americans; being a history of a family's
progress* (Contact Editions, 1925), reprinted by permission of David Higham Associates.

Robert Stewart: introduction to the chapter 'Linear Theory of Ocean Surface
Waves' from http://oceanworld.tamu.edu/resources, reprinted by permission of
the author.

Tom Stoppard: extract from Author's note from *Rosencrantz and Guildenstern Are
Dead* (Faber, 1967), copyright © Tom Stoppard 1967, reprinted by permission of
the publishers Faber & Faber Ltd and Grove/Atlantic, Inc.

Although we have made every effort to trace and contact all copyright holders
before publication this has not been possible in all cases. If notified, the publisher will rectify any errors or omissions at the earliest opportunity.

Any third party use of these extracts outside of this publication, is prohibited,
and interested parties should apply directly to the copyright holders named in
each case for permission.

The publisher would like to thank the following for their kind permission to
reproduce the following copyright material:

Cover: Tribute to Edward Bawden, 1992 (acrylic on canvas), Fisher, Jeffrey
(20th century)/Private Collection/Photo © The Fine Art Society, London, UK/The
Bridgeman Art Library. **P8**: Samhita Arni & Moyna Chitrakar/Tara Books; **P12**:
Ollyy/Shutterstock; **P12**: Ollyy/Shutterstock; **P12**: OUP; **P12**: OUP; **P12**: OUP;
P12: Doglikehorse/Shutterstock; **P15**: George Herri-
man; **P32**: Michael Maslin/The New Yorker Collection/Www.Cartoonbank.Com;
P35: Christopher Weyant/The New Yorker Collection/Www.Cartoonbank.Com;
P39: David Bradley/Plains Art Museum ; **P48**: Snap Stills/Rex Features; **P52**: The
Metropolitan Museum Of Art/Art Resource/Scala, Florence; **P53**: Scala, Florence -
Courtesy Of The Ministero Beni E Att. Culturali; **P54**: The Metropolitan Museum
Of Art/Art Resource/Scala, Florence; **P54**: The Museum Of Modern Art, New York/
Scala, Florence; **P54**: National Gallery, London/Scala, Florence; **P55**: De Agostini
Picture Library/M. Carrieri/The Bridgeman Art Library; **P56**: Sean Gallup/Getty
Images; **P59**: Santa Maria Novella, Florence, Italy/The Bridgeman Art Library;
P59: Scala, Florence; **P60**: The Metropolitan Museum Of Art/Art Resource/Scala,
Florence; **P61**: Victoria And Albert Museum, London/V&A Images; **P62**: Deagos-
tini Picture Library/Scala, Florence; **P100**: Maj. John Strahan/U.S.Army/Army.
Mil; **P100**: REUTERS/Jean Philippe Arles ; **P74**: Stockbyte/OUP; **P83**: Courtesy Of
Admongo.Gov; **P83**: Courtesy Of Admongo.Gov; **P84**: Courtesy Of Admongo.Gov;
P87: Ernest Hemingway Photograph Collection, John F. Kennedy Presidential
Library And Museum, Boston; **P96**: Alexander A. Sobolev/Shutterstock; **P96**:
Virinaflora/Shutterstock; **P96**: Lisa F. Young/Shutterstock; **P97**: FUN HOME By
Alison Bechdel. Copyright © 2006 By Alison Bechdel. Reprinted By Permission
Of Houghton Mifflin Harcourt Publishing Company. All Rights Reserved; **P104**:
"Book Cover" Copyright © 1989 By Vintage Books, A Division Of Random House,
Inc., THE STRANGER By Albert Camus, Translated By Stuart Gilbert. Used By
Permission Of Alfred A. Knopf, A Division Of Random House, Inc. Any Third
Party Use Of This Material, Outside Of This Publication, Is Prohibited. Interested
Parties Must Apply Directly To Random House, Inc For Permission; **P104**: "Book
Cover" Copyright © 1954 By Vintage Books, A Division Of Random House, Inc.,
THE STRANGER By Albert Camus, Translated By Stuart Gilbert. Any Third Party
Use Of This Material, Outside Of This Publication, Is Prohibited. Interested
Parties Must Apply Directly To Random House, Inc For Permission; **P104**: THE
OUTSIDER by Albert Camus (Penguin Classics, 2006). Reproduced by permission
of Penguin Books Ltd. **P111**: Roman Polanski Film Company Pathe/AF Archive/
Alamy; **P111**: Lebrecht Music And Arts Photo Library/Alamy; **P111**: Oliver Asking
For More, From 'The Adventures Of Oliver Twist' By Charles Dickens (1812-70)
1838, Published By Chapman & Hall, 1901 (Engraving), George Cruikshank
(1792-1878)/Private Collection/The Bridgeman Art Library; **P207**: Henry Holt And
Company, LLC; **P184**: Brandon Wright/Rob Fehr; **P184**: Moviestore Collection/
Rex Features; **P193**: Tom Gauld; **P198**: Julia C. Lee; **P198**: Oregon Shakespeare
Festival's Production Of William Shakespeare's Titus Andronicus (2002).
Ensemble. Photo By David Cooper.

Contents

Introduction

There is no formula for writing the perfect essay. There is not a definitive list of the five indispensable literary features. There is no perfect scheme for understanding a poem. There is, however, a formula for success in IB English A: Language and Literature. The formula is careful reading and viewing, thoughtful reflection and sharing ideas. The classroom (online or face to face) offers you the perfect opportunity to discover a wide range of texts, explore topics, and learn to negotiate the ins and outs of an academic community. The goal of this book is to supplement your classroom experience, offer some guidance, and give you an opportunity for additional practice.

When you play a sport or a musical instrument, you often learn and improve through play itself. This may be the best strategy for improving in an English course. English class is about engaging with texts, as you do on a daily basis, in a more formal and intensified manner. Just as with sport and music, the skills of reading, viewing, listening, writing, producing and speaking can be broken into parts. Sometimes you need to spend some time in practice pointing your toes, tossing the ball or going through the scales. For this reason, this book is designed to give you practice on smaller points of reception and production. While the topics in this book are interesting in and of themselves (and can suggest areas for further study), they are meant to help you isolate skills you need to build so that, in the end, your whole experience of actively approaching texts becomes stronger. You could approach the topics in the book as daily mini-lessons or think of them as assistance for when you are having a difficult time with your reading and writing.

The IB has designed the assessments in English A: Language and Literature to see if you meet the outcomes and aims of the course. The best way to prepare for the assessments, then, is not to cram or memorize, but to *take* the course: be an active learner for two years. The many topics in this book will help you to remain focused and practised.

Instructions

IB English A: Language and Literature Skills and Practice is an old-fashioned, print-bound, multi-access codex. In other words: this is a book. It is designed so that you can, through the completion of a variety of activities, develop the skills that are inherent in any study of language and literature and that will, in turn, prepare you for important assessments. Because this book is arranged as a series of topics, you can approach the activities haphazardly and still gain valuable skills or insights. Used correctly, however, with an attention to the possibilities in the format, this book can be a tool for endlessly exploring language and literature in an interactive way.

Building a repertoire of skills in reading and writing can be tough. English (or another language) has been part of your formal study since you entered school. In addition, you have surely noticed that the topics of study and even the methods haven't changed much since you first entered a classroom. Essentially, you read, think and write in your English classes. The depth and complexity of the reading, thinking and writing has increased over the years. A simplistic way of thinking of your schooling is to see it as a straightforward progression from easy to increasingly more difficult texts, questions and writing tasks. A less kind way of looking at the past years is to see them as a varied set of demands that have serendipitously brought you prepared to the last years of secondary school. More interesting metaphors for your study of language and literature may be the spiral or the network. Over the years you have constantly revisited texts, genres, authors, issues and questions. Repetition and revision helped you to grow so that you could do more and do it better. Or, to be more 21st century, each activity you have done in school is a node in a network of reading, writing and responding that is connected to another activity. Each activity, or node in a network, teaches you something new, reflects and strengthens something you have already known, and pushes you to yet another node. It is best to think of this book as a spiral or a network.

You can, if you want, read this book from cover to cover. The basic organization is to take you through a reasonable progression of the four parts of the IB English A: Language and Literature course. **The first parts of the book roughly correspond to ideas and problems you may encounter in language in cultural context. The book then moves through language and mass communication, literature: critical study, and literature: texts and contexts. You could easily use these sub-sections for review while you are studying a given section.** Teachers could easily use these sub-sections with their activities as mini-lessons for a given part of the course.

It would be more interesting and effective to use this book as a dispersed network of topics as if you were approaching it on the computer screen. As the media critic Lev Manovich has suggested, the reader of the web "is like Robinson Crusoe, walking across the sand, picking up a navigation journal, a rotten fruit, an instrument whose purpose he does not know; leaving imprints that, like computer hyperlinks, follow from one found object to another". While some of the objects found along the way may seem useless, the accumulation, the relationships and the play of ideas can lead to something valuable or at least interesting.

Getting started with a logical study of language and literature can be tough, but we encourage you to start anywhere and to build your own connections. This book encourages action. Every activity can be helpful but some may be more helpful to you than others. Some of these activities will take a few seconds of thought, others may take time, rereading, or a little bit of research.

Within the main sections of this book (1: Language, 2: Literature) you will find six different types of sub-section: Background, Reception, Production, Issue, Insight and Text. These six types of section are spread throughout the book. The idea is to pick up the book and play with an activity. Do you want to work on your writing skills? Find a reception section. Is it related to literature but you are studying language? No problem, make connections. Take an idea from reception in the first part of 1: Language and apply it to literature you read near the end of the book. The book is designed for mixing and matching. Pick it up, put it down, sit it next to your tablet, open it next to your computer, read an insight from a graduate or a professor, text your friends while you read.

Our advice is not to use this book as a crutch for two weeks before an examination or to use it in a panic when writing a written task. Pick it up for 15 minutes one night, an hour one week later. Approach it like Robinson Crusoe and turn random finds into something thought-provoking.

Background

What do you do in the various sections of the course? What ideas or approaches have informed the work in the discipline? How can the history of English inform your own study?

Reception

What do we look for when we read? How can we become more critical readers of texts? If practice involves breaking actions down into small components, what are some components you can examine? What are some broad features that bring you to a text from another angle?

Production

How do you write for assessments? How do you sharpen your oral presentation skills? What are some ideas for producing written tasks? How do you improve the quality of your production?

Issue

What are some of the main concerns of the topics you will study in class? What are some issues raised by the texts you study? What is the lens through which you will approach texts or reach the outcomes of the course?

Insight

What tips do fellow students have to offer? What is some advice from someone who has been through the IB English A: language and literature course? What advice would an examiner offer? What do other teachers think about preparing for assessment or developing your skills?

Texts

Text sections in this book contain pieces for you to use as the base of your practice. These texts are listed below. Read them. Reflect on them. Some of the activities will refer you to these texts for further practice with a certain technique. Feel free to use another text in this list for the same activity. The more you mix and match, the more flexible your skills and understanding will be.

100	Newspaper article: *Men in Battle*, 2012
101	Blog: armedforcesjournal.com, 2012
202	Novel: *Wuthering Heights*, 1847
206	Poem: *Recuerdo*, 1920
91	Song: *Somebody That I Used to Know*, 2011
199	Poem: *The Author to Her Book*, 1678
199	Poem: *Grief*, 1844
207	Graphic novel: *Waltz with Bashir*, 2009
199	Essay: *How the Poor Die*, 1946
200	Short story: *Preservation*, 1983
201	Novel: *Tess of the D'Urbervilles*, 1891
201	Poem: *Quashie to Buccra*, 1912
202	Autobiography: *Open*, 2009
203	Novel: *White Teeth*, 2000
204	Novel: *Self-Help*, 1985
204	Novel: *Huckleberry Finn*, 1885
205	Poem: *The Dream*, 1941
205	Play: *Top Girls*, 1982
206	Play: *Titus Andronicus*, circa 1590

Language

Background | Language in Cultural Context: An Overview

Language in cultural context is one of the four sections of the IB English A: language and literature course. Some teachers may clearly divide the course into four parts while others will integrate the four sections, choosing to approach themes or issues through the lens of two or three sections at once. The four sections of the course can be taught at any time and mixed in any way depending on your school structure, the expertise of the teacher, the needs of the community or even the reading interests of the students. It is important to remember, though, that certain course objectives and certain assessments are tied to each section of the course. One of the trickiest things about the IB English A: language and literature course is understanding that though there *are* parts of the course, though there *are* some assessments tied to the parts, and though there *are* some skills or issues that seem particularly relevant to a given part, there is considerable and consistent overlap of ideas, content, skills and texts.

This section of the course is meant to be a broad study of language in action. As the IB English A: language and literature guide states, you will be "given the opportunity to explore how language develops in specific cultural contexts, how it impacts the world, and how language shapes both individual and group identity." In this section of the course you will be asked to look at how audience and purpose affect the structure and functions of a text and you will analyse the impact of language changes over time. Also, you will show that you have a broad, and particular, understanding of how the meaning of the texts we encounter are shaped by culture and context. In order to do this you will look at a wide range of texts – and a text here could mean a spoken conversation, a poem, a newspaper article, a blog post, a cartoon or even a painting – and study them through the lens of wide-ranging topics. Some of the broad topics that will shape your study include, but are not limited to, the following: gender, community, the individual, history of language, translation, belief, knowledge and power.

In this section of the course, you will consider how texts relate to issues and how texts themselves are both part of culture and in turn influence culture. You will also have the opportunity to look closely at texts to consider how they operate. Some of the methods discussed in this book will be quite familiar, such as looking at imagery in a poem or considering bias in a newspaper article. Other elements of close reading, such as looking at the interaction of image and text, may be newer to you in the context of a language classroom.

Activity

As an introduction to the close reading you will do in this section of the course, the variety of texts available for study, and the cultural concerns related to textual analysis, look at the illustrated text on the next page. Consider how its various elements work to create meaning and effect, and how it might be important in relation to cultural contexts.

- What is happening in this text?

- What cultural information would you want or need to know in order to better understand this text?

- When do you think this text was created? Why?

- How are images and words used together in this text?

- Is there a relationship between this text and any text you have seen before? Is there a relationship to graphic novels you have seen or to children's story books?

- How is this text related to belief, to story-telling and to gender?

Assessments in language in cultural context

As part of the study of language in cultural context you will be asked to complete for submission to the IB:

■ a further oral activity.

Most likely you will also be asked to do some of the following which may also be submitted to the IB:

■ a written task 1
■ a written task 2 (at higher level).

The skills and ideas you develop in this section will also be particularly relevant to:

■ paper 1 textual analysis (standard level) and paper 1 comparative textual analysis (higher level).

Reception   Dialect

Dialect is a regional or social variety of a language that has a distinct pronunciation, grammar or vocabulary from the standard variety. There are regional and social variations of almost all languages and the differences between a dialect and the standard variety of language can vary greatly. The classification of a dialect is not straightforward. Some dialects are so different from a standard variation as to sound like a separate language; some, because of their geographical spread in a politically defined area can be officially classified as languages. In general, though, a dialect has to have **mutual intelligibility** with the standard language. A dialect is usually not granted official **political status** by a government, is not used in official state communication and, unlike slang or the use of an accent, is **rule governed** in its variations from the standard.

Dialect is an interesting aspect of language use to study because it offers us insight into regional and social relationships, insight into the attitudes of various speakers to each other, and an example of the ways language changes over time and place. Consider just the use of dialect in fiction. While many authors use dialect to reveal character, to give readers an idea about background, education and class, the use of dialect in fiction can sometimes be seen as patronizing or as a shortcut to characterization rather than as a close investigation of attitudes.

Activity

Consider the following excerpt from Flannery O'Connor's short story *The Displaced Person*.

> From *The Displaced Person*
>
> "…Why, when I come 'ere first we 'ad a butler and a cook, and eight maids—competent maids mark you, not a couple of village girls what ought to be still at school."
>
> "What's wrong with village girls?" asked Doris pertly. "Me and Joan do our work all right, don't we? You was brought up in the village yourself and only kitchen maid forty years ago."
>
> "I was brought up proper—to respect the gentry and to respect myself, and not to be gidding and gadding out to dances and pictures every night."
>
> What a life you must have had! Glad I wasn't born in those days."
>
> "You'd 'ave been better if you 'ad been."
>
> "Sez you."
>
> FLANNERY O'CONNOR

● What do we know about the characters from this short passage?
● What is your attitude toward the characters in the passage?
● Is your reaction tied to the use of language? Is it tied to the social status of the characters? Is it tied to both?

Dialects often start and thrive because of geography. Dialects are often preserved because of their deep connection to a culture. A dialect can demonstrate an affiliation with a group of people with shared art, music and other traditions. A first step in understanding dialects can be linguistic research. What are the dialects of a language spoken where you live? Who speaks these dialects? If you are able to record speech, what are the rules of the dialect you can recognize (perhaps in the formation of tense, or in the use or dropping of "ing" or other endings, in the abbreviation of articles).

Activity

Choose an aspect of spoken language that you have noticed varies from speaker to speaker or according to context. This could by *in* for *ing* or pronouncing or not pronouncing the *l* sound in words like "walk," "almond" or "Falklands," or the use or dropping of the *h* sound at the beginning of words. This variation could also be a matter of construction such as using double negatives ("I ain't never seen…"). Spend time taking notes on the variations you hear in 10-minute conversations with your subjects—friends, family members and neighbours.

- Record or note the speech of an individual in both formal and informal contexts. What variations do you see in speech in different contexts? Are there differences in pronunciation in these contexts?

- Compare the speech of four people from different groups (girls and boys, adults and children). Note carefully the differences you hear in terms of pronunciation, word choice and grammar. Are there differences between the different groups?

- Listen to language variations in your favourite television show. Pick one language variation (dropping *ing* for example) and note the preferences of a particular character. Note when, if ever, this preference changes and why. Do the characters seem to be consistent in their speech patterns? Are particular speech patterns used to portray particular characteristics related to social class or regional identity?

How can I talk about dialect in a written task?

Use the activity above to design a study that you might do to incorporate in a further oral activity. Think of role playing and discussion that might investigate the effects of or biases against dialects. Write an editorial for or against the teaching of dialect in a school. Use dialect in an original story, in a journal entry or in a blog.

How might dialect be an issue or concern in the examination?

While you may not be able to identify a particular dialect (is a text in a particular dialect of English from Africa? Is it one of many varieties of Indian English? Is it British English?), you may well be able to discuss the way the dialect is used or the attitude of the speakers of the dialect, the other characters or participants in a text or of the author or narrator.

Pidgin and creole languages are closely related to dialects in that they are variations of a wider-spread standard language. Pidgin and creole languages, however, hold special interest for some linguistic researchers because they represent a concrete example of our need to communicate, a way of studying how languages develop, and a strong connection between among culture, global events and language.

A pidgin language is a means of communication that is no one's native language; it is a new language that develops when two groups of people, speaking mutually unintelligible languages, need to communicate. Many pidgin languages developed because of the forced interaction of peoples during times of exploration, colonialism and slave trade. Because pidgin languages are born out of immediate necessity, the variations do not often follow consistent grammatical rules and are unstable in terms of vocabulary. Interestingly, these *ad hoc* languages frequently borrow the structure of one language and the vocabulary of another. Sometimes these languages are so "needs based" that they are considered "contact specific". A pidgin language, for example, may be based solely on the language needed in a marketplace where two groups meet to buy and sell.

A creole language is born of pidgin. When the children of pidgin speakers begin speaking pidgin as a native language, the language essentially develops along with the group of speakers, taking on more stable grammatical structures and more varied vocabulary. While a creole may borrow its vocabulary from another language, the grammatical rules are often quite distinct from those in the original tongue. In addition, while a pidgin may be limited in scope, a creole, like any language, is more flexible and adaptive.

Activity

In order to begin thinking about the cultural importance of pidgin and creole languages consider the two maps below and the questions that follow. The first is a map produced by the project for The Atlas of Pidgin and Creole Language Structures which has attempted to describe and analyse both the most widely studied creole language communities and some lesser-studied communities as well. The first map represents the locations of communities studied. The Trans-Atlantic Slave Trade Database produces a graphic representation of the volumes of slave trade in the Atlantic region before the 1900s, shown in the second map.

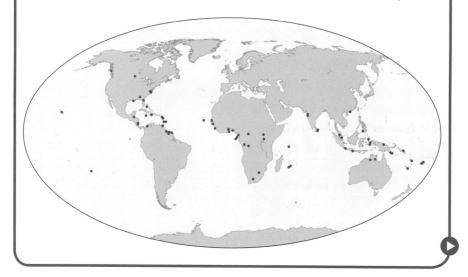

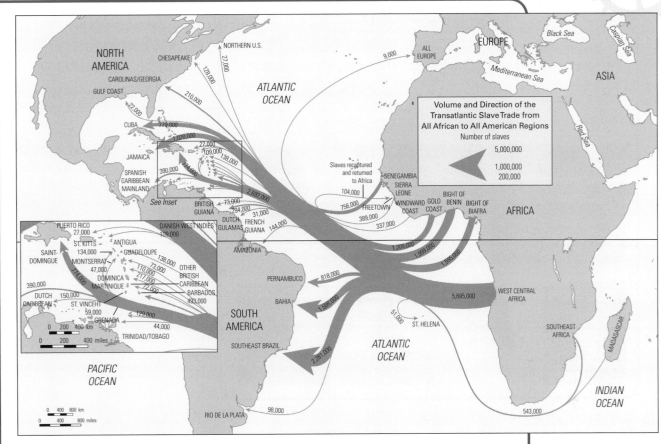

- What is the obvious overlap in the two maps?
- What does this overlap suggest about the cultural or historical importance of pidgin and creole languages?
- Speakers of creole languages are often subject to negative bias. How does this map suggest historical or cultural origins for this bias?
- Pidgin languages often developed through forced contact. Can you think of other situations where pidgin languages might arise?

Extension

- The internet is a great resource for listening to varieties of pidgin and creole. See what you can find to actually listen to the varieties in action.
- Turn to page 201 and read the poem *Quashie to Buccra* by Claude McKay. How is this poem a celebration of creole? Who is the intended audience of this poem? How much of this poem can you understand? Try to write a brief commentary on this poem, using what you understand about creole development to help you in your analysis.

Reception | Gesture and Expression

Language is expressed through writing and through the spoken word. Other types of communication, such as facial expression or gestures, may be called language (body language) but they are not governed by rules in a complex system in the same way that language is. At the same time, facial expressions and gestures do communicate and often communicate across cultures.

Some researchers have suggested that there are seven basic emotions that can be communicated through facial expressions and that these are universal. Some researchers suggest that there are up to 11 of these emotions. Look at the facial expressions below and see if you can accurately match the emotion to the expression.

A. anger B. disgust C. happiness D. fear E. sadness F. surprise G. contempt

Thinking about the nature of expressions and gestures can help us to consider the complexity of human communication. While speech and writing are conscious acts, expressions and gestures can often be subconscious. Expressions can work in conjunction with or against verbal communication. While many, if not most, of the texts you encounter in this course will be written, it is worth thinking about expressions in relation to images, film and drama. An actor can artfully create expressions to be used in either art or advertising. Expressions can work to communicate emotions in a way that seems beyond words.

Extension

- How easy is it to lie with expression or gesture? Is it easier than lying with the spoken or written word? Look through magazines or other images: how can you tell when a smile is fake or genuine?

Production   Note Taking

"Learn how to listen and you will prosper even from those who talk badly" Plutarch (CE 46–120).

The work students do in class has changed over the years and most likely in your classroom students do almost as much talking as the teacher. Especially in an English class dedicated to engaging with texts and ideas, the teacher is rarely standing in front of the classroom relaying information. If you need content information, you have resources at your fingertips. In addition, the content of this course is essentially the set of skills you develop. At the same time, listening to the advice, thoughts and recommendations of the teacher is important. Sometimes it is better to listen to something from someone you know in order to learn. It is also important to listen to fellow students so that you can use their ideas to build your own.

Listening is an essential skill if you want to be an engaged learner, and simply someone who wants to remember as well as understand. Before you even enter the classroom or a guest lecture you need to have the right attitude and know that listening and learning is your responsibility (no matter how dire the speaker, just convince yourself that the material *is* interesting). Keep your focus. Jotting down ideas and facts can help you keep your attention, but do not be a slave to every detail.

Why take notes?

Many teachers distribute their lecture slides, post their own notes to a website or put key points in a document, so why should you take notes?

- Taking notes makes you listen and listening is not only taking in information but is processing, thinking and making connections.
- Taking notes gives you something to review or something to jog your memory. Notes can also be the springboard to real learning – making connections beyond the classroom, giving you the ideas to create something of your own.
- Taking notes is a reinforcement of learning in the moment.

What do I record?

- First, remember that in a contemporary classroom you are often not simply concerned with facts but with ideas, challenges and curiosities as well as moments that have personal relevance.
- If a teacher writes something on a board or puts it up on a slide, it is worth writing down. And remember that a packed slide, given to you later, is not a time saver and does not give you the chance to be an active recorder.
- Record anything that you hear repeated.
- Listen for other verbal cues and summarize what is said (tone change, literal statements such as "this is important" or "you could use this in an examination," or "always remember to dot your 'i's."
- Important information often comes at the very beginning or very end of class.

How do I take notes?

- Record ideas in your own words. It is easier to remember something that you have essentially synthesized or understood by saying it to yourself.
- Do not worry if you miss something, the idea is often to remind yourself of what you have heard.
- Be brief, use abbreviations and use outlines.

- Use the space of the page (or the tablet or screen). Later, you want to be able to add ideas, add some quotations from a book you have read, or throw in some circles and arrows. Give your ideas space to wander while you take notes.

- Do not record a class in order to listen later. This takes too much time and takes away the benefit of being active and engaged in the moment. You will find that later it is difficult to be engaged listening to a disembodied voice and you will be less likely to take notes based on the recording.

Once again, do not forget that understanding and remembering are different things. Even if you understand what you hear in the moment, this does not mean you will remember it. Once you take notes and remember, you are also one step closer to making the connections that are needed to better understand and communicate your understanding (on an assessment for example).

Finally, keep in mind the famous five "Rs" of note taking (often attributed to the Cornell method of taking lecture notes).

Record	Record what you think is important.
Reduce	Reduce the notes to highlights you can remember, take out the superfluous, and learn by thinking about what you need to know.
Recite	Recite your notes aloud, especially the highlights.
Reflect	Reflect on your notes. This is most important when you are building your own ideas (trying to decide what to do on a written task or in a further oral activity).
Review	Review your notes for 10–15 minutes every week. You will find that studying for an examination means quick review of ideas you understand rather than a learning or re-learning of a mass of material.

Insight   Class Work

"This may be a cliché nowadays, but I know I am teaching poorly when I am doing all of the talking. I like the IB exams and other assessments because they give students a chance to think and to work with texts they know and texts they have never seen before. Isn't this what we want everyone to be able to do when they go on to university or later into the workplace? Based on the IB syllabus and the main aims of the programme, I think that my primary responsibility in the classroom is to give students and opportunity to work with texts and develop their ideas. Of course, I became a teacher because I love reading and thinking so sometimes I like to think that when I talk too much about a work, at least I am modeling a passion! In the end, the best way to understand a text is in a community of learners, and my job is to help create that community."

An English teacher

"I have been an IB examiner for a long time and I am often struck by how I start to sense the culture of a classroom when I read exam responses. While every school has a range of candidates from great down to not-so-great, certain classrooms seem to have more 'flexible' candidates than others. I am often impressed by what students are able to memorize or how well

taught students seem to be in terms of structuring a response or firing off lists of literary terms. I am often more impressed, however, when a personal engagement with a text seems to show through everything else. In the past, when I have written subject reports and tried to give advice for "the preparation of future candidates" I have stressed establishing a classroom where students highlight their own interests in a text, take leads in class discussions, or even memorize things they alone think are important. The most important exam preparation is reading a text, sharing ideas about the text in class, and listening to other ideas about the text."

A senior IB examiner

"I have to admit that sometimes I like sitting and listening to a teacher. Class discussion can get boring to me if I have to listen to my classmates drone on and on or repeat what the teacher says. Sometimes a good lecture helps me to relax and helps me to learn content in a new way. At the same time, though, it really depends on what we think the content of the course is. In English class the teacher can give us some background and give us her interpretation of the text we are reading, but beyond that, there doesn't seem to be content in the same way that there is in a science class, for example. I realize that English class is interesting because every English class is a chance to do English. When my teacher talks, she is just showing me one way to look at a text or the way people usually approach texts. In cases like this, what the teacher says makes me a bit more confident about my own thoughts and helps me to think about how to approach the next text I see. I guess, in the end, the best English class is a class where I am reminded of what we are supposed to be doing (reading, thinking, communicating), I try to do it on my own or in a group, and then I have a chance to share my ideas. I really think that the IB exam, in the end, is something that I don't have to worry about. Even though I haven't taken hundreds of mock exams, I have had the chance to 'do English' every time I've come to class so it should be easy enough to talk about a text for a couple of hours in an exam room."

An IB English student

Background — What is Language?

You will never be asked "What is language?" in an examination. You will not have to define language as part of a written task. This is a course, however, on language in action and the work you do is about exploring language in depth. Some of the texts you study *involve* language, combining image, sound and words. Other texts you study may be communicative (such as a photograph) but not include what we think of as language at all. It is probably worthwhile considering a basic definition of language while beginning to think about the complexities of how language works in the brain and how language is learned and used.

Language is the human method of communication and can be thought of as the vocabulary and rules for construction (grammar) that exists in our minds. Speech, writing and sign language are the ways through which language is communicated. We can say that language is a system because it consists of patterns, or rules, for putting together elements, such as sounds to make words and words to make sentences, that when violated results in loss of meaning. Within this complex system called language there are many elements: sounds are combined according to rules in order to create words, words are put into relationships with each other, following rules again, in order to form sentences. When we follow the rules of language we can meaningfully communicate. It is important to note, though, that these rules do not limit us to a finite set of utterances.

Human language has a few characteristics that make it unique compared to what we know about animal communication or other means of communication.

- Language, partly because of its rules of construction (as opposed to being restricted by these rules) is creative and can be used to combine sounds and words into an infinite variety of sentences.

- Human language is not only used to communicate information but is used to share, dream, argue and joke, for example.

- Language is intentional: we purposefully use language to communicate, unlike subconscious gestures that may accidentally communicate feeling.

- Some scholars have suggested that language involves a complex "theory of mind", meaning that when we speak we consider the possible reactions of other people, we imagine their thinking, and we imagine the thought and intention behind their use of language.

- Human language is a learned system of communication as opposed to the inherited biological functions such as the crying of babies or the barking of dogs.

- Many researchers believe that the ability to have and use language is inherent.

- Language is a complex system that relies on duality of patterning. Contrasts in sounds make words possible; contrasts between words make them intelligible.

- Language is also a redundant system that ensures that important sound distinctions are particularly clear to native speakers of a language.

Issue   Knowledge

The relationship between language and knowledge is an important issue in this course as well as an important link to the theory of knowledge course. Language in and of itself is something that we can come to "know" and understand but because we are immersed in language and because it is a mental activity as much as it is the speech act or written act that results, it is very difficult to study objectively. Language is also a tool for the attainment and communication of knowledge. Language allows us to explain the world and to transfer knowledge but language also, through its flexibility, is able to transform or create knowledge.

Activity

Using the picture shown here, try the following activity with a group of people. Only the group leader is allowed to look at the picture. The other members of the group, working together but not allowed to talk to each other or to ask questions, attempt to recreate the picture based solely on the leader's directions.

As a follow up, the leader can draw another picture on graph paper but this time the group is allowed to ask questions of the leader and to communicate with each other. Here are some examples of follow-up questions.

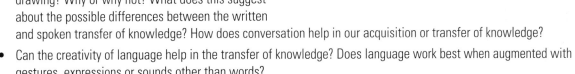

- How does this activity expose the limitations of the transfer of knowledge through language? How can the transfer of knowledge in this case relate to that in the classroom or in the pages of a science journal?

- Would this activity be any different if you were to follow written instructions for completing the drawing? Why or why not? What does this suggest about the possible differences between the written and spoken transfer of knowledge? How does conversation help in our acquisition or transfer of knowledge?

- Can the creativity of language help in the transfer of knowledge? Does language work best when augmented with gestures, expressions or sounds other than words?

Reception   Register

In common usage register generally refers to the level of formality in a variety of language use. While register is a type of language variety, it does not have the formal, rules-governed attributes of a dialect and can vary from speaker to speaker. Generally, speakers or writers purposefully vary their register for a particular purpose or in a particular setting. In fact, some linguists suggest that the level of formality of language, determined by word choice and sentence structure, could be described as **style**, while register refers strictly to language use governed by situation and incorporating a particular **jargon**, or the vocabulary of a profession (using the jargon of law, medicine or auto mechanics, for example).

Speakers tend to vary language use through vocabulary, sentence structure and pronunciation. In general, speakers tend to use what they think of as more standard or "correct" language in more formal situations. Of course, what people consider formal can vary from community to community. In an attempt to sound more formal, speakers will be careful not to use slang, will be attentive for the use of "who" or "whom" and will replace words like "mom" or "mum" with "mother."

Register can be somewhat vague to define as it can have so many variations and involves a holistic evaluation of a range of effects.

In practical terms, however, register can be useful to consider in the writing of a paper 1 **textual analysis** or **comparative textual analysis** or in approaching any text. It would also be very important to consider your imitation of register when working on a **written task**. It is useful to consider register, often a conscious choice of the communicator, when thinking about the intention of an utterance (ranging from a plea to advertisement). Also consider the implied audience: who is the speaker addressing? Is it, for example, the speaker's superiors, peers, a judge or an audience of young school children?

In 1961 the linguist Martin Joos attempted to address register as levels or formality by describing five styles of spoken English. Though these descriptions of style are not in prominent use today, they suggest a way of thinking about possible levels. Use the following terms as a starting point and then explore your own ways of describing register. Is the register uptight or relaxed? Is it elegant? Is it academic? Sometimes your own apt description works best when describing a feeling you recognize.

- **Frozen** register is pre-determined or scripted language used in prescribed, often ritualistic contexts such as a court of law or a church.
- **Formal** register is used in speeches and presentations, as opposed to discussion, that demands precise technical jargon.
- **Consultative** register is language more often used in dialogue that includes some off-hand, informal language, impromptu corrections and non-technical explanation.
- **Casual** register is used in group discussions with friends that can include gaps, interruptions, pauses, errors and personal "inside" words.
- **Intimate** register is used in private conversation between close friends and family where tone, volume and unspoken hints or suggestions may be just as important as the denotation of words.

Activity

How would you describe the register of the following statements?

- "Honored guests, members of the board, Superintendent Johnson, and most importantly, graduates of the class of 2012, it is an honour to speak to you on this occasion."
- "While I was pleasantly surprised by the menu selections for dinner service, I was disheartened by the lukewarm eggs at breakfast."
- "Yeah, right."
- "I doubt it."
- "I'm tired of your rubbish."
- "I'm tired."

Activity

Try identifying the register of as many of the texts in the text sections as possible. Start by considering the register of the blog post on page 101 and the editorial on page 85. See if you can first categorize the register using Joos' terms for spoken language situations above. More importantly, though, stretch yourself by coming up with your own terms.

Extension

If you do not think register matters, consider the times when the register just is not right (unless its use is sarcastic or joking).

A wife and a husband in the early morning:

"Good morning, John. How are you today?"

"I'm fine, thank you, and yourself? I have made a pot of coffee. Can I pour you a cup?"

"That would be fine."

An employee asking for a rise:

"Dude, I've got freakin' nuthin. You gotta give me more cash."

"As if."

Reception   Idiolect

Idiolect is an interesting term in that the issue of its very existence goes to the heart of our understanding of what language is and how it operates. Idiolect is a personal variation of language based on the particular elements of usage of an individual speaker. An idiolect can include individual preferences for vocabulary, pronunciation or even certain consistent errors in construction. In addition, idiolect can include aspects that may be more physical such as pitch, intonation or the presence of a lisp. An idiolect would include not only our linguistic slips and stumbles but our use of personally made-up words or preferences for certain clichés. Theoretically, an idiolect is based on the intrinsic attributes of an individual. This is where the difficulty in defining and describing an idiolect starts. It is easy enough to say that idiolect is our personal language use, but how do we know our usage is personal? Certain linguistic choices we make (conscious or not) are determined by geography or class (as in dialect), the communities to which we belong (jargon, argot), or the situations we encounter (register). Even peculiar words we may have inherited from family members may have derived from older cultural traditions. Looking at someone's language from one perspective, we could consider all language acts idiolectical in that the utterances are a mix of very particular conscious and unconscious choices, dialects, jargons and contexts. On the other extreme, no language choice is personal: external forces and context predetermine language use.

Extension

Language is a main concern of philosophy and the notion of idiolect figures in debates about language and knowledge, language and truth, and the very existence of language. Do a web search of the philosophy of language and see what you can find about idiolect. In what way does the notion of idiolect lead to the idea that language itself does not exist?

Activity

Answer the following questions in an effort to describe your own idiolect as completely as possible.

- How would you describe your pitch and tone. Is it, for example, high or deep, pinched or rich?
- To which dialect group do you think you belong? Do you speak more than one dialect? How would you describe the dialect of your family?
- Do you speak other languages or have you been exposed to other language communities?
- To which communities with their own jargon do you belong? You might be surprised at the specialized vocabulary you possess and use frequently (for example, think of the jargon of a sports team, a debate club, a science class or a band).
- How would you describe your accent?
- Can you think of any words, slang or otherwise, that you tend to use frequently (or more frequently than other people you know)?

Write a brief "report" about who you are as a language speaker. Is there anything about your language that is particularly yours, or is all language somehow shared?

Assessments

Idiolect would be something you could notice in the language use of a character in a novel or a witness quoted in a newspaper article. An idiolect can aid characterization. You could also use the notion of idiolect when creating a written task in a distinctive voice.

Marking a text with a pen, pencil or marker (or with comments or notes on a computer or tablet) forces you to be an active reader, helps you to make connections between various elements in a text, and helps you to remember later what you noticed while working with a text. Some students balk at the fact that their teacher requires them to mark a text; they tend to read then haphazardly underline or circle in order to "get credit" for doing homework. Other students take lengthy notes in the margins even of texts they read in their own time. No matter what your attitude towards writing in a text is, you need to keep the true end in mind: becoming an active reader.

An understanding of any text develops over time. If you are approaching the **paper 1 examination** or any text in class, it is important to read and reread. In relation to text marking, most teachers recommend, when approaching a short text or passage selection, to **read first without a pen**. Reading without marking can keep your attention on the text as a whole, on the basic situation or the overall meaning. It is only after initial reactions that you can begin thinking about the ambiguities, subtleties and intricacies of technique.

Sometimes the most basic text-marking technique works best. One recommendation is simply to look for three elements: highlights, questions and confusions. The following bullets suggest elements you may mark in a second reading.

- **Highlights** – these could include sentences that resonate with you, sentences that seem to introduce or summarize. Sometimes you can look for important cues: first sentences, last sentences, sentences in a different font or format. Highlights could also be individual words: look for striking words, repeated words or isolated words.

- **Questions** – one of the best ways to approach a text is to interrogate it. Questions in the margin can help you to think about what a text means or suggests and how it operates. Ask questions in the margin ranging from "What does this mean?" to something more related to intentions such as "Is this image supposed to be funny or disturbing?" or "Why didn't they give the name of the city?"

- **Confusions** – these are simply the places where you are confused. While these can relate to questions you ask, they may be words you don't understand, ideas that don't make sense or gaps in your background knowledge. It is important in a textual analysis or comparative textual analysis at least to attempt to deal with these confusing moments.

Some people like to stop with these basics when marking a text. The next step in marking, however, can be very useful. One approach is to jump right to your own **marginal notes**. Especially if you are preparing a passage for analysis on **paper 1** or at higher level preparing a text for analysis in a **written task 2**, some marginal notes can end up as key parts of your final analysis. While reading, marking, making connections, coming up with ideas and drafting is a sensible process, it is never an orderly process. The notes you take on a text may be final draft quality.

A final step of marking will most likely be very personal. The key to a third reading or marking of a text is to look for patterns and to **make connections** to ideas you have discussed in class. You should try to come to some holistic ideas about a text that are based on a wide variety of elements from the basics of what is being presented, to the complexities of metaphors, image patterns or symbolism. At this stage, many students like to have a system: circle verbs, use a highlighting pen for adjectives or use a different colour pen to keep track of important themes or issues. This type of marking can be very helpful in any analysis, but may particularly help with comparative analysis.

Activity

Look at this short example of a text marked by a student. Can you see any system in the marking? This particular student has been asked to read first without a pen; to do a second reading looking for highlights, questions and confusions; and to apply a more complex system on a third reading (or at least to mark in more detail). After examining this paragraph, try marking any one of the extracts in the text sections found throughout the book. Try your hand at a non-literary text, a literary text and a text that includes images.

The text is a short passage taken from a news story in the *New Zealand Herald*.

New Zealand recorded its biggest loss of migrants in a 12-month period since August 2001, as kiwis continued to jump the ditch seeking a better standard of life and higher-paying jobs in Australia.

> **Comment [c1]:** Interesting to use slang here... may be just the local audience?
> **Comment [c2]:** More slang...why?
> **Comment [c3]:** Is this more because of a rivalry between NZ and Australia than anything else?

Some 4,700 more New Zealanders left for Australia than arrived in January, taking the annual loss to a record 38,100 in the 12 month-period, according to Statistics New Zealand. That drove a monthly net outflow of migrants to 500, and pushed the net outflow of migrants to 3,134 in the year ended Jan. 31, the highest net loss since August 2001.[1]

a lot?
a little?
does it matter?

Insight   Active Reading

"It is commonplace for teachers to say this, but I think it is true: I didn't really understand my subject matter until I was forced to teach it. Having to stand in front of a class and be an 'authority' of some sort is a lot of pressure. When I first started teaching English I thought it was my duty to know as much about the books I was teaching as humanly possible so that I would never be stumped in front of class (self-preservation) and so that I would have all of the information I needed to help the class succeed (a misguided notion of my own importance). While I soon learned that teaching was not about delivering content, one lesson stuck with me: to help others work with a text and to be truly thoughtful about a text, you have to read with an urgent sense of responsibility. When I was a student at university, I skipped pages. Sometimes I skipped whole books. Not so when I became a teacher. When I read for fun, I am seldom driven to take notes. In university, I took notes on things that I thought would serve me well in an exam. As a teacher, as someone who feels responsible for a book and its reception, I find that every sentence is a possible spur to discussion, or something worthy of notice. Over the years, I have realized that active reading is the key to being the best possible student, the best possible teacher, and the best possible scholar. I like to think of those roles as thinker, thinker and encourager, and professional thinker. All of these roles involve reading, making connections to other texts and to the debates that surround us, and communicating ideas about texts to those around us. When I think about the role reading plays in an intellectual life I realize what 'active reading' looks like: it is three books open

at the same time, pages of notes sticking out of one, scraps of paper written on and tossed by a bedside lamp, notes scrawled on a tablet computer, a host of secondary readings and a couple of relevant articles bookmarked or thrown into a Diigo account. An active reader not only notes, but reads the back cover, finds similar books, shares, argues and maybe even re- reads."

Former secondary school teacher, now college professor

"Before taking literature classes in school—and before I knew what 'annotation' meant, I placed much more importance on understanding texts as opposed to appreciation. I admired writers' play on words and certain moods or vivid characterizations. But as I was limited in my conscious understanding of literary techniques, I was more disengaged with the text. To me, reading actively means paying close attention to what the author—or the narrator—is doing with the text. It means paying close attention to form, structure, breaks— especially in poetry—and also to the effect of words. For instance, when Ondaatje opens with the line 'It was a bright bone of a dream…' in the beginning chapter of his book Running in the Family, *his uncommon use of the word 'bone' de-familiarizes it and makes us probe deeper into the text. In paying special attention to such imagery throughout the novel in English class, I was able to come to a deeper appreciation of Ondaatje's narrative style and the English language, overall. The word combinations that writers conjure to create a lasting, sometimes felicitous image, contribute to the whole idea of the amazing variety and nuances present in language— sufficient to capture a colored snapshot of a mood or moment.*

In my first English literature class, the question of whether de-constructing and analysing the text destroys our ability to appreciate it came up. In my opinion, engaging with the text by surfacing the issues—should it be related to the readers' society in context—and by being conscious of the techniques employed by the author, a reader can pick out the deeper intricacies of a text that might otherwise have been missed. In learning about the different types of metaphors and sound devices, I was actually able to appreciate a poem or a passage as a whole, as opposed to being trapped within the minute details of the text. I think this is applicable in almost any field—without any knowledge of what to look out for, appreciation is impossible."

An IB student

Background   The History of English

To study the history of English is to study its present and its future. Understanding how language changes over time is one of the main outcomes of the language in cultural context section of this course and investigating the history of English could help you to understand the scope and depth of language change. In addition, the history of English is a possible topic in and of itself. The study of the history of English offers a chance for reflection not only on change but on social and cultural forces, the roles of various national groups, the intricacies of audience and purpose, and the details of individual texts. Most importantly, the English language today is tied to its varied history, and this history points to a future that is dynamic and global.

The origins of English

It is almost impossible to talk about the birth of a language (and this in itself is interesting to consider: what languages are being born right now?). The history of English, though, usually begins with the arrival of the Angles, Saxons and Jutes, three Germanic tribes, in England. As the Celtic tribes were pushed towards Wales, Scotland and Ireland, an "anglisc" language took hold that was to form many of the roots of future English. This period of English, from approximately 450–1100 CE is known as Old English and if you have ever attempted to read the epic Beowulf in the original Old English, you know that it is almost completely unrecognizable to a Modern English speaker. By the 900s the language began to change under the influence of yet more visitors to the island: the invading Norseman. By late the late 1000s English was taking root as an interesting hybrid.

The Norman invasion

The Norman conquest of much of England in 1066 brought with it the influence of French on the language. It was common during this period that a form of French was spoken by the upper classes while English was spoken in lower class households. By the end of this period (Middle English, ranging from 1066–1500) English itself regained its dominance, but forever marked by borrowings from French. A look at Chaucer's *Canterbury Tales* shows us that though drastically different from Modern English, Middle English has many recognizable words and structures.

The Renaissance and early Modern English

The period from the time that Queen Elizabeth started her reign (1558) up until approximately 1800 was a time of growth, expansion and standardization for English. The Renaissance was a time for the expansion of the arts and it was a time of exploration and budding colonialism. For many, this period marked the beginning of what we now think of as "global English". English not only began to spread around the world, but its spread meant that the language itself changed to allow for an ever-widening vocabulary. At the same time that the language was experiencing this expansion, the printing press was also causing a push for a greater standardization of spelling and construction.

The late modern period

The late modern period that we are still in today is marked by further change brought about first by the Industrial Revolution and then with continued growth of technology and the shrinking of the globe through accessible travel. New technology, trade, political upheaval: all of these forces affect a language.

As the basis of a further oral activity you could research a side issue in the development of Old English: where is the Celtic influence? Very little of Celtic language is evident in the English that developed from the languages of the Germanic tribes. Some scholars do suggest that there may have been some structural influence on the language though. When English developed through the mixing and mingling of so many languages, what happened with Celtic languages?

As a topic for a written task (either task 1 or 2) or for a further oral activity, consider exploring the links between early colonialism and the growth of English and the current use of English on the internet, or the changes in a variety such as American English in relation to the expansion of Indian English. This work could be the seed for a response to one of the questions for a written task 2, or could be the start of a "language change website" for written task 1, or an interesting film documentary and follow-up discussion for a further oral activity.

Extension

The history of English given above is only the briefest outline of the dynamic forces that have shaped English over the centuries. In-depth study of the history of English can be fascinating simply because of the content itself and the topic is, in fact, one of the most "content heavy" topics that you could study in IB English A: language and literature. The history of the language, however, clearly points to interesting ideas that are up for consideration or debate such as those mentioned in the side panels above. Linguists tend to study language either **synchronically**; that is, how a language is used at one particular moment in time, or **diachronically**; that is, looking at how a language element changes over time. A diachronic investigation sheds light on our particular moment in time and allows us to realize that language today will not be language tomorrow. What do you imagine for the future changes of English?

Issue | Community

We all belong to a wide range of language communities from the broadest categorization (of speaking English) through groups defined by dialect, wide-ranging groups related to gender, all the way to the local clubs we join. Many communities overlap (10-year-old boys in a scouting club talk like 10-year-old boys and use the language of the scouting community) and it is easy enough to find situations in which we can communicate with others easily about a certain topic. When the topic changes and specialized language seeps in, we feel out of place. Because language communities are so ubiquitous, the issue of community identity and its effects is important in the IB English A: language and literature course. Language and community could be a major unit at your school and even if it is not, the idea of community will be important in a discussion of almost every linguistic topic. The idea of community gets to the heart of the most basic issues in language: understanding and misunderstanding.

Activity

Read the following blog post. It is easy enough to understand but there are moments when being a member of one community or another may help in terms of depth of understanding. While the dialect here is standard, the overlapping of various communities may make the audience quite specific. See how many communities you can identify based on use of language.

Check Me Out: One Lucky Girl

Have you ever had the realization there wasn't a single thing you'd want to change about your life, even if a billowing Angela Lansbury emerged from a magic teapot to grant you a wish? Well, maybe *after* a jillion dollars (and a burrito) rained down on me, I'd feel that way. Still. I call myself damn lucky.

Reason 1 My new boyfriend is sweet, talented, adventurous, grows one helluva beard, and actually *likes* hanging out with my mom, taking time to watch every single sunset, and taking photos of me. I'm still convinced he immortalizes my days just to show his friends the hilarious jokes I call "outfits." This one involves combining black with brown, mixed metals, mixed leathers, and a DIY hairdo. Salons in LA are defined as dodgy if they don't charge at least one limb for a haircut.

Reason 2 In spite of my best efforts, my hair150 color manages to look like I may still have salon connections – or at least that's what I've been getting. But! There were no actual skills involved – I literally pinned up the top layer of my platinum locks and slapped a foolproof sample of John Frieda Precision Foam Color (in Dark Cool Pearl Blonde) onto the under layer. This stuff is brilliant. The haircut was inspired by Joan of Arc, Louise Brooks, and Jamaica's self-inflicted bowl-cut (Experimentation + Luck = SKILLUSION).

Reason 3 Just over a *week* after arriving in LA, I scored a meeting with the VP of Online Marketing for Lucky Brand. He said I was their quintessential Southern California Girl. "Huh! SURE!" I agreed. Among other things, he ended up sending me these gorgeous art nouveau earrings, and a pair of leather platform dream shoes. Little does he know that after just over 3 months here, I'm a total convert. Charlie, you're a prophet.

Source: *"Check Me Out: One Lucky Girl"*. 28 February 2012. www.painfullyhip.com.

Activity

Use your own creativity and knowledge of language use in various communities to complete the following exercise.

First, see how many examples of words or sentences you can come up with that would be typical or indicative of a speaker who is:

1. a professional soccer (or football) player

2. a doctor

3. a snowboarder

4. a lawyer

5. a 12-year-old boy.

Now see if you can imagine a humorous scenario in which a member of one community is placed in a different, perhaps unfamiliar, context. Mix and match the speakers above with the contexts of:

1. a sports stadium

2. an operating room

3. a ski slope

4. a courtroom

5. a school corridor.

Extension

We are often not aware of our language communities until either we enter an unfamiliar community, or someone from another community enters ours. How could your expand the above activity into something that you could use in a **written task** or a **further oral activity**?

Also, while it may be fun or humorous to explore the difficulties of communication across communities, how might you explore the serious side of this issue? What is it like to be part of a linguistic community that is discriminated against? Can we be negatively marked by the language we speak or by the varieties of English that we do not speak? An essay exploring this issue in relation to a single linguistic community could lead to an excellent response in relation to one of the questions for written task 2 at higher level.

Reception   Syntax

Syntax is the part of the rules of grammar that describes or indicates sentence structure. The structure of a sentence is essentially the order in which we place words and syntax is the study of how we make meaning out of particular word orders. There are times when English speaker may not understand a word or particular meaning but that speaker can gauge a sentence as "correct" because the syntax follows grammatical rules.

Other sentences may be deemed as complete nonsense simply because of a difference in syntax. Consider the following examples.

1. Happy green dreams sit firmly.
2. A pronoun flew over the water.
3. I gave the moment a hog-tied tree.

Though these sentences do not make sense, they are grammatically correct because they follow logical syntactical rules.

Now look at the sentences below.

1. Firmly sit dreams green happy.
2. Water the flew pronoun over a.
3. The moment I a tree hog-tied gave.

These sentences obviously do not follow syntactic rules and would not be judged as correct.

Noticing syntax

Other than the fact that recognizable word order is necessary to create meaningful sentences, how can syntax matter in our analysis of language acts? The most reasonable answer is that syntax can be employed for various purposes by speakers and writers and can affect meaning or the receiver. Awkward yet understandable syntax can call attention to a particular sentence. A particular syntax can be used to indicate the level of formality. The syntax used in an advertisement, political speech or literary text can highlight a word or an idea. We often do not consciously recognize syntax when dealing with a text. In many cases, this may be because the syntax is relatively standard or straightforward. Syntax, other than helping to communicate ideas clearly, may be unremarkable. If we think about syntax, however, and if we notice it employed in an unusual or interesting way, then it is worth some analysis. In the study of texts, syntax is first an element that we may recognize and, once recognized, it is an element to consider in relation to meaning and effect.

Classifying words

Practising your ability to discuss syntax might start with what seem like old-fashioned grammar lessons. Being able to identify types of words and their uses helps us talk about the effects of word order. Every word in a sentence essentially has a **syntactic class** and a **syntactic function**. The syntactic class of words is what we generally think of as a "part of speech". These include the following: nouns, verbs, adjectives, adverbs, pronouns, conjunctions, prepositions, interjections and articles. The syntactic functions of words indicate the role played in the sentence, for example subject, object or modifier. In the sentence "I hit the ball" we have pronoun, verb, article, noun used as subject, verb, modifier and object.

The key for your study is, again, that changes in usual syntax lead to particular meaning and effect.

Activity

The following speech by Abraham Lincoln is famous for its brevity and effect. The speech was delivered from the back of a train as Lincoln was about to leave his home town to take up the presidency in Washington, DC in 1861. Many people have noticed the rhetoric employed in the speech including antithesis, parallel structure and anaphora. Read the speech and consider the purposeful use of syntax or word order. Why would Lincoln have made the choices he did?

"My friends: No one, not in my situation, can appreciate my feeling of sadness at this parting. To this place, and the kindness of these people, I owe everything. Here I have lived a quarter of a century, and have passed from a young to an old man. Here my children have been born, and one is buried. I now leave, not knowing when or whether ever I may return, with a task before me greater than that which rested upon Washington. Without the assistance of that Divine Being who ever attended him, I cannot succeed. With that assistance, I cannot fail. Trusting in Him who can go with me, and remain with you, and be everywhere for good, let us confidently hope that all will yet be well. To His care commending you, as I hope in your prayers you will commend me, I bid you an affectionate farewell."

Source: Abraham Lincoln. "Farewell Address at Springfield, Illinois". *The Collected Works of Abraham Lincoln.* Vol IV. Basler, RP (ed.) 1953.

Extension

Shakespeare is considered a master of the artful employment of syntax. Turn to the excerpt on page 206 and note places where the syntax seems unusual or important. What is the purpose or effect of this unusual syntax?

Production | Analysis and Comparative Analysis

Giving advice on how to do an analysis of a passage (as in **paper 1 standard level**) or a comparative analysis (as in **paper 1 higher level**) is simply giving advice on how to read and how to communicate your understanding and appreciation to a quite specialized audience (an examiner). This entire book is meant to break the elements of reading and communication into as many small parts as possible so that, over time, your overall reading and communication habits will improve. In this brief section, however, we will outline some basic steps to approaching the analysis and comparative analysis of paper 1.

Here are some **steps to take in the examination room**, and some **approaches to take to the passages**.

1. **Read all of the passages without making a mark**. You will probably be nervous in the examination and more than anything else you need to get an overall sense of what the passages are about. In the standard level examination you will choose between two passages, in the higher level examination you will choose between two pairs of passages. Read the available passages, ponder briefly, then go with your gut instinct and choose a passage to analyse. Do not over-think your choice: pick the passage or pair you understand the best or find most interesting.

2. **After choosing, note basics such as text type.** If you recognize the text type (letter, editorial, blog, advertisement) or genre (poem, graphic novel)

note it at the top. If you have already recognized a possible audience and general purpose (to inform, persuade, sell), note this as well.

3. **Reread and mark main points, confusing points, concerns.** The second time you read the passages you should be looking for the most important elements that get at meaning as well as the elements that seem confusing. Remember, too, simply to note what you find interesting. The chances are that if you find something interesting, important or confusing, the examiner does too, so you will be expected to comment on the element. At this point you may also note the important overall qualities of the passage such as the **tone** or any obvious elements of **structure** (for example long paragraphs, captions and images, dialogue, short sentences.)

4. **For the comparative commentary, repeat step 3 with the second passage.** Some of the elements you note at the beginning (key points, major issue, audience) are **likely to be important links between passages**.

5. **Read a third time.** Now you should really pick a passage apart. What do you notice in terms of stylistic or literary devices? What elements do you notice about any images present? This is when you start to make notes about the meaning and effect of elements that you see throughout this book. Remember, if you notice something, it is important.

6. **Take notes and begin to outline.** While you may want to read again, at this stage you are probably ready to make some summative or evaluative notes and to work towards an outline. This will help you tie together all of the elements you have marked or commented upon.

Here are a few warnings:

- **Embrace ambiguity.** Keep in mind that ambiguity or the lack of a clear "meaning" or "answer" can be a purposeful rhetorical strategy on the part of the author. Passages are not puzzles to be solved nor do they often have one meaning or intent.

- **Beware of theme.** Yes, stories, poems and even pieces of journalism can have themes but it is rare that a passage has one basic theme or intent. In the IB examination, candidates often use theme as a crutch, resorting to a broad, vague idea such as "love", "the cruelty of man" or "hope" rather than looking at the complex issues and questions raised by a passage. A discussion of theme can be both reductive and general. At the very least, think in the plural: a passage may raise many issues, ideas or themes.

- **Always integrate technique and meaning.** When you write, you should talk about what is going on, what it suggests, and how the writer has managed to convey these notions. Literary or linguistic features should be discussed at the same time as you are discussing meaning, intent or effect.

Finally, here are some big questions to consider:

- What is the text type, purpose, audience?
- Who is speaking?
- Whose eyes do we see through: do we see through a character in the piece or the narrator?
- What is the general situation?
- What is most striking?
- What is most surprising or confusing?
- What questions are raised?
- What does it mean?

- What does it suggest?
- Why is it interesting?
- How is it all put together?
- How is the writing itself interesting?
- How do images contribute to meaning and effect?
- How are the images visually interesting?
- How are the two pieces similar?
- How are the pieces different?

The writing itself

While there are other sections of this book that deal with particulars such as writing a good introduction or integrating quotations into the body of your essay, here are a few things to consider when coming up with an outline and writing your analysis.

- Always structure your writing with an introduction, a body and a conclusion.
- There is no "correct" formula for an introduction. Let the reader know what you will talk about, what your main focus is (a passage analysis can have a broad thesis that incorporates a couple of ideas and some main techniques, or it may focus on the element that you found most interesting and will eventually branch to other elements).
- Be sure that you are writing a coherent, continuous essay rather than a list of disjointed points or observations.
- Let the examiner know from the start, either in the introduction or in the next paragraph, that you know the basics in terms of what the pieces are about or their type or intention.
- It is often helpful to start with a holistic view of the passage and then move to an analysis that goes from beginning to end. Some students organize by issue or idea instead, which is fine as long as important elements of the passage are not skipped over in order to adhere to particular ideas.
- Remember, the passages in front of you are interesting. Tell the examiner how and why the passages are interesting.

> **Activity**
>
> For a good practice at the skills of passage analysis or comparative analysis, use the texts found throughout the book. For the analysis of an individual passage, try looking at the war reporting on pages 99–102. If you are taking higher level, practise by comparing this passage to the graphic novel on page 207. Feel free to move on from there by mixing and matching passages in this book.

Reception   Semantics

Semantics is the linguistic study of the meaning of words, phrases and sentences (as opposed to syntax, for example, that focuses on structure). While the field of semantics can be quite complex, there are some key notions in the field that can help to draw your attention to the complexity of making meaning with words and may help in your close analysis of texts. The following key concepts in semantics clearly relate to principles you encounter throughout this course.

- Language communicates information about our world.
- The meaning of words and sentences resides in the minds of senders and receivers.
- The meaning of language is social and depends on context.
- Meaning depends on a variety of relationships between and among words, phrases and sentences.

The activities below focus on some key semantic issues that will give you an introduction to the method of study as well as provide practice in thinking about the particulars of meaning in a text.

Activity

1. Dictionary definitions

- Write your own definition of the word "hero". How would you define the word "hero" as used in your English class? Now look up the dictionary definition of "hero". How do the three definitions compare? What does this suggest about the contextual definition of a word? What does this suggest about the ways we combine **denotation** (explicit meaning of a word) with **connotation** (implied meaning or feeling evoked by a word)?

- How would you define the word "aftermath"? Look up "aftermath" in a good dictionary that also shows the origin or original meaning of the word. Does the original meaning relate closely to how you use the word? Do we need to know or understand origins in order to understand a word fully?

Activity

2. Background information

Sometimes, the meaning of a word assumes a particular background or context. For example, the word "surrender" assumes that at one time two parties were in conflict or battle and that one party gave in to the other. This surrender of one party has caused the other party to be the victor and the surrendering party has given up the conflict and perhaps certain rights.

Explain the background or context of the words:

1. procrastinate   2. trustworthy
3. patient   4. kind   5. respect

Activity

3. Relationships

List as many **synonyms** (words with the same or nearly the same meaning) as possible for:

1. stingy   2. fat.

Now rank your list in terms of positive and negative connotation from most negative to most positive (showing the **scalar** relationship between words). How easy is it to order the words? What determines the connotation of these words?

Other important relationships between words can include **antonyms** (words with opposite meanings) and the **order** of words (in the following list, "house" is superordinate, while the other words designate subordinate types: "house", "hut", "shack", "cottage" and "mansion".

Activity

4. Multiple meanings

A polysemic word is a word with different but related meanings. A homonymic word is spelled the same, sounds the same, but has different, unrelated meanings. The word "bank" is homonymic in that one "bank" is a place to keep money while another "bank" is the side of a river. Are the following words polysemic or homonymic? For some of them you will need to use a dictionary or the internet to see if there is or is not a relationship between meanings.

1. Fine   of high quality
           money paid as a penalty.

2. Spell   to write the order of letters in a word
           a magic formula
           a period of time.

3. Pilot   the operator of a ship or plane
           the first episode in a television series.

Activity

5. Truth assumptions

The use of certain verbs can imply the actual or probable status of events in a statement. In the sentence "I know the dog died" the verb "know" is **factive** as it assigns the death of the dog as true. In "I believe the dog died" the verb "believe" is **non-factive** as the clausal object (the dog died) may not be a true fact.

Are the following statements factive or non-factive?

- I thought that today was your birthday.
- I forgot that today was your birthday.
- The teacher scolded me for not studying hard enough.
- The teacher acknowledged that I hadn't really studied.
- The teacher realized the student had cheated.
- The teacher assumed that the student had cheated.

Activity

6. Idioms and ambiguity

Meaning can often be complicated through the use of metaphors, idioms, or simply through ambiguous relationships between words. What are the actual meanings of the first two idioms below? What are the possible meanings of the next ambiguous sentences?

- Bite your tongue.
- Pull my leg.
- He is my English teacher.
- I saw the person with a telescope.
- She doesn't like short men or women.

Issue   Grammar

Grammar is the set of rules that describe how a language functions to make meaning. A **descriptive grammar** is used by linguists as a way to understand the patterns and relationship that enable a language to function as used. The underlying grammar of a language would enable a native speaker to understand that the following sentence, though it contains meaningful words, does not make sense in English: "The hit John ball." Many of us, however, when we hear the word "grammar" think of **prescriptive grammar** which is the set of rules that we follow not simply to be understood but in order to speak what would widely be considered "proper" English. It is important to remember that these prescriptive rules change over time and are, in fact, even originally based on typical usage in a variety of circumstances (how constructions appear in early novels, for example).

Knowing grammar

First, "knowing" grammar can mean having a grasp of standard English constructions or it could mean understanding the complex rules that make meaning possible in English. But either way, why would we want to study grammar? And what does it mean to study grammar in the first place? While many schools no longer work through exercises in prescriptive grammar, an argument could be made for the idea that studying usual language rules for the construction of meaningful sentences can help us with communication. Sometimes the reason behind a rule immediately clarifies the linguistic choices we make and helps us to make our own pronouncements more exact. Another argument for learning these "rules" is that using a standard, accepted version of English is helpful when moving from community to community (or from school to a job). From a completely utilitarian perspective, being accurate in your use of acceptable grammar can influence your mark in this course. Consider the highest language criteria from paper 2: "Language is very clear, effective, carefully chosen and precise, with a high degree of accuracy in grammar, vocabulary and sentence construction; register and style are effective and appropriate to the task." Reading often and paying attention to construction in what you read are probably the best routes to improving your own language use.

The basic elements of grammar (from the sounds of phonemes to morphemes—parts of words—up to sentences) can be useful to know when analysing the effect of language. Being specific about words and their relationships can help you not only to consider meaning in a text but to communicate your understanding to someone else.

Understanding the grammar of language is fascinating in and of itself. If we think it is valuable to understand the mechanics of communication in any text, then we essentially admit to thinking that it is valuable to understand grammar.

This cartoon gives an example of prescriptive grammar at work.

"Sorry, but I'm going to have to issue you a summons for reckless grammar and driving without an apostrophe."

Issue | Belief

One broad topic that you may use at your school in order to explore language in cultural context is the close relationship between language and belief. In this instance, belief is taken in its broadest sense to mean anything that a speaker thinks is true rather than thinking of the narrower area of religious beliefs. In a very theoretical way, many philosophers have argued that we may not be able to even have beliefs without having language. In a more narrow, practical sense, linguists have also suggested, in a somewhat related context, that understanding theory of mind—understanding that other people have thoughts and beliefs different from our own but formulated in a way that is similar to our own—and what other people believe may also not be possible without language.

Can belief exist without language?

The philosophical debate about the necessity of language to belief is quite complex. It is worth, however, summarizing a few key points here in order to raise debate. **Arguing a side** of this issue would be a good starting point for understanding the connections between language and our beliefs and could also branch into other topics such as knowledge and the nature of language itself. Thinking about this debate could also lead to further research and an interesting topic for a **written task** (especially a written task 2 at higher level) or an engaging presentation or debate for a **further oral activity**.

In a series of influential essays in the 1980s the philosopher Donald Davidson made arguments about the necessity of language for belief. He started with the idea of the interpretation of the speech of other people. On the one hand, interpretation involves understanding, at least to some extent, the meaning of words. On the other hand, interpretation involves understanding the particular uses of the words or the complex intentions of the speaker. In a sense, in order to interpret the language of others, we need a full understanding of all of the complex thoughts, concepts and relationships behind all of the elements of communication.

Davidson's argument is that beings without language (very young children, animals) cannot have belief. In order to have a belief with specific content I have to already have a rich network of other beliefs and concepts. If I am throwing a ball high in the air near the edge of a forest and the ball does not fall back down to me I may say, "I believe the ball is in the tree." This belief may seem simple but it presupposes a number of other ideas and beliefs (the notion of gravity, thoughts about trajectory, the nature of trees, an understanding of wind and its effect, a disbelief in magic, for example). Davidson argues that very young children and animals, because they do not have language, are not capable of setting up such a complex system of relationships.

Language and religion

What we believe is often codified and regulated through religion, a broad system of beliefs. The connection between language and religion is a broad topic of its own and is clearly connected to any discussion of how language is connected to culture. Religion often creates standard uses of language (rituals, prayers) in order to create a common bond or understanding. The language of a particular religion can affect, in turn, what we think and how we make judgments in every aspect of our social relations. Religion often functions like a language, like a shared means of communication, at a more basic level as a collection of signs, symbols and shared understanding.

Activity

What are some possible avenues for arguments against Davidson's notion of belief or language?

Davidson also argues that beings must have a conceptual understanding of the notion of belief itself in order to believe. In the above example, if I believe that the ball is in the tree, then I must be able to understand that, based on a conception of what belief is, the ball may not be in the tree; it may have disappeared or it may, contrary to what I believe based on complex understandings of nature, blown in a different direction and be hidden in the nearby meadow. Without an understanding of what belief means, expressed in language, I cannot have belief. If you trick a dog by pretending to throw a ball, the dog runs off and is incapable of reasoning a false belief or other possible scenarios.

Understanding false belief

Based on the above notions, you may have argued that you can believe something without having language, but can you have notions about what other people believe without language? Many linguists would argue that you cannot. Many linguists argue that understanding the possible thoughts and intentions of others (theory of mind again) is closely tied to the development of language. Consider the following sequence.

Activity

Do I have to know what belief is to believe I am hungry? Is believing I am hungry really a belief? Chew this over.

33

The boy took the ball from the girl.

The boy put the ball in a box.

The boy left the room.

While the boy was out of the room, the girl took the ball from the box and put the ball under the couch.

Question: when the boy returns, where does he believe the ball is?

We all know that the boy would think the ball is still in the box because we would understand in him the nature of his beliefs about the situation. Children who do not have developed language abilities (those younger than 3 years old), do not understand this possibility of false belief and assume the boy will look under the couch. Understanding true belief (take the situation above only the boy watches through a window as the girl moves the ball), may only relate to what *we* already believe. Researchers have conducted a very similar experiment with adults. In the experiment, the adults watch a language-free video depicting a scenario like the one above in addition to a language-free video showing the boy with the true belief. Adults usually correctly identify both the false belief and the true belief. When distracted by annoying sounds (buzzers or knocks), the adults still tend to identify the beliefs properly. When the adults are distracted by spoken words and sentences, however, their identification of false beliefs falls greatly. Language, perhaps, is a necessary condition for understanding the beliefs and intentions of others.

Extension

All of the issues outlined above are not only fascinating areas of investigation but show how the study of language and literature branches into other areas of study that might interest you in the future including philosophy, psychology, linguistics, language learning, the treatment of disabilities and even law. Research into these topics is the perfect base for **written tasks** and **further oral activities** and this basic understanding of intentions behind speakers' statements can also serve you well in **paper 1**.

Background   Language Acquisition

Though technically IB English A: language and literature is not a language acquisition course (the primary concern isn't for you to learn English but to study language. Though happily, as you work through the course your language skills will surely improve), an understanding of how we learn language is important. The study of language acquisition gives insight into the biological and cultural aspects of language and how these interact.

Mother-tongue language acquisition

Instead of reading one of the passages in the text sections in order to understand, appreciate or analyse, read one of the passages and consider this: what do you have to know and what skills must you have mastered, in order to understand the text? If we think of a baby staring blankly at the page (or perhaps drooling on a corner) or ignoring our instructions, we realize that learning language is a phenomenal achievement. Perhaps most amazingly, it is an achievement that most people accomplish and that does not come without a great deal of assistance from family members, friends and teachers. The learning of a mother tongue is also a process that is necessarily intellectual, physical, social and cultural.

The first three years of language development for children is the beginning of a very long process. The development of language is not only about learning vocabulary but also about forming sounds and then establishing a grammar through naming and single words up to three- and four-element sentences. Even at the final stage, it is evident that children have a long way to go through daily language use, pointed informal instruction, and formal training (as in school) before they become adult language speakers.

These are the common stages of the first three years.

- **Babbling**—a prelinguistic stage that takes place from the age of 3–9 months and consists first of strings of vowel sounds followed by the addition of consonant sounds ("da-da-da", "ma-ma-ma" being sounds strings rather than actual identifying words).

- **Holophrastic stage**—from the age of approximately 12–18 months children begin to use one-word utterances. These words usually are used to identify or name common objects while up to 20 per cent can designate an action. During this stage children often use one word to communicate an entire sentence-worth of information ("ball" could easily mean, "I want the ball"). By the end of 18 months most children have learned about 50 words.

- **Two words**—from the age of 18–24 months children begin to string together two-word combinations. This is the beginning of a much more complex grammar as children learn combinations such as subject + verb ("dog bite") or verb + object ("give ball").

- **Three to four words**—at the age of 2–3 years children reach this stage, which involves fleshing out the basic patterns that were learned in the previous stage. Instead of "go bed" a child may now say "I go bed."

Activity

Look at the following cartoon that involves a strange use of language by an early language learner. Why is it relevant to make a joke about change here? Why is this joke funny beyond the fact that babies can't speak like this? How does this play on the elements necessary for language development and its relationship to cultural context more broadly?

"I know it's just a political buzzword, but the idea of change really resonates with me."

Lexis is a linguistic term that refers to the set of all possible words in a language. Within the vast lexis of the English language, words have myriad relationships to one another. Thinking about the relationships between words helps us to understand the ways in which the meaning or effect of an individual word is established through the play of relationships with other words. A **lexical field** is a set of related words that helps to denote a concept or idea. An example of a lexical field could be "clothing" and would include words such as "shirt", "trousers" and "socks". Lexical fields are related to synonyms but extend from this relationship in that any term associated with the particular field, not just synonymous with the word, are included in the field. Another example could be the broad field of "agriculture". Words in the field could include all of the following: "farmer", "seed", "plant", "corn", "cow" and "soil". Lexical fields can also include "unmarked" or broad members, such as the previous examples for agriculture, but may also include what are called "marked" or more specific or technical members such as the following: "farmhouse", "hydroponics", barbed wire fence", "milking machine" and "crop insurance". Lexical fields become particularly interesting when we consider metaphoric language in an text. A sports article, for example, could use words from the lexical field of battle in order to create a dramatic effect. In a sense, looking for the use of words within a lexical field is a way of looking at dominant metaphors, purposeful comparisons, or the creation of a desired tone or attitude. Just a quick warning though: it may be more interesting in your analysis to note the use of one lexical field in relation to another (using the lexical field of dance to describe football, for example) than it would be to find the use a words from a field in a text with closely related subject matter (using the lexical field of the farm in an article about animal husbandry).

Activity

There are many different ways to represent the relationships between words in a particular lexical field. The first lexical field represents a hierarchy of categories, the second (on the next page) is based more on loose association. Play with the two lexical fields in order to explore word relationships, the variety of possible relationships, and the possibility for metaphor and creativity when the two lexical fields below are mixed.

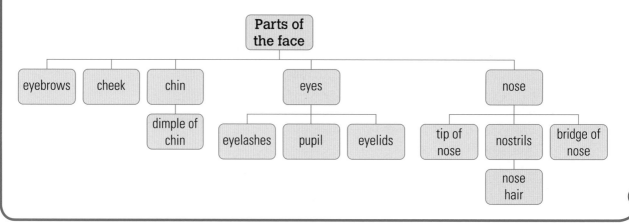

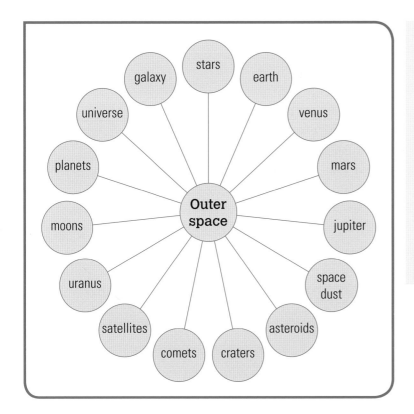

Extension

What lexical fields can you identify in the passage from Shakespeare on page 206? While in an **analysis** you might not necessarily say "the lexical field of x is used…" noticing this type of pattern or these relationships between words might help you to see something interesting in the passage. How does Anne Bradstreet use a particular lexical field to her advantage in the poem *The Author to Her Book* on page 199?

Production Rationale

Technically speaking, the rationale on written task 1 is only worth two points. If your rationale manages to demonstrate a "clear explanation and understanding of the aspects being investigated" in your task, then you will get those two points. The rationale, though, is a key component of your written task. However, because it is a justification of the work you have undertaken it can help an examiner understand your choice of topic, your choice of text type, and how these together demonstrate that you have met the outcomes of the assignment and the course. The rationale is a rare opportunity in an assignment to explain yourself and guide your audience. In other words, the rationale is worth much more than just two points.

Here is an overview of what you need to include in your 200–300 word rationale.

- You need to include the title of your task.
- You need to explain how the content of the task is linked to a part of the course. Remember that you are judged on how well you understand content. Content in this course relates to either the texts you study or the language topic you are exploring in class. Your content, then, is language in action—analysing a text (content of the course), addressing a language issue (content of the course), exploring the use of language in a particular setting (content of the course). Content is *not* terrorism, for example man versus nature, power. It *could be* the use of metaphor and hyperbole in the discussion of terrorism, the portrayal of conflict between man and nature in *Into the Wild,* or the exploration of jargon and register in relation to power.

- You need to include an explanation of how the task will explore particular aspects of the course.
- You need to state the nature of the task chosen in terms of text type or genre (a letter, an advertisement, a web page).
- You should give information about the audience, purpose and context (social, cultural or historical) in which the task is set.
- You need to demonstrate your knowledge of the formal conventions of the text type and how they relate to the aims of your task.

Sample student work

Read the following sample and see if it meets the criteria above. Remember that there are no specific formal requirements for the format of the rationale. Between one and three paragraphs could easily comprise 200–300 words. Your rationale should be as clear and logical as any essay you write and should be sure, again, to help the reader along.

www.rideon.com.au: kooks welcome

Surfing looks like fun: you paddle out, catch a big wave, and then effortlessly rocket towards the shore. At the same time, the size of waves and the strength of an undertow can be intimidating to a beginner. The Australian surfing community is similar to surfing itself. While surfers are very laid-back, warm and welcoming, they have a culture and language all their own that can paradoxically communicate a very open or closed, ritualistic community. This written task will explore the close relationship between language and the characteristics of the young Australian surfing community, along with the sometimes paradoxical attributes of its image, with close attention to the use of jargon and register.

For my task, I have chosen to create the homepage of a surfing website. The website is the perfect medium of communication for the surfer community because it is youthful, dynamic, and allows for a variety of types of language use on one page. While the text on the web page will not directly explore the issues of community, certain elements (such as the forum link, the personal photo uploads, and the overall register) will clearly welcome the kooks (beginner surfers) while other elements will indicate that the surfer community can be an elite, insular club (some of the advertisements, the jargon, the presentation of surfing skills). In this way, the audience of the website, even though the homepage states that beginners are welcome, consists of experienced contemporary, young surfers especially from Australia.

Issue Identity

Language and identity may be one of your main topics of study in the language section of this course. Even if this topic isn't explicitly studied at your school, you will find that personal identity, and the way that language is both part of that identity and a product of identity, is not only important to you as an individual but is tied to almost all language topics such as idiolect, dialect, language and gender, and language and power. While it is almost impossible to separate your personal language use from who you are, it is equally difficult to consider any form of linguistic social relation without thinking of its effect on you as an individual.

Simply put, how we speak reveals a lot about ourselves. Personal language can reveal heritage, geographical location, social class, membership in official organizations and education. Language also, of course, reveals our hopes, dreams, fears and desires. At the same time that we may unwittingly—or quite purposefully—reveal something of ourselves in language, we use language to make judgments about others. At the very same time that these complex relationships are forming, language itself is acting as a force on our personalities, convincing us to watch movies, vote for politicians, hold certain beliefs, buy clothes, or study a particular subject.

Extension

As practice for a **paper 1 comparative analysis** (at higher level), compare this image to a text such as the poem *Quashie to Buccra* by Claude McKay on page 201.

How could you use an image like the one above as the basis for a **written task 1** exploring language and identity?

Some people have noted that identity is **performative**, that we make conscious decisions about who we are and how we want to portray ourselves with others. How could a **written task 1** explore identity as part of the performance through language?

Activity

Image is an interesting way to represent the way we communicate identity and the way identity is shaped by culture. Consider the painting by Native American artist David P Bradley. This "text" borrows from the Mona Lisa, beauty pageants, Native American dress and contemporary culture. How does this painting address issues of identity? How does the painting itself represent the complexities of our memberships in various linguistic and cultural communities and how they influence who we are and how we represent ourselves?

Reception   Tone and Mood

Tone is the author's attitude in a piece of writing in relation to the content such as the topic, the characters or the general situation. Mood refers more appropriately to the **atmosphere** created by a text and its general emotional effect on a reader. There is quite a bit of overlap between tone and mood since the author's tone or attitude—and the words or images chosen to express that tone—obviously affect the overall mood of a piece. The most important fact to remember is that the tone of a piece matters. If we do not understand a communicator's attitude, it could be argued that we do not understand the meaning of the utterance. Just think of a short post on a social networking site commenting on a friend's new sunglasses: "great look!" can be construed as sarcastic and mean, or cheerful and complimentary, depending on a wide variety of contextual elements.

Students often ask for lists of possible "tone words" without thinking that almost any adjective related to feeling or emotion can describe tone or atmosphere. The difficulty in describing tone is that you need to find the word that best describes a feeling or attitude that might be complex, nuanced or even ambiguous. So sometimes looking at a list of words can help to give you a sense of the endlessly fine distinctions of tone and mood.

Tone words: admiring, amused, angry, anxious, celebratory, cheerful, confident, clear, determined, dignified, direct, encouraging, euphoric, formal, gloomy, hopeful, humorous, ironic, matter of fact, ominous, passionate, resigned, pessimistic, playful, sad, serious, wistful, witty.

Mood words: depressed, desolate, disheartening, eerie, fanciful, frightening, frustrating, gloomy, happy, jolly, optimistic, romantic, sentimental, solemn, sorrowful, suspenseful.

Activity

Identify the tone and mood of these short excerpts, the words that helped you determine the tone, and any contextual clues that helped you identify the tone and mood.

- From *How the Poor Die*
  "No doubt English nurses are dumb enough, they may tell fortunes with tea-leaves, wear Union Jack badges and keep photographs of the Queen on their mantelpieces, but at least they don't let you lie unwashed and constipated on an unmade bed, out of sheer laziness."
  GEORGE ORWELL

- From *House Rules*
  "My sixteenth birthday is today, but I'm not expecting much. We're still waiting, six days later, for the jury to reach a verdict. I'm guessing, actually, that my mother won't even remember—which is why I am struck speechless when she yells "*Breakfast*" and I come downstairs with my hair still wet from my shower and there's a chocolate cake with a candle in it."
  JODI PICOULT

- From *Open*
  "Philly walks in. I see in his eyes that he doesn't just sympathize—he lives it. This was his defeat too. He aches."
  ANDRE AGASSI

Activity

In order to think about mood and how it is created, try an atmosphere translation game. Think of any movie and try to translate it into another genre, creating a trailer for your new movie. Can you turn the comedy *The Hangover* into a horror film? Can you make the movie *The Hunger Games* into a slapstick comedy? This is a good exercise to make you think about generic conventions but it also helps you to understand how small elements of presentation, from word choice to sound and image, show tone or create mood. This would be a great activity for a **further oral activity** or to work into a **written task**.

Reception   Modality

Modality in linguistics refers to the extent to which a given proposition is possible, probable, likely, certain, permitted or prohibited. Modality is a way of indicating the **illocutionary force** of a statement, or in other words a combination of the point being made and the degree of commitment to that point. Modality is frequently indicated in a sentence through the use of modal verbs (also known as auxiliary verbs, or you may know them from the early years of school as "helping verbs"). The words "will", "may", "can", "should" and "must" function to indicate the various moods within a range of likelihood or intention. Modality is interesting to note when considering various persuasive or informative texts. Politicians who frequently use modal verbs such as "may," "should" and "could," for example, would perhaps be said to be "hedging their bets".

While modality is frequently indicated by modal verbs, modality may also be indicated using nouns, adjectives or parenthetical expressions. In the statement "it is a necessity to learn to swim," "necessity" is a noun that indicates the modality of the sentence (the fact given here that one must learn the skill). "He is ugly, I think," is also a statement with a particular modality (closer to "may" than "must"), this time indicated by the parenthetical "I think". Again, the importance of these modal functions is that they give us, the readers, an insight into the attitude of speakers or the level of their commitment to whatever they are stating.

Types of modality

Though there are many variations of modality there are three main types to consider: **epistemic**, **deontic** and **ambiguous**. These terms refer to the type of commitment rather than to the degree.

- Epistemic function is concerned with whether or not the given proposition is true.
- Deontic function is concerned with the possibility or necessity of the proposition in terms of freedom to act.
- Ambiguous function indicates that the proposition can be taken as either epistemic or deontic depending on the context.

Examples (using the modal verb "must")

- **Epistemic** You must be tired. (It is the case that you are tired based on the effort you exerted.)
- **Deontic** You must go outside now. (It is required that you go outside.)
- **Ambiguous** You must do your homework. (This is either epistemic: based on your success it is necessarily the case that you do your homework; or ambiguous: it is required that you do your homework.)

Activity

See if you can identify the modality of the following sentences as deontic, epistemic or ambiguous.

1. You may be sick.
2. I must be tired.
3. Fred must leave now.
4. You can leave.
5. She must be discouraged.
6. The second draft could be better.
7. Only graduates can go to the party.
8. You must be kidding.
9. He might want to study a bit harder next time.

Extension

Try writing two political speeches, one in which you address the issue of government funding for university education (something you support) to a group of retired people who want education cuts and a second in which you outline your agenda before taking the office you have won. Highlight your use of modal verbs.

Background Linguistics

Linguistics is the study of language and is focused on the structure of language as a system of communication, the physical attributes of language production, the role and use of language in society and the ways languages change through time. The study of linguistics not only enriches our understanding of language but can enhance our understanding of other fields such as computer science, law and even physical rehabilitation.

A good way to think about the vastness of the field of linguistics is to consider the questions that linguists ask about language. These questions include the following.

- What are the basic features of a language?
- How are the individual sounds of languages produced?
- How do individual units of language have meaning?
- How do the elements of language interact to create meaning?
- What do all languages have in common? How do they differ from each other?
- How do we learn language as a mother tongue? How do we learn second languages?
- How and why do languages change over time?
- How does the history of a language relate to language use in the present or to our predictions of language use in the future?
- How does language influence the way we interact in society?
- How do social and cultural values influence our use of language?
- How does our knowledge of language inform the way we learn?

At the very core of linguistics is the close analysis of language as it is used. The following core areas of study in linguistics (some of which are addressed in other parts of this book) help lead to broader concerns:

- phonology: the study of the sounds of language
- morphology: the study of words and how they are formed
- syntax: the study of the structure of sentences
- semantics: the study of meaning in language.

In contemporary linguistics students and scholars have expanded the field of study so that from the close examination of sounds and patterns, further fields have emerged, such as:

- historical linguistics: the study of language history and change
- sociological linguistics: the study of the relationships between languages, individuals and societies
- psychological linguistics: the study of the mind and the creation of language and the influence of language on thinking
- neurological linguistics: the scientific study of the brain and language function
- computational linguistics: statistical and computer-based modelling and understanding of linguistic relationships.

How is the study of linguistics useful in this course?

While the language sections of this course do not function as a traditional introduction to linguistics, you will find that the concerns of the course, because the focus of the investigation is firmly based on language as it is used, are inherently linked to the concerns of professional linguists at every level. At times in this course you are acting as a historical linguist, at others as more of a social linguist. Perhaps one difference is that in this course you don't have to be as concerned with the smaller building blocks of language and its function (phonology, for example) but you immediately immerse yourself in some of the larger issues of the field.

Answers to the activity question on page 42

1. Epistemic 2. Epistemic 3. Deontic 4. Deontic 5. Ambiguous
6. Epistemic (both "the second draft is not as good as it could be"
or "possibly the second draft of this will be better than the first")
7. Deontic 8. Epistemic 9. Ambiguous.

This useful chart suggests the value of the study of linguistics.

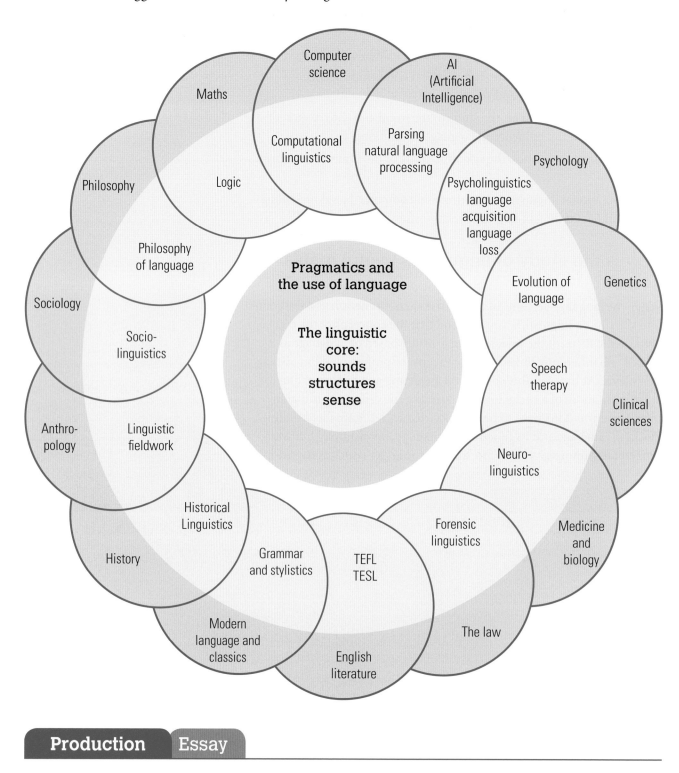

Production   Essay

One of the most common questions asked by students is "How do I write an essay?" Perhaps this isn't a very serious question, because most students have been writing essays of one form or another for a long time. What most people want, though, is reassurance that they are on the right track or basic steps to follow when they are feeling nervous, frustrated or overwhelmed. Whenever we are given a rather complicated task to complete, we look for something solid to hold on to or at least somewhere to start. In various production sections of this book we will look at some of the particular elements of essays (such as writing sentences or conclusions) but here we will simply put you at ease and outline some steps to follow when you approach an essay.

Sometimes you have to generate topics from scratch when you are given an essay assignment. A teacher could simply tell you to choose a topic and write an essay in relation to a book you are studying. Since we will cover "generating a topic" in a later section, let's look instead at essays that you may write in relation to a prompt. The written task 2 prompt and the paper 2 essay question below are not only types of essays that you will have to write in this course, but could be the kinds of prompt you are asked to respond to frequently in class.

- A **written task 2 (for higher level) prompt:**

How could the text be read and interpreted differently by two different readers?

- A sample **paper 2 essay question (based on part 3 of the course):**

"Family holds society together and gives authors something to write about." Discuss how and to what effect family is represented in at least two works that you have studied.

Step 1: Read carefully

The very first step of writing an essay is to understand the prompt. Take some time to pick apart the prompt and take notes. In relation to the above prompts, what does it mean to interpret? Who are the two different readers? What kind of assumptions would they make in relation to different texts you have encountered? Are there families in the texts you have studied? Why is family important to society? Can family help structure a work?

Step 2: Focus on texts

Pick the texts you will use to answer the question and begin writing down the big examples. Which texts are clearly related to these prompts? What are some of the key elements you remember? What did you talk about in class? What are your key thoughts in relation to the texts and the prompt?

Step 3: Focus on examples

Write down as many examples as you can think of. Be as specific as possible. If you can use the texts (in a written task, for example) find quotations, scenes, key moments. Keep generating ideas and write some in relation to your examples. What do they show? How do they relate to the question? How do they offer interesting insight?

Step 4: Make connections

If you are using more than one text, decide how the texts, in relation to the prompt, are similar or different. Try to connect all of the various ideas you have had. Are they beginning to gel into an "answer" to the prompt?

Step 5: The introduction and thesis

Now that you have written extensive notes, you are probably starting to come to an interesting and particular response to the prompt based on the work or works you have studied. Try to sum up your main idea in one statement. Perhaps this will become your thesis or focus. What do you think you need to say in the introduction?

Step 6: Building the body

Try to organize your notes into important sections that will become your body paragraphs. Perhaps you have four points to make about one text and each main point will be a paragraph. Perhaps you have two points to make about three different texts and these will form your body. If you have an idea that you think will make a paragraph, be sure you have evidence in the form of specific examples or quotations from texts.

Step 7: Write

If you have been generating ideas, taking notes, organizing and taking more notes, the writing of the essay should be the easy part. Tell the audience what you are thinking, why it is interesting and why it matters.

Some important thoughts

Enjoy it

Just as you approach a text for analysis making the assumption that it is interesting, think about how your thoughts about a prompt are interesting. Take the time to enjoy thinking or coming up with an original or striking answer. Have fun taking notes and thinking "out of the box". Enjoy the words you choose, the sentences you put together, the sounds and rhythm of what you are writing. Enjoyment and engagement show in an essay.

Writing is learning

You learn as you pick apart a prompt, as you take notes, and as you craft an essay. The whole process of writing is a chance to refine your thinking and to learn.

Think, speak, write, shape and revise

Almost any topic or text, taken at face value, may seem simple. Thinking about a prompt can reveal its complexity but thinking, perhaps, doesn't give you a coherent idea that is ready to share. The essay should be the end of a process that includes thinking, speaking (even if in your own head), writing, shaping and revising.

Think of your audience

Your actual audience is most likely your teacher or an examiner and you should keep this in mind when you consider your register. Your teacher, however, usually knows what you are "getting at" when you talk about a text. An examiner seems like a distant teacher. It is best to think of your audience, then, as the general reader. The intelligent general reader is the person who reads the kinds of texts you are studying, thinks about the kinds of prompts you are considering, and is in tune to the way you and your teachers at school think. The general reader wants to be informed, amused and pushed to think. The general reader assumes that you are going to say something that matters.

Insight	Writing at Home

"I never kept a journal when I was a kid except for one time when I was 13 and my teacher made me write one. She said that I would eventually enjoy recording my thoughts and I have to say that she was wrong. When I took IB my English teacher suggested again that we should keep a journal, but

this time it was a reading log. To be honest, I didn't enjoy that writing either. Most of the time, I wrote very quickly in my journal right before class just so that I would get credit for doing my homework. I also thought that we did enough writing in English class and I didn't want to spend time writing something that didn't really matter. It wasn't until I entered university that I realized that writing in a journal could be helpful. During my first year in university I ended up taking two English classes and two political science classes. I soon realized that I had hundreds of pages of reading every week and then, at about mid-semester, I would have to produce about fifty pages of writing on ideas that had come up in my courses. I felt like a giant wall was standing between me and the rest of my university career. After making it through all of my papers, I realized that I needed a new system. So I started a "thinking journal." I was going to use my laptop but instead I decided to be a bit retro and use a black notebook I had with completely blank pages. Whenever I did a reading for class, I would write ideas I had or quotations that I thought were interesting. If I was feeling very inspired, I would write a page or two. Usually my notes were just giant scrawls across the page such as "PARANOID" when I read the book The Crying of Lot 49 *by Thomas Pynchon. Soon, however, I started to not only take notes but based my responses to texts in political science on ideas that I had got when I had taken notes on my texts from English. By the end of the semester I had a pretty complex web of notes and ideas that could have generated twenty papers. I was actually excited to write about the things I had discovered. In one class, I had to tell the professor about all of the ideas that I had floating around. The essay just wasn't going to be enough. When my first semester ended, even though I had got off to a bad start, I was in great shape and I realized that all along that was why my teachers had wanted me to respond to texts in writing. Eventually, my black reading notebooks—notebooks that grew to contain drawings, ripped out pages of magazines, reading suggestions from friends and the occasional late-night ramblings based on a conversation at a party—became the generator for my senior Honors Thesis."*

Former IB student, graduate of University of Chicago

"My most important writing strategy is bedside scraps of paper. You would think that I would have the foresight to put a notebook next to my bedside table, especially when I am in the process or working on a book or a journal article but I tend to plan my writing better than I plan my thinking. I tend to spend a fixed amount of time in my office each day dedicated to writing. I also tend to end my day mulling over a problem in my writing. The most important seed for my writing and the solutions to my toughest problems, however, seem to come in the first hour or so after I go to bed. I can't count the number of nights that I have sat up straight in bed, fumbled for a pen, ripped a corner off any piece of paper at hand, and then written something that would one day wind up in print."

A professor of philosophy

Issue   Sexuality

Language and sexuality is another area of study within 'language in cultural context' that can lead to an investigation of a wide range of language issues. The study of sexuality differs from the study of gender in that it is specifically focused on how we as humans approach the act of sexual intercourse. It may not seem as if sexuality is related to language until we start thinking that even the word "sex" has different meanings to different people. While "sex" may simply denote a way of categorizing living beings in relation to reproductive function, to most "sex" is intercourse—but what counts, in a particular community, as a sexual act? The study of language and sexuality is concerned with how we talk about sex, how we define or judge sexual acts (which may then further relate to issues such as the definition of sexual harassment), and how we construct or exhibit our sexuality through language. In a very innocent way, "flirting" is a sexualized use of language. In a more blatant way, language and images tied to sex or the notion of being sexual are used all the time to communicate, convince and sell. The study of language and sexuality can lead to discussions of community norms, the changes of language use over time, the connotation of words, the use of slang, the construction of identity and a host of other language and cultural issues.

Activity

As a way to begin thinking about language and sexuality, consider the complex issues raised by the book *The Hunger Games* by Suzanne Collins and the subsequent movie version. *The Hunger Games* is a dystopian novel for young adults that is set in a future where children from oppressed and defeated districts in the country of Panem are forced to compete to the death in a televised gladiatorial contest. The novel has been praised both as an exciting "page turner" and as a work that explores oppression, the rise of an exploitative upper class, the exploitation of children and the rise of a voyeuristic reality TV-addicted populace. Some critics have noted that the book criticizes a society that forces young adults and children to wear provocative clothing, get into relationships that will be followed by avid fans, and worst of all, to kill each other for the pleasure of an audience. Some of these same critics have also said that the book takes advantage of our own desire to read about a young girl who is exploited, falls in love and kills. Are we cheering to see exploitation end or are we cheering along with the voyeuristic audience depicted in the novel?

The movie version brought more of these broad cultural issues to the fore. What would the movie show and not show? How would the film handle scenes of killing or scant dress? How is the audience of the Hunger Games in Panem different from the audience of *The Hunger Games* the movie?

Look at the poster and consider how relevant a study of language and sexuality is in culture at large today. How does sexual language in magazines or movies influence us? How do posters, books and movies define sexuality for us or, at the very least, suggest or create what is acceptable in a community?

Background   Performativity

Throughout the study of language in cultural context you will come across the idea that language both shapes and is shaped by culture. This may seem like a simple enough proposition but it is linked to the nature of language, our intentions, the restrictions of our language use and our ability to be creative with language, so it is quite complex. The inextricable link between language and culture can be understood (and also made more theoretically difficult) when we think about the performative nature of language.

Words do

In the 1950s the linguist J L Austin shifted the study of language from the properties of language as a descriptive force with certain truth values (for example, "the table is brown" is descriptive and can be either true or false) to the idea that language can be an act in itself, that some language performs. The famous example would be that as opposed to statements such as "the table is brown" we have statements such as "I now pronounce you man and wife" that are not describing a situation but actually creating something. When we look at certain uses of verbs, we can see how some sentences enact an intention or state of being: "I promise", "I bet", "I warn" and "I declare".

Performatives and ritual

Since the 1950s linguists and anthropologists have continued to investigate the ties between performative language and cultural practice. Many examples of language that creates a state of affairs or performs an act through its utterance come from religion and law. These language acts are codified by a culture and are passed down to users. In a sense, we are constrained by these creative acts of language. On the other hand, we can create a state of affairs with our language. Politicians, for example, are always making vows and promises, creating a situation or a desired situation through their use of words. Whether or not these words will come to fruition is another story. What is interesting is what the linguist John Searle has suggested and that is that our performative utterances sometimes fit the world but often our world and our interactions within it change to fit what we have uttered. Using the marriage example above, the ritualistic language of marriage that in many societies is considered to be between a man and women can be transformed so that the performative language can apply to, and constitute, same-sex marriage. Performative language can be both restrictive and creative.

Performative identity

The idea of the performativity of language and how language helps to constitute individual identity has pushed beyond linguistics into broader cultural studies. Scholars such as Judith Butler and Eve Sedgwick have shown how our gender identity, for example, is something that we perform but that also this identity is prescribed by language acts and rituals that have been handed down through culture. They also offer the possibility for the transformative nature of performative language or the ability of speech acts to create a new identity that stands outside or in opposition to repeated cultural rituals.

The investigations of the performative nature of language and identity are not without controversy. What is important for this course, however, is the notion that what we say, why we say it and what this means is influenced heavily by cultural traditions and that, at the very same time, our language can create an individual presence within culture and shape culture as a whole.

Extension

Research into some of the challenging theory behind performativity can lead to interesting **further oral activities** or even topics for the **written task 1** or **2**, or as a way of approaching a written task 1 question. Try doing some research on one of the following theorists: J L Austin, John Searle, Pierre Bourdieu, Judith Butler, Eve Sedgewick.

Background Language and Mass Communication

Language and mass communication is one of the four sections of the IB English A: language and literature course. Some teachers may clearly divide the course into four parts while others will integrate the four sections, choosing to approach themes or issues through the lens of two or three sections at once. As you study language as it is used on a daily basis, it will become clear that it is almost impossible to separate language from its means of dissemination. In this section of the course, even if it is integrated with language in cultural context, you will gain the skills necessary to consider the effect of medium, or the means of communication, on language as well as the importance of "the media" in our exposure to language.

This section of the course, like language in cultural context, focuses on language and how it is used on a daily basis. This section tightens the focus, however, on mass communication and the various media that affect the sending and receiving of messages. Mass communication is any form of communication that goes beyond the conversations between two people. Mass communication, then, can range from a presentation given in front of a class to a televised sporting contest that reaches viewers all over the world. Mass communication obviously shapes our lives and there are various issues to consider when investigating the relationships between language and the medium of delivery. First, the choice of medium (from print to digital devices) affects the way we use language, and second, institutions such as the government or the broad "mass media" such as news organizations control much of our mass communication. Through the study of topics such as bias, stereotypes, popular culture, political campaigns and advertising, you will develop an understanding of different forms of communication, show an awareness of the influence of the media, and understand the many ways various media use language and image to inform, persuade and entertain.

This part of the course will offer you a unique opportunity to compare the effects of communication in various media. Just consider the advertising campaigns designed for films. How are different types of information in different formats delivered about a film through talk-show appearances, opening-night parties, posters, associated toys at fast food restaurants, trailers on the internet and the release of songs from the soundtrack? While the marketing of a film might be an interesting case study for the study of advertising, it also offers a way of looking at how language is used in different media or the various ways in which images can be used to enhance communication. Film marketing is both a fascinating cultural topic related to the mass media and popular culture, and a fascinating exploration of media use of and impact on language.

Assessments in language and mass communication

As part of the study of language and mass communication you will be asked to complete the following for submission to the IB:

- a further oral activity.

Most likely you will also be asked to do some of the following which may also be submitted to the IB:

- a written task 1
- a written task 2 (at higher level).

The skills and ideas you develop in this section will also be particularly relevant to:

- paper 1 textual analysis (standard level) and paper 1 comparative textual analysis (higher level).

Reception   Image

Images are part of the way we communicate and though the IB English A: language and literature course is not an art appreciation course, it would be impossible to talk about how language operates in our world without considering the operations and impact of images. Many of the texts we encounter include images and some texts, such as road signs (to give just one example), are made up of images alone. Here are just a few questions that we might ask about images.

- How does an image work with or against written text in a poster, advertisement, magazine article or website?
- How does an image on its own communicate information, an idea or emotion?
- How do the elements of an image work together to create meaning or effect?
- How are subject matter and artistic elements related in an image?

This course will give you the opportunity to analyse and create images in an effort to understand better the way we use images in the texts we encounter every day, from advertisements to more "literary" texts such as films and graphic novels.

Art historian Michael Lewis has suggested a way of concentrating on image as opposed to broader narratives. As an introduction to looking at and thinking about images, let's consider the image below. To start, write a brief, open-ended commentary on the image. What kind of work is it? What is the subject of the piece? What feelings are produced by the image? What is most striking or interesting about the image? Does this image engage with any ideas?

You could easily produce a wide range of responses about this image. Some notes or ideas that students have raised in relation to this image include the fact that this is a painting, the subject is dancers, it is relatively spare. Others have noted the muted tones and the delicacy of the dancers. Still others have noted the strength of the dancers, the facial expressions. Many students have noted that this image is "about" dancing and practising and it raises issues of beauty and dedication.

But let's step back a minute. One simple question may change the focus of our initial response: why is there a watering can in the painting?

Many students have told possible stories about the watering can, including the correct idea that watering cans were used in wooden floored dance studios to manage the tackiness of the floor—if there is not enough moisture dancers slip and fall. While this is a good narrative explanation of the image based on reality, is there another possible reason for the presence of the watering can?

The watering can mirrors one of the dancers. As much as the watering can plays a particular role in "real life" the watering can

in this image is an echo and creates balance. This balance, then, has a range of effects. Perhaps it draws our attention to the difficulty of the dancer's stretch, or to its mechanical nature. Conversely, perhaps the balance created by a tin can highlights the light gracefulness of the dancer. Regardless of the answer, the watering can is as much a formal element as it is part of a story.

Extension

Throughout this course, it will be important to step back and consider how images operate. We may be used to doing this with written texts but it will be important to be active readers with images as well. Investigate some of the images in the texts found throughout the book. How do the images in the graphic novel on page 207 operate? Are they simply illustrations to go along with text? How do the images and words work together on the poster on page 48?

Reception | Line

Before a picture represents something it is a collection of visual elements, just as a page of writing is a collection of letters, words and sentences before it is about anything. One of the most basic visual elements of an image is the line. A line may be the first thing we are able to scribble as a child and a line is the basic element of our alphabet. A line is essentially the drawn or even implied distance between two points and in art a line is used to define shape or to create edges. While this definition may seem obvious, it does not do justice to the functions of a line in any image. A line can be strong, bold, silent, sensual or jagged. A line can give the eye directions. A collection of lines on a flat surface can create depth, space, light and shadow.

Examples of lines in action

Horizontal lines can suggest rest while vertical lines suggest height. In this image the sleeping person may be dreaming of the heavens:

Diagonal lines can give a sense of activity and movement:

Curving lines may help to create energy:

Collections of lines can create shading, depth, volume and light:

Activity

Look at the images throughout the book and take note of the use of lines. Do the lines communicate any of the feelings or ideas suggested above? What other attributes can lines communicate? What about the thick lines in the graphic novel on page 207? How do lines draw our attention to particular aspects of an image? How do lines or implied lines function as an organizational device on a web page, in a graphic novel or as part of a magazine cover?

Reception   Light and Colour

Two important visual elements to consider when analysing an image are light and colour. While it is not necessary for the purposes of this course to understand all of the properties of light and colour it is an important fact that light not only allows us to see but that the source, direction and intensity of light changes the appearances of objects. A light shone from in front of an object tends to flatten the appearance of the object while highlighting shape, whereas a light shone from above or below tends to highlight form. Painting and drawing use variation in colours and shades from light to dark to give the appearance of real light and to give flat objects the illusion of shape. This variation in lightness or darkness is called the **value** of an image and is also a property of colour. **Hue**, or the particular wavelength of light that produces colour, can have a value that ranges from light to dark. Colours can also have a range of **intensity** from a pure red, for example, to a less saturated red that could be made by adding the colour white. Both light and colour are used in images ranging from hand-drawn sketches to blockbuster films not only to mirror reality but also to draw attention, create a focus and portray or elicit emotion.

Activity

While you can't analyse colour in this black and white reproduction, what are the effects of light on the image? How would you describe the variations in **value**? What is the effect of the supposed source of the light? Its direction? How does variation of light affect the appearances of the objects in the painting?

Activity

The graphic novel on page 207 makes dramatic use of light effects. Write a brief analysis of the use and effects of light and dark and the possible relationships to the text.

Extension

The use of light and colour in images used in conjunction with text can be the focus of a **written task 1**. How could you focus on the delivery of a coherent message in an advertisement or on a webpage using colour? Light and colour would often be an important visual element to analyse in relation to an image used as part of **paper 1** analysis (standard level) and comparative analysis (higher level).

Reception   Shape, Form and Texture

Shape, form and texture are important visual elements that can communicate a variety of feelings or ideas. Shape is the outline of a two dimensional object (or the outline of our view of a three-dimensional object). Form, or mass, is the actual or implied volume of an object. Texture is the actual or simulated feel or tactile quality of an object. While these are basic elements of visual art, their interplay can create a variety of sometimes conflicting responses and can call attention to underlying meaning and emotion in a work or even inherent tension.

There are two general types of shapes: **geometric** shapes—such as circles and squares—and more free form **organic** shapes. In many images we often find that geometric shapes can convey order, rigidity or a man-made quality, while organic shapes imply a sense of freedom or closeness to nature. On any flat surface of an image, a shape plays out against a background. In fact, we can think of the main subject matter shapes as

positive shapes while the resultant background becomes a **negative shape**. The eyes of the viewer are automatically drawn to the positive shapes that are foregrounded in an image. At the same time, negative shapes are often used to create a dynamic tension in a piece, to suggest unity in an image, or even to make subtle allusions or hints. The artist M C Escher famously worked with the relationships between positive and negative shapes. His prints call our attention to the way the eye (and the mind) negotiates the relationships between shapes in an image. Search for images of his prints on the Internet.

The mass of an image is best understood when thinking about sculpture. Obviously, a sculpture in three dimensions has actual volume and mass. By looking at a sculpture, we are able to perceive how much space it takes up. Also, without touching or lifting the piece we are able to sense or imagine its weight based on an estimation of the materials or the look of bulk. In the two-dimensional space of an image, the artist uses light, shadow, colour and shape to indicate mass. Just as in a sculpture, an artist is able to express mass and a variety of effects based on the viewer's impression of mass. Large, heavy objects often give a sense of monumental permanence. A squat, heavy object could also suggest dullness or an elemental quality. Fine, long objects can suggest refined delicacy or they can suggest weakness and decay.

The texture of an object (or the implied texture as depicted in an image) can also affect the viewer's impression. Just as we have a notion of mass from our experience of objects in the real world, our ideas about how an object in an image *might* feel can give us an impression closely associated to our response to the actual object. A picture of a furry kitten might evoke warmth while a shiny, metal surface creates a feeling of hard coolness.

Activity

The image on the right is interesting in relation to shape, mass and texture. This image here was shown at an exhibition of art meant to comment on the medium of the print newspaper. Before thinking about the actual objects (a deer, newspaper) and possible meaning, consider the following questions.

- What shapes do you see?
- What is the effect of the shapes or the juxtaposition of types of shapes?
- What is the mass of the objects in the work of art?
- What qualities are evoked by the mass?
- What possible paradoxes are suggested by the mass of objects in the work?
- What textures can you discern in the work?
- Are there feelings associated with these textures?
- How do all of these qualities contribute to the possible meaning of the piece?

Insight   Working with Images

"Every day, our world becomes increasingly technical. Objects all around us are being replaced by pixel-based representations of themselves that appear on our laptops, smartphones and tablet computers. For me, my days are particularly made of bits, bytes and pixels. As a software developer I develop pixel-perfect graphical user interfaces that are used by millions of people around the world. These graphical user interfaces are pixel-based metaphors that represent tactile objects. In order for these metaphors to be effective, graphical user interfaces need to be intuitive and feel natural for users. In order for this to happen, graphical user interfaces need to be quick and responsive. This is done using efficient programming paradigms and algorithms. However, creating graphical user interfaces goes far beyond using efficient programming paradigms and algorithms. Effective writing is also essential. Before any code is written or any pixels are drawn, a large amount of planning must take place. To document this planning, everyone on my software development team must clearly and concisely describe their thoughts and ideas in very detailed writing, which is read by numerous people including project managers, consumers, vice presidents, CEOs and other software developers. Working with images ends up being a recursive process that involves writing, speaking, drafting, drawing and writing code. I loved programming when I was in high school but I never thought about how my work with code would be so intertwined with every sort of symbolic representation and communication."

IB graduate, graduate of Dalhousie University in Canada, Software Developer at Research In Motion (makers of the Blackberry)

"We know that it is cliché to say that a picture is worth a thousand words, but for us that is true. Both of us really enjoyed English, especially when we could have a class discussion and say what we felt about a novel or a poem but we really looked forward to art class every day. In art class we liked looking at as many works of art as we could. We watched slide shows focusing on different artists almost every day. But what we both loved even more was doing our own paintings. A painting was absolute freedom and we really felt like we were getting a chance to express emotions. While one of us really likes writing poetry, we would agree that the images we created really were worth a thousand words. As we were studying IB art and especially as we began to put together portfolios for application to art schools, we better understood the connection between writing as an art and the painting and sculpture we were doing. Every image tells a story and we needed to understand how to put everything together—the colour, shapes, lines—to tell the story that we really wanted to tell or to create the right emotion. There is nothing worse than painting something that no one gets at all. We realized that the way we had to be so careful about our art must be the way that writers need to be careful about their stories. Even when we made mistakes that worked, mistakes that would become part of the final piece, we knew that there was no such thing as a chance detail. We also started to see that all of the art we had been viewing over the years influenced our work with images. We saw how Picasso could be part of the images we create even if we are not purposefully imitating and that helped us understand the way authors seem to share ideas and inspiration. From now on, when we read, we will think about writing the way we think about an image: some many elements come together, it must be magic."

Two higher level art students (enrolled at art school in London, enrolled at art school in Hong Kong)

Space is all that surrounds us. On a daily basis we recognize, mark and move through space. In a two-dimensional image the illusion of a third dimension can be used not only to replicate our experience in the world but also to draw our attention to important objects or create depth both of space and emotion. By recognizing a few of the techniques used to create the sense of space of depth in an image, we can see how artists and designers are able to make us perceive something deep in an object that is flat—or in a sense, to feel a world on a page.

The four drawings below are ways in which an artist can manipulate shapes in order to create spatial depth.

Overlap:

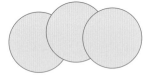

Overlap and diminishing size:

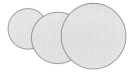

Vertical placement:

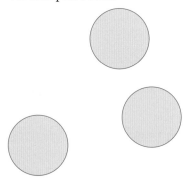

Overlap, vertical placement, and diminishing size:

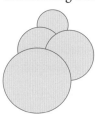

These basic methods of creating the illusion of depth are also a way of creating the illusion of reality. In art (whether in a painting or in an advertisement) artists are able manipulate our perceptions of depth, and play with our concurrent knowledge that what we are viewing is flat, in order to create purposefully the real, the imaginary or the surreal. What is important when approaching an image for analysis is to think of space and depth as part of the purposeful construction of an image rather than an accidental effect. In the second image above, the circles may be carelessly strewn on a table while in the fourth image the circles are steadily moving towards us.

Linear perspective

The method of depicting the way the eye sees objects in space, diminishing in size as they reach the horizon, was formalized by architects and artists during the Renaissance in Italy. When we look at a painting that uses linear perspective we "see" in the space of the painting from a fixed *vantage point*. Our eye then follows what should be parallel lines (the edges of a floor, the sides of a road) as they converge towards a *vanishing point* on the horizon.

Activity

What are the effects of a space and perspective in image A, completed before the formalizing of linear perspective? What is the centre of attention? What is the feeling of the space? What feelings are generated and where is the focus in image B (on the next page) where carefully planned linear perspective is used?

Image A

Image B

Atmospheric perspective

Another way of creating a dramatic sense of space, while perhaps creating a different focus, is to use atmospheric perspective. Artists use changes in colour, light (value of light), texture and detail to create space. In the real world, if we were to look over a vast panorama, perhaps a landscape without defining lines, our sense of space would come through these similar changes in intensity.

What are the effects of space created in this image using atmospheric perspective? How is the general effect, and perhaps meaning, of this image different from images A and B above?

Reception   Unity

Unity is one of the key elements of overall design of a work of art or image and can be attributed to a combination of various visual elements such as line, colour, texture, shape and perspective. Unity, as the word suggests in everyday usage, is the sense of a work of art fitting together as a whole rather than as a collection of haphazard elements. In contrast to unity, **variety** is the sense of diversity in an image that can keep a work from being too bland or predictable. A diverse group of objects in an image creates interest for the eye while elements of design tie some of these objects together to create unity or a sense of a coherent effect.

An artist or designer can create unity by using some of the following techniques.

- **Repetition** is using repeated colours, textures and shapes to help create unity in an image. Some have suggested that groups of three help create sense of unity in an image (as some have suggested groups of three terms creates strong effects in a speech).

- **Continuation** is tying various elements in a work together using similar effects. Continuity is a trickier concept than repetition. An artist could create continuity by using a single colour in a range of intensities in an image. An artist may also show a progression in shape such as using shapes from perfect circle to oval. The key to continuity is progression and connection rather than repetition.

- **Alignment** is simply grouping objects together to create unity in an image.

- **Balance** While balance is an element of design in its own right, balance in painting can lead to unity. A balanced painting, even of an active or disturbing scene, can feel finished, convincing, forceful, or stable. An unbalanced image can seem haphazard. An image can have **symmetrical balance** when elements (shapes, colours) are parallel in a work.

- **Asymmetrical balance** can be more subtle and difficult to achieve through the near juxtaposition of elements that create close symmetry through weight, texture, and light.

Activity

How is the painting below an example of asymmetrical balance? Which objects, on either side of an imagined centre line, balance each other? How have shades (or the colours you imagine) contributed to balance?

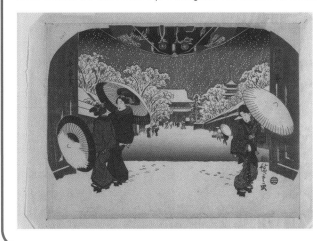

Extension

Unity is something to consider in your analysis or comparative analysis in **paper 1**. A discussion of unity can naturally lead to a discussion of the overall effect of an image. Unity is also something to consider in a **written task** or a **further oral activity**. Basic elements of design, such as unity, can help in your own creation of an advertisement, a film or a website.

Reception Contrast, Repetition and Proportion

There are many elements of design that combine to create the overall impression of an image (or any visual art work including sculpture and film). To gain balance, disturb balance, create symmetry, disturb symmetry or generally attract the attention of the viewer, works of art often use the basic principles of contrast, repetition and proportion.

Scale, or the relative size of a work of art as compared to the size of things in the real world, is one of the first decisions an artist must make. A larger than life-size statue in a nation's capital creates different effects for different purposes as opposed to a miniature decorative carving made for a child's bedroom. The artist's decision about the size of a work sets into motion all of the other elements of design. Within the work itself, **proportion** is the size of objects relative to each other. Proportion can be consistent and related to proportions in the real world or, more often, proportion is manipulated for effect. The statue of David by Michelangelo is a famous example of the use of proportion because the hands and head of the statue are noticeably large or out of proportion when compared to usual human proportions. In the case of this work, the proportions may have been changed to emphasize David's noble face or the surprising strength in his hands or proportion may have been changed because the statue was to be displayed at a great height and the hands and head, in usual proportion, would seem insignificant from below.

Contrast is the juxtaposition of differing elements in a work. Just as language is not possible without the opposition of elements, an image is not possible without contrast (of course, a completely black canvas has no contrast within it but it could be argued that a contrast is created between the canvas and the frame or the surrounding gallery space). Contrasts of colour, shape, texture and technique keep an image from being monotonous and can create interest and energy in a work. Repetition of elements works in a similar way, giving logic and consistency to contrasting elements. Like contrast, repetition can be created with shapes, lines, colours or almost any visual element.

Activity

Images – other than images in film, of course – are static. One of the most interesting things about a static image, however, is that it can give the impression of movement or passing time. Many paintings can be described as being dynamic. Look at the painting opposite and consider how the design elements of contrast and repetition – as well as other elements – have possibly created an impression of **time** and **motion**.

Background   Communication

Communication is at the heart of the entire IB English A: language and literature course. While mediated, mass communication may be the particular focus of the language and mass communication section, every text that is studied in this course is a means of communication between a creator and a broader audience. In order to study mass communication—

in order to study every text in this class—the most important thing this course can do is, perhaps, make communication seem bizarre to you. Communication between two people is strange enough but the desire to communicate with a group of people and the attendant effects of this communication should seem almost magical. We are so immersed in a culture of easy and constant communication, however, that we too often ignore its complexity. One of the goals of this course is to step back from something you do every day in order to think critically about its means and effect.

A basic model of communication, while it may break the communication process into steps, also suggests the complexity of the various components. When two people communicate (also known as dyadic communication as opposed to mass communication) the process can be described as follows.

- An individual reacts to stimulus and formulates thought.
- Thought is translated into code or language and sent along a channel (or, in the most basic case, spoken).
- A message is perceived by the receiver.
- The receiver translates code into thought.
- The receiver can reverse the process.

While this model, which describes a basic "turn-taking" model of communication, is a logical step-by-step explanation it does not explain the complex contextual considerations of basic two-way communication. For one, it is assumed that the two participants speak the same language. Beyond this, however, there are other factors: some parts of the utterances may not be important to understanding, others may be key and cannot be left out; the participants are also, in this model, assumed to be in close proximity and can understand paralinguistic features such as gestures and facial expressions. Difficulties in communication arise as soon as people are separated by distance or as soon as participants begin to rely on a medium, such as paper and pencil, for communication.

Mass media communication

While the use of a particular medium such as a pencil and paper or a telephone as a channel clearly complicates dyadic communication, the process becomes more complex when an individual, through a particular medium, is able to communicate to a large, distance audience.

Over the years many theorists have suggested some key elements of mass communication. These include the following.

- Mass communication often requires formal organization (from a television station to a telephone network).
- Mass communication is usually focused on a large audience.
- This communication tends to be public and can reach people over a wide geographic area.
- While the audience of mass communication comes together because of common interest, there is often not extensive interaction or communication between audience members.

Mass communication is interesting in that it often involves what is called **reification** which means turning a complex process into a fixed product. A spoken message, for example, is reified by being recorded then broadcast. While a spoken utterance in a conversation may be "off the cuff," a mass communicated, reified message is often planned by a number of people, rehearsed, edited and transmitted with effects. A reified message also doesn't usually allow interaction and response. On the other hand, contemporary digital media is interesting in that it allows for interactivity despite the fact that it shares many traditional attributes of mass communication.

Broadcasting

Broadcasting was one of the most important developments for communication with a large audience. Broadcast media technologies allow organizations to communicate with a widely dispersed audience via public airwaves. Television and radio broadcasting allows for communication in the form of movies, news programmes and songs directly to listeners and viewers in their homes, offices and cars. The advent of radio in the 1920s and the television soon after (with the first fully scheduled programming in the 1940s) is one of the most significant developments in the history of mass communication. While broadcasting too is changing today with satellite and cable taking over much of the television programme access, our ideas about access to instant media communication are forever changed by broadcasting.

Noise

Noise is the enemy of communication. Noise is unfiltered information from which we must discern a message. As soon as a message leaves the sender, it is subject to noise: messages from other sources, background sounds and irrelevant chatter. Think about being at a party where four conversations are taking place around you at the same time. As a listener, you can filter the mass of undifferentiated information (the noise) by turning your head and focusing your attention on one conversation. However, this filtering system is imperfect and it would be easy to lose parts of the conversation or to misunderstand. Media designed for mass communication are made to reduce noise during the sending and receiving process (headphones are an example of a device that can help to filter noise and accentuate a message on the receiving end).

Activity

Noise is interesting in that it serves as a good metaphor for the complexity of communication. Thinking about all of the steps in the basic communication model, and considering the addition of noise, at which points along the continuum can a message deviate from its original intention as thought? Does an institutionalized mass communication apparatus (such as broadcast television) help to clarify or confuse messages?

Background   Semiotics

Semiotics is the study of signs and of sign systems and has been a useful field of study in relation to the analysis of meaning and effect in media works. The study of semiotics arguably started with Ferdinand de Saussure in the early 1900s with his work in linguistics. Concurrent work by Charles Sanders Peirce and later work by the French theorist Roland Barthes pushed the study of signs into the broader study of how signs of all kinds have meaning in culture. Taking a semiotic approach to text – that is, broadly considering words and images as elements that stand for meaning beyond themselves – can be a useful way of considering how texts in any medium work.

In Saussure's discussion of language, he describes the relationship between the signifier, or the spoken word, and the signified, that abstract concept a word stands for. For Saussure these signifiers (the word "dog", for example) are completely arbitrary and do not necessarily relate to an actual dog but an idea of "dogness". Pierce, on the other hand, suggested that signs have a close relationship to actual objects. He also suggested that images could act as signs. In Pierce's model an image of a cat (a *sign*) could represent an actual cat (an *object*) which would then create an idea in a listener or viewer's mind (an *interpretant*). The relationships that both theorists describe are significant because they suggest that there are complex relationships among the signs we see and hear, objects in the real world, and the images or ideas evoked in our minds. If we take this idea further, as Roland Barthes did in the 1970s, these signs operate in complex relationships with other signs and with the broader cultural sign system, creating meaning for a listener or viewer.

Some useful ideas

Some terms or ideas from semiotics can be useful in your analysis of media texts throughout the course. First, Pierce classified signs into the following categories (and suggested, importantly, that signs could function in more than one category at one time).

- **Icons** are signs that work through similarity or likeness and usually structurally resemble the objects they stand for. Some examples of icons are maps, photographs, or the drawing of a man or woman on a lavatory door.
- **Indices** (indexical signs) are closely associated to the object they represent. A moustache on a men's lavatory door, for example, would be indexical. Smoke would be an indexical sign for fire.
- **Symbols** are linked to objects only through social agreement or cultural understanding. In this way, words are considered symbols because they are learned and have only an arbitrary link to the objects or ideas they represent.

Looking at images and words, how can these individual signs work in ways that are iconic, indexical and symbolic? How can the word "hot" be both symbolic and indexical? In what way is the image of a person iconic? In what way is the same image indexical?

A few more ideas that are useful (of course, there are many more in the writings of all of these theorists and in the field of semiotics in general) come from the work of Roland Barthes.

- **Surrounds**—a surround, also known by the literary theorist Gerard Genette as a *paratext*, is all of the extra information and clues in a work that influence meaning but are not part of the "main text". These elements could include titles, by-lines, footnotes, prefaces or even the cover of a book. Though we may not always consider these elements in a literary analysis, for example, they certainly influence our reading.

- **Syntagms**—a syntagm is a chain of signs. A single sign seldom works in isolation either in a written text or in an image. Rather, a collection of signs operates to create meaning and the relationship of one sign to another has as much influence on meaning as the relationship of one sign to the viewer.

- **Paradigms**—while in a syntagm there may be a dominant sign, it is interesting to consider that this one sign was essentially "chosen" from a number of other signs that could be in the same category and could have been used instead. A commercial for a snack food, for example, may feature someone's apartment where there is a dog, the family pet. The sign of the "dog", however, could have been replaced from any number of signs from the paradigmatic set such as a cat, a hamster or an iguana. The choice of the dog as a sign in the particular television commercial may not have seemed significant or particularly meaningful (except to suggest "home with pet") until we consider the choices that were *not* made. The consideration of what is not chosen can lead to interesting analysis.

Reception — Print Media

The invention of the movable type printing press in 1450 by Johannes Guttenberg brought about the birth of the mass media as we know it today. Before the printing press, access to printed materials was rare and with the relative ease of printing came the ability to widely disseminate information, opinion and entertainment. The popularity of printed material began with the publication of religious works but soon branched to novels and to newspapers, magazines and daily or weekly "almanacs" that collected both local information (such as the weather) and opinion. The influence of print media on society is obviously strong but the features of the print media landscape have changed throughout the centuries. In the United States, for example, newspaper circulation peaked in 1973 when 92 per cent of households received a daily newspaper while by 2005 only 49 per cent of households did so. Magazine circulation has seen a similar decline, especially since 2000. On the other hand, book readership seems to be strong. To use the United States as an example again, in 2004 the number of new titles published was 2.5 times what it had been in the late 1990s.

Perhaps most interesting for students of IB English A: language and literature is the way in which early print media differed greatly from the spoken word. It is also interesting how conventions of print media have still influenced communication in the digital age. The differences between the written and spoken word (to go back even to handwriting) exist on a continuum of extremes depending on the particular medium used (from pencil to face-to-face speech; from a newspaper to a personal story; from word processor to a Skype meeting). The following oppositions, outlined by media theorist Jenkins, shed light on interesting attributes of the print medium.

Writing	Speech
objective	interpersonal
a monologue	a dialogue
durable	ephemeral
scannable	only linearly accessible
planned	spontaneous
highly structured	loosely structured
syntactically complex	syntactically simple
concerned with past and future	concerned with the present
formal	informal
expository	narrative
argument-oriented	event-oriented
decontextualized	contextualized
abstract	concrete

Activity

Every medium has generic features readers can easily recognize. In print, for example, we can recognize a newspaper article from elements such as a headline, by-line and location line. A news article has certain stylistic elements such as brevity, clarity, an objective stance and an informational slant. When considering texts from various media, regardless of generic qualities, to what extent do you think they fit into the dichotomies between speaking and writing listed above? Do these characteristics always hold true? How is e-mail an interesting blend of the spoken and written? Is it legitimate to call e-mail a kind of electronic speaking in digitized print? Analyse the print media texts throughout this book and see where they fit in relation to the attributes above. How do attributes of the print medium that date back to the days of the first printing press influence communication in a digital environment? How do you think the digital environment changed attributes of the print medium beyond issues of sales numbers?

Reception   Film and Sound

The two most significant advances in mass communication after the invention of the printing press would be the ability to record sound (with the phonograph invented in 1877) and the ability to display motion pictures. By the 1920s the two advances led to the synchronization of sound and image to create "motion pictures" as we know them today. Just as in the medium of print, the way we send and receive sound and moving images has changed drastically through the ages. The ability to record moving images has moved into the hands of everyone with a cell phone and sound recording has been revolutionized and personalized in the digital age. Recorded image and sound is still produced on a large scale by the movie industry but the medium is also exploited in television, on the internet and in private homes. Moving images and sound are so ubiquitous that literacy today is necessarily multimodal—combining some aspects of text, image and sound.

In relation to this course, though you will not have to respond to moving image and sound on paper 1 of the examination, you will certainly study recordings of all types in class as you investigate how language is used in practice. Recorded sound and image represents a significant text for study and presents the student with a complex mix of features and effects. The study of a film (ranging from a blockbuster movie to a viral advertisement on the internet) will give you a chance to explore important contextual language issues as well as important issues related to mass communication. You could also be studying film and aspects of remediation in relation to the novels or plays you study in the literature sections of the course.

Aspects to consider

Purposefully, this book focuses on the analysis of written language and on images. With your skills of analysis in these media, however, you should be able to extend your thinking into film and sound. While the study of film is a specialized field, there is broad overlap with the analysis of images and the broader language concerns of this course obviously apply.

The following aspects are worth considering when analysing a film and could also be interesting areas for further study. You may consider the investigation of one of these elements for the topic of a **further oral activity** (including the production of your own film), or for presentation in a **written task 1** (perhaps a film review) or a **written task 2** (an analysis of a film in relation to specific aspects that address the given prompt).

- **The auteur**—sometimes a director of a film has broad artistic control over a project and manages to give his or her artistic stamp to a film. It is worth thinking about the role of a director in the artistic choices made in a film or, at the very least, to consider the fact that a film is made by a large team of artists ranging from screenwriters to camera operators.

- **Mise-en-scene** refers to the broad representation of space in a film that determines the mood or feel of the world created on the screen. Elements of mise-en-scene can include depth, proportions, space (closed or expansive), lighting, costumes, décor and even the style of acting.

- **Cinematography** is the means of creating a particular look in individual shots in a film through specific camera effects. Elements of cinematography include colour, contrast, focus (highlighting the attention of viewers on near or distant objects), types of shots (a shot is one continuous camera view and can range from a telephoto close-up to a panning view of a landscape), framing and movement (a steady shot versus short, jerky camera movement).

- **Editing** is the process of putting individual shots together to make a continuous film. Careful editing can draw the viewer's attention to the most important elements in a scene. Editing can serve to make fluid or abrupt transitions. Smooth editing can give the impression of seamless reality while noticeable editing can draw attention to the artificial nature of film much as a post-modern novel draws attention to its own writing.

- **Sound**—part of the analysis of sound involves the analysis of the quality of sound. Elements such as volume and timbre can affect mood or enhance action. Sound can be *diegetic* (happening in the world of the film) or *non-diegetic* (happening outside the world the film, as with a theme song played as background). Diegetic sound could include speaking, delicate sounds or explosions. Much like a shot or focus, sound can draw the viewer's attention to important elements. Other elements to consider in relation to sound are theme music, musical transitions and voice-over.

Activity

Try to find a clip from one of your favourite movies that shows an entire important scene. How do you notice the working of the above elements in this one scene? How many individual camera shots are there? How would you describe these shots? How is the world of the film portrayed? How would you describe the costumes or décor? How would you describe the nature of the camera angles? How is sound used? What are the most important or effective elements of construction in the scene?

Reception **Digital Media**

In general, when we use the term "new media" we are referring to any media that is produced or distributed with the assistance of computer technology. While it may seem easy to say that digital media is simply any communication via the internet, this definition is both too narrow and too broad. First, thinking of digital media as just the internet means that we don't include digitally produced "films", e-books or digital music that are different, maybe more flexible or efficient, media than their analogue cousins. Second, if we think about the wide range of genres and types of communication available over the internet, we realize that the internet is coming to resemble a conglomeration of all media types including websites that look like magazines, internet telephones, live video conferences, downloadable television programmes and live streaming radio.

The digital media revolution has managed both to enhance certain media types and encourage **convergence** where multimedia devices and individual media all share the same platform. Smartphones and tablet devices alone allow us to see that the age of media convergence is here when we can participate in dyadic communication (one to one) in writing, video or audio. We can be the receivers of mass communication (in writing, video and audio from established organizations and individuals), and we can both create and send a wide range of messages in digital format. While the types and genres of communication explode (chat, Twitter, video) the devices and tools for receiving and sending shrink to something the size of a deck of cards (that is, about the size of a cell phone).

Mobility and fragmentation

Digital media are changing the nature of mass communication. First, because of the portability of devices and access to information over the internet, communication (speaking, watching movies and downloading books) can happen almost anywhere at any time. Second, because such a wide variety of information is available to us at all times, the individual consumer has greater choice than ever before. Before the advent of digital media, a viewer may have had the choice of only a few television stations, the local newspaper, stores that sold music, and cinemas. Choices were limited in terms of access and because relatively few organizations controlled and distributed content. In fact, with the increased fragmentation of the media market, nothing tends to reach a viewership or readership quite the size it would have been before fragmentation. On the other hand, because of global connection and ease of personal communication through the internet, we have seen small, homemade music videos reach audiences in the millions.

Background   Media Institutions

While the content of messages sent through various media are influenced by audience, purpose, genre and the medium itself, another way of considering media messages is to investigate the institutions or organizational structures that allow for production and dissemination. It is easy to see that many media texts come to us through advertising agencies, vast print media companies that create both magazines and websites, and news organizations. All of these institutions have their own agendas and rules of conduct that affect the messages they produce. In addition, while we may be tempted to suggest that media communication through a video sharing website such as Youtube is not affected by organizational structure because individuals post on their own, the format itself, created by Youtube, affects the quality and length of videos. In addition, organizational decisions about appropriateness of content, commenting structure, copyright and advertising affect both production and sharing. Both government and corporate culture shape our reception and production of mediated language acts.

Government communication

Every organization has a unique culture that is both created by and displayed through its internal and external communication. A ruling political party can create a coherent impression of itself through official proclamations, written platform statements, formal speeches, planned television appearances by party members, press conferences and even leaks to news organizations. Internally, a government, like any organization, can create a culture through communication: informal e-mails may encourage camaraderie, formal directives keep staff professional and careful, stand-up meetings keep people informed but active. A working government is a multifaceted communication machine.

Governments, of course, also have an important role to play in communication beyond setting or maintaining a political agenda or an impression of competence. Governments have the responsibility of keeping the public informed, making health recommendations, warning of impending natural disaster and helping to educate. While governments often rely on private news organizations to communicate information, governments usually have access to their own media outlets or have the ability to take over public airwaves for important announcements or events. An important issue to consider when analysing any governmental communication, from a health awareness poster to a broadcast in the event of a national tragedy, is whether we can separate political motive from governmental responsibility. While it is difficult to say when a government is being helpful and when a government is being helpful to gain political mileage (and it may, to some, not matter whether the two go hand in hand), the issue is further complicated by the political views of the receiver.

News organizations

News organizations are perhaps the best example of the way institutions affect the messages we receive. If we look at news uncritically, we think of it as informational and unbiased. We can think of news as the events and information that are simply "there" in the world and think that news organizations uncover this information for us. In reality, however, the relationship between news and reality is far more complex. News organizations are affected by how they themselves receive news and information and then news organizations must determine, based on their audience and even their advertisers, how and what to broadcast. The following are just some of the organizational structures (not factors such as political bias, the influence of advertising or community context), outlined by media theorists Brian L Ott and Robert L Mack, that affect how news is gathered and disseminated.

- **News agencies**—most news organizations such as newspapers and television news stations rely on large media corporations to gather news. Organizations such as Reuters and the Associated Press have their own news gatherers, photographers or freelance journalists who collect "news" for the organization. This content is then sold to media outlets for dissemination. The size and ubiquity of these agencies accounts for much of the similar content seen in newspapers, for example, throughout the English-speaking world in relation to international events.
- **Journalistic beats**—media organizations also have their own reporters who gather news and these organizations often restrict themselves to "beats" or important areas of coverage. A local newspaper might have beats such as the city government, crime and local sports. A British news organization may include the United States as one of its beats and place a reporter in Washington DC to cover news from a closer perspective. While beats assure that news organizations are close to a story, they also take reporters away from quirky, less popular or less profitable sources of news (poor neighbourhoods, small countries or popular sports).
- **Pundits**—news organizations also rely on pundits ("experts") to offer opinion in news programmes. Pundits are often specialists in their field and can offer complex information in a digestible format to the viewer. These pundits can also, through the strength of their own delivery or conviction, offer convincing opinion in the guise of straightforward information.

- **Press releases**—news organizations rely on carefully constructed informational releases from the government, sports and entertainment agents, and corporations to put together the news. While as reported these statements of information can seem like straightforward news items, they are carefully controlled by the organizations who release them and often serve a political or economic agenda.

Some news conventions

Every organization also has certain conventions of delivery. While these conventions are often established through use over time, they are often developed or refined based on positive or negative audience reception. Part of the organization of news, then, is the mode of presentation of news stories and this, in turn, affects what is considered news. If information does not fit into a conventional model, it may not be deemed "news worthy". Some of the conventions of news include the following:

- **Mystery**—the reporter is the investigator who will uncover the truth. For example, what is the secret behind this company's success? Why did the government fail to respond to threats in time? What is the source and prognosis of the illness spreading through part of the country?

- **Therapy**—the reporter becomes someone we trust who will sympathize with us, allow us to find solace in times of disaster, and help to explain confusing situations such as terrorist attacks, natural disasters and economic turmoil. Therapeutic reporters often represent their audience when confronting government officials, questioning the motives of business leaders, or finding out about the love lives of celebrities.

- **Adventure**—the reporter often take us to new places where travel is difficult, lives are different, and we can gain new perspective on our own lives. While the piece of "news" itself might not be urgent, the reporter gives us access to lives that we can see as real, quaint, strange or exotic.

- **Arbitration**—the reporter plays the classic role of neutral observer of a complex or at times ambiguous story. Arbitration often does not produce a story with an easy answer but lets us see the complexity of a story and lets us view the news organization itself as intelligent, unbiased and willing to take on difficult issues.

Reception   Objectivity and Bias

While we may have been well trained to understand the intentions behind advertising or even to recognize the "spin" that politicians can put on their discussion of events, at times we take for granted the objectivity of news media. It can be argued, however, that every act of mass communication has some form of bias simply because there is an underlying intention that spurs the desire to communicate. Even if the intention of a speech act is to inform, the question becomes: Who decides what is information and why? Being on the lookout for bias is part of being critically literate and is arguably more difficult in today's media-saturated world when the lines between fact and opinion, news and entertainment, and public and private become increasingly blurred.

The following list suggests how bias can be detected in news media.

- **Selection and omission**—all news organizations have some kind of gatekeeper – whether it is an owner, editor or bureau chief – whose job it is to decide what goes in the news and what stays out. Decisions about what to report can be influenced by sales projections, the needs and sensitivities of advertisers, or the supposed importance of a news item based on ideological leanings.

- **Placement**—where and when a news item appears in a newspaper or on a television news programme matters. Important events appear first or near the top of a page, less important events are saved for the inside of the paper, a bullet on the side of the web page or the end of a broadcast.

- **Headline**—the size and content of a headline affects the way we read a story or may push us to a certain opinion without even reading the article. Choice of headline can reveal ideological bias even when there is a policy in a news organization to be consistent and objective in headlining practice.

- **Photographs and captions**—images can reveal bias in many ways. First, the choice of whether or not to include images in a story affects the way the story will be perceived or deemed important. Second, photos can be chosen to make stories more or less dramatic or emotional. Photos of people can be chosen that are either more or less flattering. Captions can be simply descriptive or can create irony.

- **Names**—the naming conventions in news can affect how we value a source of information. Bob Johnson sounds less impressive than Dr Robert Johnson, Director of the National Institute of Economics.

- **Statistics**—numbers can be used in a variety of ways. News organizations often estimate crowd sizes at political events, for example, and these numbers can vary widely. Saying that "many" people attended an event is different from saying "over 2,000".

- **Source control**—sometimes news organizations are very specific about their sources while other times the source is "a highly placed official". It is not always clear from whom we are getting our news. Much information is sourced from press releases issued by the organizations that are hoping for news placement.

- **Tone**—diction and general attitude that is created through language (through **mode**, for example) often indicates bias or point of view.

Blurring boundaries: infotainment and infomercials

When watching the news it is sometimes difficult to distinguish between editorial opinion, the opinion of a guest or analyst, and the news itself. The distinction becomes even more problematic in the case of infotainment and infomercials. Infotainment is a genre that is distinguished by the attempt to both entertain and inform. While infotainment can be part of a news programme (a human interest story, for example, that tells the tale of a lost bear or a young person's success in a spelling competition) entire networks now exist that create programming to explore history, geography, the weather, biography or sports stories in a way that educates and entertains. The problem, however, becomes distinguishing the line between truth and exaggeration for effect. In a similar way, but perhaps one easier to identify, infomercials are extended advertisements that are created to resemble a news programme or an informative talk show. A celebrity host and guests may discuss a miracle diet for a full 30 minutes without clearly letting viewers know that the whole programme is a paid advertisement for the diet product. While viewers may know they are watching an extended commercial, the packaging of a sales pitch in the genre of informational broadcasting can be misleading.

Activity

Choose a significant story in the today's news and compare how it is reported in three newspapers either from the same city or from very different markets. Look at the elements above and make a chart comparing the way the story uses or reveals the different elements. What does your comparison suggest about bias? What are the possible reasons for the different biases (economic, political, cultural, market size)?

Production   Advertisement

Creating your own advertisement could be an interesting in-class project that sheds light on issues in any part of the course. For a **written task 1**, an advertisement could be your choice of text type for an investigation of a language issue or even of an element in a work of literature. You could also consider working on an advertisement, or even a whole mock advertising campaign, for the basis of a **further oral activity** (here you would have to be careful to remember that you are being judged on the oral part of your presentation while the advertisement you create may be background, a spur for class discussion or part of a larger presentation). In any case, it is always important to remember that on the one hand you are demonstrating your knowledge and understanding of the text type and on the other hand you are showing your knowledge and understanding of "content". But **what is content**? If you are working on a written task for language and mass communication your content may actually be the elements of advertising themselves (manipulation, layout, use of language). If you are studying language in cultural context, while the advertisement itself could be for sporting goods, your "content" could be the connection between language and gender. An advertisement designed for the literature: critical study section of the course may explore a theme in one of your novels, or highlight aspects of a particular character.

Without reading a rationale, which would help to explain the student's intentions in this piece, consider this advertisement a student created and developed for a written task 1. The piece is meant to explore the use of narrative elements in advertisement. For more on advertising copy see page 81.

When you know where you've come from...and where you're going.

When you were you thought you knew it all. You were proud, energetic, daring and maybe a bit brash. Now that you are older you are all of those things still. But you have a bit more. Some call it wisdom, some call it humility. We like to say you have a story. And you understand that as time goes on and you have victories and defeats large and small, you reach a have a little catharsis, become a more complex character. And you understand that sometimes great things come our of small places where attention is paid and personalities are nurtured. In 1789 Fergus McCullen knew the value of telling a complex tale that only the attentive listener could fully understand. In 1789 Fergus McCullen turned his attention to a small and precocious whiskey that would grow through the ages.

PERFECTLY AGED   PERFECTLY BALANCED   PERFECTLY COMPLEX

YOUR STORY

Examiner comments

While this advertisement is a promising idea for a **written task 1**, it is not fully or carefully executed. First, exploring the notion of the use of narrative in advertising is interesting but does this advertisement itself do anything but copy the style of using narrative? Other elements could have been tied together to explore narrative further. There is some confusion here because the advertisement is about narrative and attempts to use narrative. Is this meant to be about how the product has an implied story or about how a product needs to fit with a consumer's story? A good rationale here, of course, could help to guide the examiner and explain the intentions. The image could also do a bit more to tell a story. Another approach here may be to create two parts for the assignment: an actual advertisement like the one shown along with a "statement" pitching the campaign to a client. This could help explain the intended use of narrative. In terms of understanding of the conventions of the text type chosen, the task is adequate but not as polished or exact as an actual advertisement would be.

Reception Stereotype

A stereotype is a commonly held idea or image of a person or group based on an oversimplification of an observed or imagined trait or appearance. In relation to mass communication, stereotypes can often slip into seemingly objective reporting because of the biases of owners, editors, writers, directors or producers. While stereotypes are by definition reductive, stereotyping stems from a need to cull information and simplify the world around us. Media of all kinds use stereotypes, at times unknowingly or innocently, to quickly characterize an individual, to create an image, or to communicate a feeling or idea in a story. While we are all familiar with hurtful stereotypes, (even stereotypes that can be hurtful despite seeming positive) such as the "nerd" or the "jock" (and others that we won't bother to elaborate here), media producers can easily take a simple image and play on our preconceptions in order to make a point. Everything from "elderly teacher" to "young schoolboy" can entail elements of stereotype that may or may not be exploited in mass communication.

In order to think about the uses and effects of stereotype, work though the activities below.

Activity

1. Categorization

Newspapers, magazine, television news programmes and other media use categorizing terms to describe a person in a way that is relevant to the piece at hand. An article about a fire, for example, could interview John Smith, a "chief fire investigator". For the purposes of the article, there is no reason to discuss other elements of John Smith's identity such as his age, appearance or level of experience. On the other hand, the same article might cite the "new, young chief fire investigator" giving us the impression that perhaps we should view his opinions with a bit of scepticism. **Using any of the articles or blogs** in this book or, better yet, a full issue or page of a magazine or newspaper, write down as many categorizing phrases as you can find. Are there any stereotypical images or ideas conjured by these phrases? Are there positive, negative or neutral connotations to these phrases?

Activity

2. Diversity audit

The media has often been criticized for either negatively portraying minority groups or for simply not portraying the diversity of a community. Use the basic format below to perform a "diversity audit" of an individual newspaper or magazine in order to consider the uses and effects of stereotyping.

Name of newspaper or magazine:

Total # of stories or articles in issue:

Total # of stories or articles featuring minorities:

For each article featuring minorities, record the following:

Headline:

Page #:

Topic:

Portrayal: Was the portrayal of the minority or minority group positive? Was the portrayal negative? Was it neutral? Discuss the complexities of the portrayal and its effect on meaning or your point of view.

Activity

3. Stereotyping and school

The school is a breeding ground for all kinds of stereotyping of students, teachers and support staff. How many "categorizing phrases" can you come up with that may be used in positive or negative ways in a school? How do teachers view students? How do students view teachers? How do students view each other? What are the positive and negative stereotypes of support staff (for example secretaries, caretakers, food service workers, security staff)?

Activity

The following excerpt from a discussion of the portrayal of the female hero of the film version of *The Hunger Games* touches on many of the complicated issues involved in the media's portrayal of gender identity. The brief discussion below touches on societal attitudes towards appropriate roles, the portrayal of sexuality in film, the responsibility of art in the representation of gender and even the change in gender portrayal over the years. Read this discussion and then, using this discussion as a model, attempt a similar analysis of gender representation (either male or female) in the texts throughout this book. In particular, you could consider the portrayal of Huck Finn on page 204 or the image of the man in the graphic novel on page 207. How do these gender representations use or perpetuate existing stereotypes? How do they subvert stereotypes?

Film critics' discussion of *The Hunger Games*.

SCOTT All of this means that, as she sprints through the forest, Katniss is carrying the burden of multiple symbolic identities. She's an athlete, a media celebrity and a warrior as well as a sister, a daughter, a loyal friend and (potential) girlfriend. In genre terms she is a western hero, an action hero, a romantic heroine and a tween idol. She is Natty Bumppo, Diana the chaste huntress of classical myth, and also the synthesis of Harry Potter and Bella Swan—the Boy Who Lived and the Girl Who Must Choose.

Ms Collins's novels are able to fuse all of these meanings into a credible character embedded in an exciting and complex story. I think, in spite of some shortcomings, that the movie also succeeds where it counts most, which is in giving new and die-hard fans a Katniss they can believe in.

DARGIS Certainly the character is strong enough to survive Gary Ross's direction and the miscasting of Jennifer Lawrence, who turned 21 around the time the film wrapped. My problem with her in the role (which, needless to say, isn't her fault but that of those who hired her) is that she looks like the adult woman she is instead of a teenager who, a few years before the story starts, as Katniss says in the first book, had been "skin and bones" and, as a consequence of those hungry years, looks like a "young girl". It's hard not to wonder if the producers cast an adult to make the violence more palatable; it's also hard not to think that they cast a woman with a rocking body instead of a young girl partly because they were worried that guys wouldn't turn out for a female-driven story.

Yet Katniss is such a sensational character that she fires up your imagination, even when Mr Ross seems intent on dampening it, and to embrace all those identities you mentioned. That she embodies these different roles at the same time makes her feel new, particularly because in contemporary American cinema, female characters are (still!) often reducible to type (mother, girlfriend, victim). That's worth looking at, as are the ways she differs from other heroines, including one of the greatest, Ripley in the "Alien" series. Katniss isn't locked into gender. She has assumed her dead father's responsibility as the family provider and is also a mother surrogate for her sister, Prim. But Katniss doesn't shift between masculinity and femininity; she inhabits both, which may mean that neither really fits.

Source: From *A Radical Female Hero from Dystopia*. A conversation between reviewers A O Scott and Manohla Dargis. *New York Times*. 8 April 2012. www.nytimes.com/2012/04/08/movies/katniss-everdeen-a-new-type-of-woman-warrior.html?_r=1.

Reception   Persuasion and Rhetorical Analysis

Persuasion

While many texts attempt to inform an audience, many attempt to persuade. It could be argued that persuasion of some sort is at the heart of most mass communication that goes beyond pure (if this is possible) entertainment. While persuasion is obviously the sole intent of **propaganda** or even **advertising**, persuasion can be seen in the lowly text message that, in its "ping" is at the very least persuading someone to "hear" the message above the noise of information and popular culture.

Rhetorical analysis

Rhetoric broadly refers to the study of how to persuade or the analysis of the ways in which texts (oral, written and visual) attempt to persuade. Rhetorical analysis, then, is concerned with how a text works to convince an audience through various semiotic strategies. Rhetoric functions as close relationships among **rhetor** (speaker, author), **text** and **audience**, often referred to as the rhetorical triangle (see below).

The job of rhetorical analysis amounts to considering the following.

- Who is the audience (implied or actual)?
- What is the context of the argument or the audience?

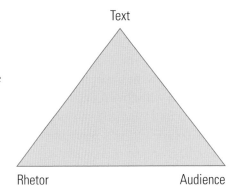

- What is the context of the speaker? (This could include the speaker's reputation or attributes such as timbre of voice in a spoken speech.)
- What are the effective stylistic features of the text?
- How do these elements work together to persuade?

In classical Greek times, Aristotle outlined ways of persuading an audience and the distinctions he made are still used in rhetorical analysis today. Aristotle suggested that an audience is persuaded in three ways.

- **Ethos**—members of an audience are persuaded by their belief in the honesty of the speaker.
- **Pathos**—an audience is persuaded by the emotional content of a message.
- **Logos**—an audience is persuaded by the actual argument or reasoning in the text.

A solid analysis of a speech act can come from considering the broad aims of rhetorical analysis along with the three methods of persuasion. Analysis should also take into consideration **kairos**, or the general and historical context of the speech act—a speech given by a king before the troops enter battle depends greatly on context for effect.

In terms of analysing the stylistic devices in a persuasive text it is important to consider the elements that you are studying throughout this book but, broadly, you should consider word choice, figurative language and structure (from overall organization to patterns such as repetition).

Using the blog entry on pages 24–25 as an example, your sentence might look like this:

The blogger's argument that you can look and feel good with a DIY haircut and experimental outfits will persuade fashion-forward young men and women, because they agree that looking good needn't be expensive (logos).

Or your sentence might look like this:

The blogger's argument that you should experiment with hairstyles and outfits will persuade fashion-forward young men and women, because they have a desire to look fashionable without spending much money (pathos).

What are other possibilities here? Think about both more specific arguments being made, images and words being used, and emotions aroused.

Activity

Use the basic outline below to write a brief statement of rhetorical analysis based on a political speech or an editorial from a magazine. You can use this same outline to analyse the texts found throughout this book (focusing first on the more obviously persuasive such as the blog entry on page 101.

The blanks here should be filled in with the particular **rhetor**, the basic **argument**, the particular implied or actual **audience** and the specific **reasons** related to ethos, pathos and logos.

_____'s argument
that _____ will/will
not persuade _____,
because _____.

Production   Speech

There are three questions to ask yourself: why would you give a speech, how do you write a speech, and what in the world does "giving a speech" have to do with the IB English A: language and literature course? First, you may find yourself in a situation, such as graduation, where you actually give a speech. More importantly (but less nerve-wrackingly), though, giving an oral presentation in front of a class is very similar to delivering a speech. In addition, a written speech could be a great text type to use for a **written task 1** or as a significant **further oral activity**. This section will give you an overview of how to go about writing a speech.

This process is important beyond production, however. Looking at how to prepare a speech can give you insight into the rhetorical strategies used in speeches in general and understanding these strategies is at the heart of this course.

First steps

Before even thinking about how to craft a speech you have to think about the why and what. The situation often dictates your topic as well as your general approach or tone. You should consider the following first.

Occasion—why is the speech being given? If you are delivering a graduation speech you know the occasion but you might want to come up with ideas specifically about the occasion: Why is it important? What elements are already highlighted without the speech? When will you speak? When creating a written task, the supposed occasion should also be considered and either implied, directly stated, or mentioned in the rationale.

Audience—to whom will you be speaking? A graduation is difficult because your primary audience may be peers but you will also address family members, guests, teachers and administrators. This audience should greatly affect your speech. Politicians, for example, often walk a fine line between appealing to a very specific and partisan audience sitting in the seats in front of them, and a varied and critical audience that will watch a short clip on television.

Topic—what will you talk about? It is important, right from the beginning, to try to narrow your ideas. It has been said that members of an audience forget 70 per cent of what they hear. Taking this into consideration you should make your main idea clear, you should be able to repeat the idea throughout the speech, and you should be able to build upon and support your idea.

Objectives—while part of your objective is to communicate your topic, you should also consider whether you are trying to inform, entertain, persuade or a bit of all three. You should also consider broader objectives. Do you want your audience to act on your speech? Or simply to consider your ideas? Do you want your audience to respond directly afterwards?

Building the speech

1. **Research**—don't forget this important stage. Support your argument or build your idea with quotations, references, details or even funny stories. Turn to the reception section on persuasion and rhetorical analysis to consider Aristotle's ideas on how audiences are persuaded (page 100). How can you find elements that will appeal to logic, or to emotion?

2. **Outline**—as in all writing, never forget the value of an outline.

3. **Write**—writing a speech is like writing an essay; but you should keep speeches short. The brevity of a speech goes beyond its overall length, however. If you look at a printed version of a politician's speech you will find the general trend today is to keep language direct, sentences short and paragraphs even shorter.

4. **Read and revise**—a speech is meant to be spoken so part of the revision process should be reading the speech out loud. If you stumble, you may want to rewrite.

Rhetorical effects

- **Repetition** is one of the most important rhetorical devices in a speech. If you want the audience to hear something, let alone remember it, you probably have to repeat it. A good rhetorical effect can be to repeat an idea a few times with subtle variation as the speech progresses to a climax.

- **Figurative language**—do not be afraid to use metaphor, interesting simile or evocative imagery. Recent studies suggest that even clichéd images (for example, the officer was "hard as nails") affect sensory parts of our brains and make a speech more evocative.

- **Delivery**—know your speech well, speak slowly, speak clearly and pause for effect.

Sample student work

For a written task 1, this student decided to write a speech to be given at a high school commencement ceremony by the character Benedick from Shakespeare's *Much Ado about Nothing*. While the student used some of the language of the play in the speech, the rationale stated that this speech would be put into in a contemporary setting: a modern day graduation. The speech would demonstrate the conventions of a speech, and graduation speech in particular, but would aim to explore as content the character's relationship with (or how the character is used to portray) the theme of man's fickle nature. Without thinking about content, consider how successfully this student has demonstrated the conventions of a public speech.

Sample student work

Honorable guest, teachers, and most importantly, members of the class 2013. It is an honor to be able to speak to you on this special occasion. While I hesitated to accept the invitation to speak today, I thought, "Hey, what harm can a few words do..." I have to admit that giving a speech is tough for me. I enjoy conversation but sitting and writing something that then you have to perform? This reminds me too much of school.

I do have a few things I can say to you today as you begin your adult lives. Don't do it!

Of course, I'm kidding. But I have had a varied life. I have fought in wars, spent lazy days at Italian villas, and courted many... or some... of the most eligible women in the land. So today I want to give you three pieces of advice: be free, stay single, get married.

An immediate recognition of text type, convention, audience.

Starting off with at least an attempt at humour fits the conventions of the genre. In addition, these lines begin to show a good sense of the character, referring to ideas brought up in the play.

Again: good in terms of conventions of the genre with another nod to the content of the play and character.

Good use of rhetorical strategy of emphasis through the use of "threes".

My wedding day was a special day for me. All the white dresses, the seductive veils, the flowers... all of the things a guy loves. The most interesting moment for me, however, came later that night. Bear with me. I had been reflecting on the revelry of the wedding party and I remarked that "man is a giddy thing". My wife Beatrice suggested that this was the most joyful things I have ever said, that I was full of light-hearted well-being. I had just meant that everyone seemed to be drinking too much and dancing with the old aunts. But today I wonder if I meant something else all together?

Giddy is whirling, spining, frivolous. Giddy allows you to do everything. Be free, stay single, get married.

The speech so far has a light touch that Benedick at times displays in the play. There is good relation so far to the play ... it will be interesting to see where the discussion goes. These last two paragraphs really work as a speech: humorous, brief, clear in repetition, an underlying thoughtfulness an attempt to give advice upon entering the adult world.

Reception   Advertisement

Advertising today takes a surprising number of forms. While print advertisements, television commercials and roadside billboards are still prevalent, advertising agencies are always looking for creative ways to sell products. Current advertising takes advantage of the viral networking possibilities of social media, the alternative quality of place-based or installation art, and the potential to exploit other media such as the television news programme or the article format (using infomercials and special magazine supplements). One of the most important skills a critical consumer of advertising can have today is the ability first to recognize advertising. Once recognized, however, advertisements still have the power to seduce and persuade.

An analysis of an advertisement is similar to the analysis of any text. All of the reception skills in this book, as you have most likely seen already, are relevant to advertising. The elements below are traditional features of print advertising and can be used as a base for any critical look at a text. It is also interesting to consider why certain advertisements may *not* use these traditional features or how either adherence to the norm or subversion of traditional techniques is relevant to intentions.

- **Headline**—often the most obvious portion of the advertisement, the headline grabs attention. The headline will not necessarily mention the name of the product but will attempt to be intriguing. Size, colour and placement, along with diction, connotation and tone, are all important in the headline.

- **Image or artwork** appears in almost all advertisements. An advertisement can use photography, drawings or simply basic design to enhance the look of the page. You will notice that there is an important synergy between artwork, headline and the angle (or particular tactic) being used in an advertisement. An image may attempt not only to attract attention but to reinforce the narrative of advertising copy.

- **Copy** is the text of the advertisement. While many advertisements purposefully avoid long copy that may not be read or may not quickly capture the attention of a viewer, long copy is sometimes used to imitate the conventions of editorials or informational articles. Interesting copy has the potential to hold the consumer's attention for longer than a headline and also has the potential to establish trust or develop narrative.

- **Slogan**—this may be different from a headline in that it is consistently associated with the brand over a series of advertisements. Slogans—short, memorable phrases—not only characterize a product or company but they are designed to be memorable.

- **Logo**—a logo often appears in an advertisement in order to further cement the symbolic image of a brand in the consumer's mind.

- **Signature**—the signature is simply the added information that can help a consumer find the product. The signature could include everything from a list of stores to a website.

The functional elements of an advertisement combine to convince a reader or viewer to purchase a product or service. The following are the basic principles behind the design of an advertisement.

- **Attention**—an advertisement can only function if it is noticed. Attention can be generated through placement (in a particular part of a newspaper or magazine, during a certain television show, on popular bus route), imagery, colours, music or celebrity images among many other gimmicks.

- **Trust or positive association**—consumers tend to buy from companies they trust. Sometimes the entire point of an advertisement is to build or restore trust in a company rather than to make a one-time sale of a particular product. Trust or positive associations can be made through good humour, a pleasant image or even the quality and professionalism of the advertisement itself.

- **Desire**—advertisements need to let consumers know why they should want a product. Sometimes advertisements provoke desire by associating a product with an existing desire such as the desires to be wealthy, to have a beautiful partner or to be a good person.

- **Action motivation**—while sometimes desire is enough to get a consumer to act (buy a product or register on a website) there are times when advertisements include specific calls to action. A call to action may be a statement ("Stop by our store soon!") or it may involve the demonstration of an action since people are often motivated by the actions of others (for example, a person stepping up to the counter at a fast food restaurant or shaking the hand of a friendly car salesman).

Activity

The following advertisements were created by the US Federal Trade Commission to teach children how to recognize various forms of product placement. In what ways do these advertisements conform to the attributes outlined above? How do they use or vary these attributes in creative ways?

A text message advertisement:

An "advertorial" (or an advertisement in a magazine that is made to look like article copy):

An advertisement in a video game:

Reception   Editorial

While much of a newspaper or news magazine attempts to offer bias-free news and information, the editorial is a place where the news organization can offer opinion on an issue, reflect on current events or promote critical thinking. Editorials are opinion pieces that attempt to reflect the ideas of an institution—of a critical, news-gathering organization—and as such often portray a consensus opinion that attempts to be balanced and thoughtful. Often, in order to clarify the differences among opinion, factual reporting and advertising, newspapers or online news sites keep editorials and opinion pieces by individuals in a separate section known as the "op-ed" pages. The editorials of large news organizations have the potential to influence public opinion and can even work as a call to action, influencing public debate, corporate culture, and local or national elections.

The editorial is an interesting text type to examine in relation to its influential position as well as its rhetorical strategies. Because an editorial does not have a single author (it may even be the result of a vote and the collaborative writing of an editorial board) it often has the air of authority and lack of personal bias that an opinion piece from a featured journalist or outside commentator may not carry. The presumption of lack of bias, however, can never be completely solid. For one thing, a newspaper is often owned by a corporation with its own interests. Also, newspapers, like many media institutions, rely on support from advertisers and these corporations need to protect their interests. And though an editorial may reflect a group opinion and careful deliberation, it is still written by people with their own leanings, hopes or motives. Rhetorically speaking, an editorial capitalizes on its own position of authority (often a very important position near the front of a newspaper, magazine or website). Editorials are known for being concise, clear and reasoned, and they usually incorporate the following contextual or rhetorical features:

- **Timeliness**—an editorial focuses on a current news event or pressing concern of the community. Editorials function through their immediate relevance.

- **Clearly stated thesis**—an editorial always makes its opinion clear from the start, often stating an argument or major decision in the title itself.

- **Reasoned argument**—an editorial attempts to make an argument based on a systematic argument that is clearly outlined in the body of the article.

- **Clear explanation or interpretation**—an editorial often informs as it argues. Facts and figures as well as key issues that influenced the decision of the editorial board are outlined in the body.

- **Balanced approach**—an editorial attempts to convince the reader of its authority and relative lack of bias by considering (and dismantling) opposing opinions.

- **Persuasion or praise**—an editorial clearly works to persuade and often becomes a call to action.

Activity

A brief editorial

The editorial below was selected because you may be able to separate yourself from the political debate being discussed. In this way, you can read the editorial for its rhetorical features. As you read, see if you can identify the features listed above. Also, take note of how you may be able to use the text type of the editorial as a model for a **written task 1**. Though you are not allowed to write an essay for **written task 1**, the editorial is a close cousin to the essay and is a permissible text type. You may want to take care if you choose to use an editorial as your text type, however. The editorial should not be a way for you to bypass the intent of the written task and simply produce an essay on some topic. An editorial on a language issue, for example, should be timely and relevant, and should clearly follow some of the features above (or some other features that you may study in your own class and you can mention in your rationale).

Break the Logjam

This has to be good news for the embattled UPA government. The main opposition party, the BJP, has sent out a positive signal for cooperation with the government three days before Parliament reconvenes its budget session. Arun Jaitley's statement that the BJP would support the smooth passage of the pension fund regulatory development authority Bill—an important item on the reforms agenda—raises fresh hopes of breaking the policy logjam at the Centre.

Given that the current policy paralysis has slowed growth, fuelled inflation and spooked business all round, it's of the very essence that the government gets cracking on reform. If and when passed, the pension Bill is expected to open up multiple savings and investment channels. Lending statutory backing to the pension regulator, the legislation will steer funding for long-gestation infrastructure sectors. Besides, it would facilitate alternative sources of low-cost retirement savings, and ensure a market-linked safety net for workers in both organised and unorganised sectors. So far the Left parties and the BJP have been instrumental in stalling the Bill. As a result, it has been hanging fire for seven years. However, things could now be looking up. The BJP decided to change tack after the government accepted its amendments to the pension Bill. If the present spirit of cooperation endures, the forthcoming Parliament session could well turn out to be a productive exercise in passing fruitful legislation. But for this we need to see robust collaboration, not only between the ruling coalition and the opposition, but also from recalcitrant allies within the UPA, like the Trinamool Congress. Of late we have repeatedly witnessed Parliament being held hostage by the BJP as well as the Trinamool Congress, stalling a range of legislations like FDI in retail, the pension Bill and so on. It's not that the Congress is a united house itself. There are rumblings within the ruling party on crucial financial sector Bills, including the banking amendment legislation, aiming to lift the 10% cap on voting rights of investors, and raising the FDI limit from

Production · Blog

The blog (from the original "web log") is a common text type and is important in terms of a critical approach to the use of language in mass communication. The blog is also likely to be a popular text type for the **written task 1** or as the vehicle for discussion or presentation in the **further oral activity**. While the blog may seem to incorporate almost any kind of writing on a wide variety of topics, some features distinguish it not only from other internet-based writing but also from traditional editorials or opinion pieces.

Features of a blog

Like a log or a journal entry, a blog is meant to be a chronological collection of reflections by the user. Because a blog exists in read–write digital format of the internet, the blog allows for the possibility of a wide audience as well as for the possibility of interaction through readers' comments. The original web logs were exactly what the word implies, a log of a user's visits to various websites. A web log was a way of keeping track of sites visited and sharing insights about them with other users. While blogs have come a long way, they remain a place to comment upon other websites, blogs and readings or viewings in general. While blogs can be very personal, as they have moved into the institutional realm of mass communication (where professional journalists, for example, might maintain blogs connected to their newspaper) rules of conduct similar to the rules that govern editorials and communication in the mass media, in general, have often been taken up by professional bloggers.

Today, the world of the blog spans from young children blogging about their summer vacations to professional philosophers blogging about the ethics of euthanasia. Some other features of a blog include:

- a posting of topics in chronological order
- a focus on response to a text (or event)
- a simple layout that highlights the topic of the day
- brevity of individual posts
- a simple option for readers' comments
- a button that allows readers to subscribe
- links to social profile sites
- category pages for the filing or archived posts
- a clear feature or menu bar.

While it was noted above that the growth of professional blogging has brought about a certain amount of professionalism in editorial comment (one frequently cited rule is "Don't say anything about a person or text in a blog that you wouldn't say in person"), blogging has become so widespread that almost any tone and purpose can be found in an individual blog. Recently, blogs have become less text-based as well, allowing users to post daily images or short messages easily.

You should take some care when approaching the blog as a **written task 1**. First, consider why the blog is an appropriate text for use in conveying your understanding. Second, you should take care to indicate your understanding of the text type and not to simply reproduce an essay and call it a blog post. The student sample work below is interesting in that the rationale suggested that if Jake Barnes, the character in Ernest Hemingway's *The Sun Also Rises*, were alive today (or if the novel were taking place in the digital age) the blog would be the medium of expression that Jake would use to express his thoughts or perhaps even to post his dispatches from Paris.

Sample student work

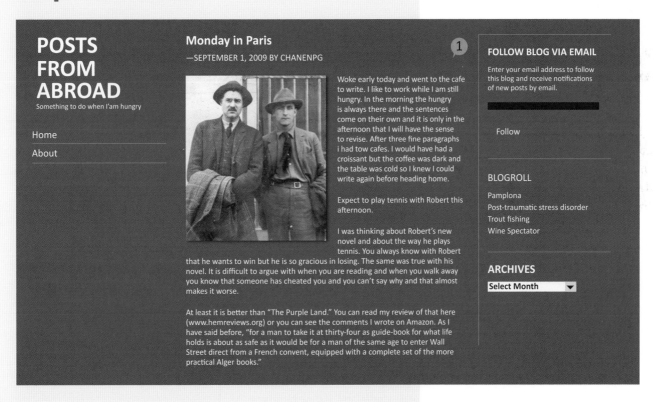

Examiner comments

The blog clearly demonstrates an understanding of the text type. Not only does the post look like a blog, both the language and the rationale show that the student has made an interesting connection between Hemingway's influential style and the style of the contemporary blog. The candidate has also made an interesting connection between Jake Barnes' attitude and profession in relation to the blog text type. The page above (and a following page not pictured) have all of the common elements of a blog from a title, date, list of links and a place to comment. The text itself and the comments (on the following page, from Brett Ashley, Robert, Bill and other characters) are all interesting, to the point and relevant both to the work at hand and the text type.

Reception Political Campaign

Attention to language becomes very important in political campaigns. During the long fight of a political campaign, it is very difficult to determine from where a message originates let alone to deconstruct – by looking at images and text – the meaning and clear intent of a message. Today's political campaigns exploit every type of medium available for mass communication from the projected human voice at a campaign rally to the Twitter post from organized supporters. For this reason, and because the political process is important to our daily lives and our futures, political campaigns are an interesting laboratory for the study of language and mass communication as well as the perfect example of where critical literacy is essential.

The analysis of mediated language in political campaigns involves putting into practice all of your reading, listening and viewing skills. While contemporary political campaigns are quite complex and are essentially an industry unto themselves, there are certain aspects to media use in the campaign process that have been seen for years in both local and national races. The categories and issues below can get you started and push you to some complex questions.

- **Political advertising** is one of the most significant forms of communication during a political campaign. With a wide variety of media available for communication, the advertisement – short and engaging – can be one of the best ways to reach an audience. Today, political advertising takes many forms (including viral online advertising) and is paid for by candidates, large organizations and even individuals.

Activity

Find a political advertisement from your community or from a political race with which you are familiar. The terms below are issues or elements that advertisements frequently use to persuade an audience or generate support. Note which of the issues or elements you can find in the advertisement you found: **patriotism** (an appeal to patriotism or a claim to strong patriotism)**, gender** (an appeal to a particular gender or gender-related issue), **family** (a focus on the importance of family), **celebrity** (either using a celebrity in an advertisement or the attempt to portray the candidate as a celebrity), **bandwagon** (giving the impression that everyone else is already supporting the candidate), **insults** (belittling or insulting the opponent), **statistics** (using facts and figures to support an argument), **populism** (appealing to or portraying the candidate as a "regular" person), **heart** (creating a story that is emotional), **integrity** (focusing on the strong values of a candidate), **fear** (generating fear in relation to the other candidate or suggesting that the candidate can alleviate fears), **stirring images or music**.

- **Political debates** are a good opportunity for potential voters to view candidates in action and to see their (partly) unscripted answers to important questions. Debates, however, generate income for media outlets and are formatted not just to be informative but dramatic. While watching a debate, consider the following. How does the opening of the debate create interest or tension? How does the set itself imply importance or drama? To what extent is a debate structured to inform as opposed to being structured to create tension and hold interest? How are topics chosen and what is the nature of those topics or questions? Are they important? If so, to whom? How is post-debate analysis handled and who has a chance to speak during the analysis?

- **Political reporting** from newspapers, magazines, television news and websites is a primary means of disseminating campaign information. The news about political campaigns can be difficult to decipher, however, because of the variety of sources for news stories. First, news often is gathered from **press releases** from the political campaigns themselves. In addition, campaigns create **photo-opportunities** for their candidates, scheduling special events at which a candidate can be photographed in a "newsworthy' situation (for example visiting a school or giving a speech at a military base). The influence of reporting on political campaigns is quite complex.

Some interesting but debatable ideas can help you to consider the influence of the news on a campaign.

- **The importance of information**—in the 1970s analysis of the influence of the media on the political process suggested that while it seems that the news shapes the issues in a campaign, there is a greater correlation between media coverage and voting results when the audience decides what information is important. The theory of "information seeking" suggests that viewers have issues in mind and look to news coverage to give them information in relation to issues. This very theory, perhaps, is one of the reasons why campaigns poll voters to find first where interest lies before generating newsworthy text. Studies may suggest that the news media is unsuccessful in persuading but successful in informing, but how does a campaign work to get the audience to look for particular types of information?

- **The two-step flow model**—in the 1940s the theorists Elihu Katz and Paul Lazarsfield suggested that there are two steps to the mass media communicative process in political campaigns. Their studies suggested that people are not directly influenced by the mass media or direct reporting during the political process but are more influenced by active audience members who become opinion leaders and in turn influence voters. We can easily imagine that at times this process can be quite personal: you, slightly disinterested (a passive audience member), watch the news with your intelligent and passionate friend. After watching a news report on a candidate, your friend distills his views and explains his opinion to you, thus persuading you to vote for a particular candidate. Today, news programmes themselves repeat this mediated process. What is more important, for example, a debate or the expert opinions that follow a debate? Grooming, choosing and placing "opinion leaders" is certainly important.

We communicate differently when we communicate with a large audience. Not only is our message mediated through some format, changing how we structure the message in the first place or changing how an audience receives the message, but the actual content of a message is affected by the very fact of communicating to an audience. Television news has a responsibility to create a programme that will not offend (for example) and, just as significantly, an individual may feel the responsibility to moderate content so that it is "appropriate" for a wide audience. When talking to a friend, you may not always say what you are thinking. The likelihood of keeping some ideas to yourself probably increases when you are talking to a group. This form of self-censorship is closely related to the institutional censorship that usually comes to mind when we think of limiting or restricting our messages. If journalists are writing for a publication with a particular bias, they may purposefully slant articles, even if they have not been instructed to do so, simply so that the article will be more likely to be published. When considering any text it is worth thinking of what forces either have influenced the creation of the message or have conspired to keep certain information out of the message at hand, whether in the form of explicit institutional censorship or more subtle variations.

The state and the money

The most well-known form of censorship is the restriction of media outlets by a government. In some countries, governments can restrict access to certain publications, ban particular websites or limit the possible content of news programmes based on an assessment that material is harmful or immoral. In countries where there is generally free speech, a government may still choose to restrict the publication of certain types of information when that information is considered potentially harmful (for example, official secrets or certain information during a time of war).

In many countries where there is broad protection of speech, another form of censorship can be evident and that is from the power of money. In a market economy media outlets depend on subscriptions, advertising or a combination of both for their income and survival. The need to keep an audience interested can serve as a form of censorship. In a similar way, stories that are critical of the interests of advertisers may not make the page or the air. This may not be a subtle form of censorship but it is a very hard form of censorship to track. The complex relationships among corporations and media outlets, though public, are not well known. For the active reader it is most important to be critical of stories and to push to think of **audience** and **purpose**. If we think about to whom an article is directed and why, we begin to uncover the sometimes conflicting forces behind the intentions.

Activity

While newspapers and television news can be easily regulated, communication on the internet is open and partially unfiltered. The internet is the perfect place to practise free speech. Many critics herald the internet as the place where uncensored mass communication can bring about political and societal change. While in many countries we are free to speak our minds, however, we are equally free to live without harassment or hatred. Most societies have laws censoring the use of "hate speech". Go to one of the websites you frequent and ask yourself the following questions. Does the internet encourage free speech? Is there any limit to what you can say on the internet? Can free speech on the internet affect speech in other forums? What are the lines between thoughtful criticism and hate? Are the viral capabilities of the internet a reason why, perhaps, speech should at times be restricted?

Reception | **Popular Song**

The popular song is a distinctive text type. While the term itself may be broad and may include a wide variety of style, including driving rock anthems, rhythmic hip-hop and synthetic-sounding electronics, the key element is an appeal to a wide audience. Musically speaking, even diverse popular songs work within relatively clear parameters. Songs that reach a wide market have a catchy melody, a clear rhythm and repetitive structure. More interestingly for the purposes of this course, popular songs serve as an example of how show business creates and sells a particular kind of message. In addition to the links between the popular song and advertising, marketing and culture, the popular song is also interesting as an example of a short but intriguing "media speech event".

The lyrics of songs are a unique case of linguistic communication. While song lyrics have much in common with poetry, as a text type that is closer to spoken poetry, song lyrics are subject to problems of intelligibility. A reader can slowly and carefully peruse and analyse a poem, or transcribed song, on the page. A listener to a song or spoken poetry, however, listens and possibly mishears in real time. Even when listening to a recording there may be problems since words that are not written are influenced by inflection and emphasis. Songs push the limits of intelligibility even further by shortening words to fit a rhythm, elongating vowels, or actually losing the words to the sound of instruments. Music can also change the connotation or effect of words. Happy words sung to a sad melody lose their pep. The misunderstanding, then, of words is interesting: how essential is the usual literal meaning to the understanding of a song?

Song case study: *Somebody That I Used to Know*

The song *Somebody That I Used to Know* by Gotye (featuring Kimbra) is a perfect example of the media event that is a pop song. The song was originally released in Australia in June of 2011. The artists singing the song brought a certain global quality to the work from the start. Gotye (the stage name for Wouter DeBacker) is Australian-Belgian and Kimbra, the featured artist, is from New Zealand. The song was almost instantly popular in Australia and New Zealand and soon spread to Europe. Long before it was released in North America, the song had gained exposure through the music video that received over 300 million views on Youtube. Its popularity grew over the course of the next year aided in part by all of the following: an encouraging Tweet from a popular actor and tech activist, another Tweet from singer Katie Perry, an appearance by the duo on the US television show *Saturday Night Live*, a cover version of the song performed on the popular musical television show *Glee*, and a popular Youtube cover by the band Walk Off the Earth. By April 2012, the song had reached number 1 on popular music charts in at least 18 countries and in charts for a variety of genre (such as "rock" and "alternative") as well as accumulating 175 million views on Youtube. The global phenomenon raises questions about the influence of media on what we find engaging. Are we as influenced by marketing as we are by the quality of a song? What matters more: musical qualities, lyrics, or a combination of the two?

Listeners and critics have commented on the attractive musical qualities of the song. Gotye's voice is described as "plaintive" and "reedy". Kimbra's voice is "clear" and "penetrating". The melody includes repetitive phrases that are easy to remember. The instrumentation of the song is sparse and clear, accentuating individual instruments and attractive sounds. Aside from the music, however, the lyrics of the song are striking, if at first simply because they are clear and easily understood. The lyrics of the song are intelligible, insistent and suggest—or even build—a narrative. In relation to language, you can analyse a song in relation to the very specific meaning and effects of the words in the lyrics. The media theorists Alan Durant and Marina Lambrou offer an interesting analysis of popular song and its effects based on listeners' reactions to what a popular song is or based on the "sort of speech event, or imagined speech event" a song enacts. The following brief analysis of "Somebody that I used to know" is based on Durant and Lambrou's analysis of pop songs.

Somebody That I Used To Know

[Gotye:]
Now and then I think of when we were together
Like when you said you felt so happy you could die
Told myself that you were right for me
But felt so lonely in your company
But that was love and it's an ache I still remember

You can get addicted to a certain kind of sadness
Like resignation to the end, always the end
So when we found that we could not make sense
Well you said that we would still be friends
But I'll admit that I was glad it was over

But you didn't have to cut me off
Make out like it never happened and that we were nothing
And I don't even need your love
But you treat me like a stranger and that feels so rough
You didn't have to stoop so low
Have your friends collect your records and then
change your number
I guess that I don't need that though
Now you're just somebody that I used to know

Now you're just somebody that I used to know
Now you're just somebody that I used to know

[Kimbra:]
Now and then I think of all the times you screwed me over
But had me believing it was always something that I'd done

And I don't wanna live that way
Reading into every word you say
You said that you could let it go
And I wouldn't catch you hung up on somebody that
you used to know

[Gotye:]
But you didn't have to cut me off
Make out like it never happened and that we were nothing
And I don't even need your love
But you treat me like a stranger and that feels so rough
You didn't have to stoop so low
Have your friends collect your records and then
change your number
I guess that I don't need that though
Now you're just somebody that I used to know

[x2]
Somebody
(I used to know)
Somebody
(Now you're just somebody that I used to know)

(I used to know)
(That I used to know)
(I used to know)
Somebody

Source: Gotye. 2011. *Somebody That I Used To Know* (from "Making Mirrors") featuring Kimbra.

The first three verses of the song are remarkable because they lack much of the repetition of content that we find in popular song. The language is relatively straightforward and clearly outlines a relationship. The speaker describes the end of a relationship and asks the listener, the implied audience, why she had to be so drastic or cold in her response to the end. The words focus on the pain and loneliness of a broken relationship. At the same time, the emotions are enhanced through an insistent rhetorical use of "threes". The repetition of the rhythmic structure musically draws out the last three words of each line. The final words focus on the variety of feeling in the song: "I still remember", "kind of sadness", "not make sense", "it was over", "used to know". These phrases highlight the singer's or speaker's perspective, his loss and his pain.

The song then switches perspectives and slightly switches tone from plaintive and questioning, to melancholy but firm. The female voice enters and gives her perspective on the relationship with the same musical qualities and the same stressing of repeated "threes". These trios of words, as throughout the song, alternate between rising and falling pitch, alternating the tone from pained and crying to more resigned and beaten. The song offers an interesting switch between the perspectives and experiences of "I" and "you" and when the voices sing in unison, it is as if the listener sees and feels from both points of view at once.

In the end the song tells a story of a male who once thought he was in love, saw his relationship end but then wonders why the break-up had to be so final, why the woman treated him as if he did not exist or as if she had never known him. The woman's response, however, suggests that she had herself been hurt, that she had doubted herself when the man had hurt her. The song suggests not only that they are now simply two separated people who "used to know" each other and nothing more, but that perhaps they never knew each other in the first place, despite their shared passion.

As Durant and Lambrou suggest in their analytic work, a discussion like this is a straightforward "reading" that we could do even with a poem. But as we listen to a pop song, how do we experience the event? How are we witness to a very particular kind of mediated and enhanced speech act? The four responses outlined below help to reveal the special nature of an emotional affective song and also suggest various ways an audience treats the phenomenon of popular music in general. These basic responses show the ways we can respond to a wide variety of media language events that are experienced at a distance and often out of context.

Response 1

This is a very personal song based on the experiences of a failed relationship. The singer has written the lyrics and the song gives his perspective on the break-up with the added insight of stepping briefly into his lover's shoes. This song is like reading a work of non-fiction. When I listen, I feel the complex emotions of the singer-songwriter.

Response 2

It feels as if the singer is addressing me in this song. When the male voice accuses "you" of being so cold, I think about how I have acted in the past or how I might have inadvertently hurt someone because of my own emotions. I then sympathize with the female voice because it is like I am given a chance to respond. This song not only speaks to me but gives me a brief chance to speak.

Response 3

I can completely identify with the voice of the singer in this song. I have had this experience before or a very similar experience. I "cry" along with the lead singer and feel a sense of guilt when the female voice begins her response.

Response 4

The song is just a song. The lyrics do not matter much because they are essentially following the typical rules of popular song in discussing love gained and lost. In addition, the story itself is basic. My enjoyment of the song comes more from the sounds. The "people" in the song are just made-up characters.

Social media is part of the driving force behind what was once considered the revolution of web 2.0 or the development of the internet as a place for production and sharing. The internet, a social media place more specifically, is a place for both extended conversation and quick interaction. It is also a laboratory for studying language change, the power of language and the relationships among language, media and culture. As the use of social media sites continues to grow among all age groups, the nature of communication on the internet expands, influencing language use in other media forms. Your study of social media, then, might take two tracks: one would be to study the way social media language use serves as an insight into social communication in general; another might be to study the distinctive features of online communication that may spur broader language change.

Language issues in social media

There are many interesting studies of social media and its effects on friendship, community building and even productivity in relation to school and work. Rich studies of language in social media are only just beginning. Many interesting studies consider the ways in which social media, and by extension language, relate to broad concerns such as gender, identity and power. Another perspective is to examine patterns in language use to see what insights are to be found. Some of the issues related to language use in social media include register, the use of jargon and the link between public versus private language. The following topics, many of which are under investigation by language and technology researchers, offer avenues for discussion, study and possible **written tasks**:

- the communication of emotion in microblogging (for example Twitter)
- modality and authoritative words and their effects in social media
- jargon and community identity on online forums
- diction and register as a means of discovering intended audience
- the choice of language (English, Arabic) as a means of identifying purpose in relation to global issues
- the importance of image to tone and intention in social media.

Activity

The hashtag (#) is a symbol used on micro-blogging sites such as Twitter to "tag" or help categorize the content of a message. A hashtag can be used to indicate location of sender (#LAX would mean the sender is at the Los Angeles international airport), a general emotion, sentiment or opinion (#FAIL), or the context or situation related to the message (#fireinperth, fire in Perth). The hashtag is an interesting linguistic feature of a message because it is a shorthand way of communicating information, suggesting who the intended audience of a message is, or building an audience for a message. Hashtags are also interesting because though they may be used by a brand (or a television show, for example), they are case sensitive, mutable and owned by no one (at least not yet) so they grow, change and die like an language or jargon in fast motion.

Extension

You could use the text type of a social media site for a **written task 1**. You could also analyse language use on a social media site as part of an essay at higher level for **written task 2**. As with all of the decisions you make in relation to the text type chosen for your written task, be sure that you have thought of an interesting reason why using a social network page, for example, would be an appropriate way to demonstrate your understanding of an issue.

Go to a microblogging site such as Twitter or Google+ and consider the language use in posts and the use of hashtags in particular. How does a hashtag indicate the intended audience of a message? Does a hashtag limit or broaden an audience? Does a hashtag indicate the purposes of a message? Does it broaden or narrow the purposes of a message? What are the effects of modifying a hashtag? Why would you purposefully modify a hashtag?

Production Oral Presentation

The oral presentation is a time-honoured means of assessment in the English classroom. You have probably had to stand up in front of the class many times to deliver a practised and polished presentation. The oral presentation, despite the fact that it may seem standard and boring, can be a very effective means of communicating ideas. For this reason, the oral presentation is often a good choice for an informative **further oral activity.** You could decide to do almost anything for your further oral activity, for example a role play, a debate or a structured discussion, and you could really push the boundaries for your oral performance in front of the class. The presentation may serve you well in the class and in the future.

The basics

Preparing for an oral presentation is, at first, exactly like preparing for writing an essay. You have to come up with an interesting topic, do your research, analyse your results and prepare your conclusions. In this course you could do an oral presentation on anything from aspects of characterization in a novel (for literature: critical study, though this would not be part of your IB assessment as a further oral activity) to the use of images in product packaging (for language and mass communication). The work you would do for a presentation would be the same as the kind of reading and analysis you do on a daily basis for the course with, of course, added depth and personal choice. The presentation itself would generally be a straightforward discussion with a clear introduction, body and conclusion and with detailed support integrated throughout. The following considerations are important to consider when planning an oral presentation.

- Is your topic engaging? Though you will have a captive audience, a provocative or interesting topic can electrify your audience and, in turn, improve your own performance.

- You should not only organize, but you should "signpost". Make it clear where you are going in an oral presentation because it is harder for a listener to follow a speaker than it is for a reader to follow the logic in an essay. While "first I will discuss" may sound mechanical in an essay, it may be the best guide for an audience in a presentation.

- Use graphics. PowerPoint is certainly not required. Nor is Prezi or any other presentation software. Since you have the chance to use images, however, and since you have studied images in this course, why not use pieces of text, images and graphics to clarify your presentation.

- Remember that you are performing. Speak clearly, watch your posture and moderate your tone and volume.

Variations

The **further oral activity** is a place for you to explore your own interests in relation to the course as well as a place to produce media content. While you need to remember that you are **marked on the oral itself**, you could base your presentation on the following kinds of groundwork.

- Create your own film. Your oral presentation could be an explanation of your intent and methods along with an analysis of your work.
- Design an advertising campaign for a product. Your oral presentation can be the "pitch" to the owners who may hire you for the project.
- Create a website based on a language issue.
- Conduct authentic linguistic research and present your findings in an oral presentation.

Sample student work

While the examiner comments are not particularly relevant here, these first two PowerPoint slides of an actual oral presentation give you an idea of an appropriate topic and the way it can be presented to a class. This student chose a topic that lends itself to an oral presentation because it is a discussion of a graphic novel and the student was able to focus attention easily on graphic detail by using the projector. The PowerPoint itself also helped the student to structure her presentation.

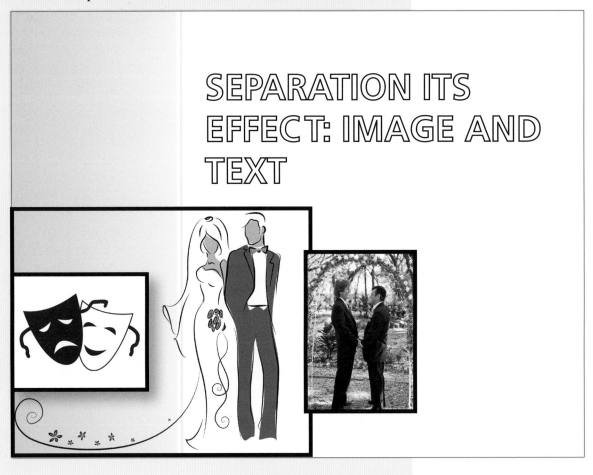

HELEN & FAMILY

- **Mother's detachment to family**
  - Use of expression to shows her nonchalance
    - **Constant expression**
  - Use of Spacing to describe the distance
    - **Alison's Adolescence**

Issue	The Future of English

Approximately 350 million people speak English as a first or native language. Another 400 million (or even up to a billion) more people have English as a strong second or other language (though this number is very difficult to estimate). English is the main language of the internet. English mass media messages circulate throughout the world in films, music and in viral internet postings. English has become so widespread, and is so frequently used as a means of common communication between speakers of different languages as a modern day *lingua franca*, that it is studied even more assiduously and used for global networking. Perhaps one of the most interesting things about this rise of English is not only that we live in dynamic times for the study of English, but that dynamic growth itself is a sure sign that this state of English will change dramatically.

The sections below provide an outline of some of the main factors in the spread, growth and change of English. While language change itself is an important topic in the language sections of this course, you can easily consider broad language changes through the lens of any topic related to language in cultural context or language and mass communication. Having some of these major points in your mind as you approach other topics in the course (or a variety of texts) will push you to consider the symbiotic relationships between language and culture.

The rise of English

- **Imperialism**—the obvious beginning of the spread of the English language was based on exploration, colonization and the imperialism of the British Empire. The language of government and trade became the necessary legal and economic language of people under the influence of the British Empire. In the late 1800s the United States began a similar expansion, creating further strongholds for English. Colonization and imperialism have many lasting effects and one of them is language change. In relation to language alone, when a country loses or surrenders control of another, it does not mean that language changes simply disappear. In India, for example, the use of English allowed people with different languages within the country to communicate with each other. In addition, the use of English gave many people an access to trade outside their local regions. Political and economic factors once again came into play, this time making it advantageous to retain English.

- **Trade**—the language of corporations spreads with the language of goods and services. Early imperialism created routes for, and was fired by, trade. As trade has increased and has become increasingly global, the need for a common language has grown.

- **Technology**—the language of the internet is English. This alone is a significant symbol of how technology can lead to language spread.

- **Education**—as trade has become more global, so has education. Important universities and the necessary communication between academics also calls for a *lingua franca*. Once again, language spread is self-perpetuation. Trade affects learning, which affects trade. The choice of a language for business affects the language of education which then further influences business to adopt a language that will facilitate growth.

The changing of English

Every one of the factors above is a factor in the spread of English but is also a factor in the changing of English. As languages are exposed to each other, they change (see the discussion of creole languages on page 10). Technology encourages new uses of a language and creates an environment for the development of new words. As different groups of people decide to use English for trade and education, their own particular uses of English change the language in terms of vocabulary, preferred usage and grammar. Growth means change.

The future of English

What does all of this mean to the future of English? While many people see a future in which English becomes more dominant as a global language, others suggest that certain factors, one of which is growth itself, may change the position of English.

- **Strength of bilingualism** As more people speak English as a second or other language, there is less dependence on native speakers as teachers, go-betweens and language leaders. In other words, English no long belongs (or will belong) somehow exclusively to first language English speakers. This may change, in many years, what English looks like.

A global English may end up looking very little like what we consider the English of today in a place such as Sydney, Australia (to pick an example at random). In addition, as more people speak two languages (Hindi and English, for example), they may be more likely to be employed by global corporations than speakers from say, the United States, who speak only English. How will the use of English change if more and more multilingual speakers from India and China fill more and more posts in multinational corporations?

- **Technology**—English may dominate the web but Chinese is getting close and Arabic is growing. Also, as automated translation technology improves, how necessary will it be to learn English?

- **Nationalism**—there is often a sense of pride in the language of a nation. English may be powerful but many nations, with changing technology and movement patterns, would be reluctant to use English as an official or encouraged language.

Men in battle: When a brotherly bond turns deadly

GRAEME SMITH

The relationship between men who go into battle together can be intense, a brotherly love as strong as any romantic bond. But when such relationships break down the results can be deadly.

France lost four troops on Friday in what appears to be a fratricidal shooting by an Afghan soldier. During the Vietnam war, enlisted men threw fragmentation grenades at their superiors so frequently that killing within the ranks became known as "fragging". In the Afghan war, the catchphrase is "green-on-blue" attacks in which Afghan forces (green) kill or injure their supposed NATO allies (blue).

The international forces recently took steps to conceal the scale of this problem but it's impossible to hide major incidents. Paris suspended training operations and threatened to withdraw its forces from the country after Friday's shooting, the second such green-on-blue incident in a month for the French troops.

French military officials immediately suggested that their men could have been killed by a sleeper agent, a Taliban member who infiltrated the ranks of the Afghan army. Such explanations are the standard NATO response in these circumstances, but a piece in Friday's *New York Times*, based on a classified report, raises the more troubling possibility that these killings indicate an erosion of the relationship between Afghan and NATO forces.

"[T]he report makes clear that these killings have become the most visible symptom of a far deeper ailment plaguing the war effort: the contempt each side holds for the other," writes the *Times*' correspondent Matthew Rosenberg. (A correction posted Friday on the *New York Times*' website notes that the classified report was described in an earlier article by the *Wall Street Journal*.)

The word "contempt" has become an important part of recent literature on relationships in the civilian world. Books such as Malcolm Gladwell's bestselling *Blink* popularized the theories of psychologist John Gottman, who claims that the emotional reaction most poisonous to the health of a marriage, the factor that consistently predicts the likelihood of divorce, is contempt.

I've seen expressions of contempt on both sides of the blue-green divide, among Afghan forces and NATO troops. Sometimes the foreign soldiers seemed willing to give their local counterparts the benefit of the doubt, and some of the Afghan troops openly admired their international allies.

More often, however, the two cultures clashed. Afghans considered their foreign counterparts disgustingly unhygienic for allowing their bare bums to touch the toilet seats in the latrines on military bases, which look nothing like traditional squat toilets—and NATO troops complained about the messy results. (One handwritten sign at a forward base contained a more vulgar phrasing of "Please do not defecate in the shower.")

Performance on the battlefield became another source of conflict. In 2007, I was riding with British troops in the Sangin valley of Helmand province when the Taliban ambushed our convoy. It was a terrifying moment: a hill beside us exploded in a shower of dirt as rocket-propelled grenades whistled from a nearby line of trees. The British troops reacted precisely the way they were trained to respond, throwing their vehicles into reverse and pulling out of the kill zone, while returning fire.

The Afghans did the opposite, charging straight forward into the oncoming bullets. I could not understand what the Afghans were screaming at their British allies, but their expression was obvious: contempt. After the battle, British officers struggled to explain to their local counterparts that tactical retreat isn't the same as cowardice.

On many other occasions it's been the NATO troops accusing the local forces of failing to stand and fight. In 2008, I obtained a classified military assessment of an insurgent ambush on a combined French and Afghan force in the Uzbin valley east of Kabul. The Afghan National Army's role in the battle was summarized with obvious contempt: "The ANA force spent much of the time lounging on the battlefield," the report said.

With feelings like that, it's no wonder the Afghans and international troops are having trouble making the relationship work.

Source: *Globe and Mail*. 20 January 2012, posted online.

Truth, lies and Afghanistan
How military leaders have let us down

BY LT. COL. DANIEL L. DAVIS

I spent last year in Afghanistan, visiting and talking with U.S. troops and their Afghan partners. My duties with the Army's Rapid Equipping Force took me into every significant area where our soldiers engage the enemy. Over the course of 12 months, I covered more than 9,000 miles and talked, traveled and patrolled with troops in Kandahar, Kunar, Ghazni, Khost, Paktika, Kunduz, Balkh, Nangarhar and other provinces.

What I saw bore no resemblance to rosy official statements by U.S. military leaders about conditions on the ground.

Entering this deployment, I was sincerely hoping to learn that the claims were true: that conditions in Afghanistan were improving, that the local government and military were progressing towards self-sufficiency. I did not need to witness dramatic improvements to be reassured, but merely hoped to see evidence of positive trends, to see companies or battalions produce even minimal but sustainable progress.

Instead, I witnessed the absence of success on virtually every level.

My arrival in country in late 2010 marked the start of my fourth combat deployment, and my second in Afghanistan. A Regular Army officer in the Armor Branch, I served in Operation Desert Storm, in Afghanistan in 2005–06 and in Iraq in 2008–09. In the middle of my career, I spent eight years in the U.S. Army Reserve and held a number of civilian jobs—among them, legislative correspondent for defense and foreign affairs for Sen. Kay Bailey Hutchison, R-Texas.

As a representative for the Rapid Equipping Force, I set out to talk to our troops about their needs and their circumstances. Along the way, I conducted mounted and dismounted combat patrols, spending time with conventional and Special Forces troops. I interviewed or had conversations with more than 250 soldiers in the field, from the lowest-ranking 19-year-old private to division commanders and staff members at every echelon. I spoke at length with Afghan security officials, Afghan civilians and a few village elders.

I saw the incredible difficulties any military force would have to pacify even a single area of any of those provinces; I heard many stories of how insurgents controlled virtually every piece of land beyond eyeshot of a U.S. or International Security Assistance Force (ISAF) base.

I saw little to no evidence the local governments were able to provide for the basic needs of the people. Some of the Afghan civilians I talked with said the people didn't want to be connected to a predatory or incapable local government.

From time to time, I observed Afghan Security forces collude with the insurgency.

From bad to abysmal

Much of what I saw during my deployment, let alone read or wrote in official reports, I can't talk about; the information remains classified. But I can say that such reports—mine and others'—serve to illuminate the gulf between conditions on the ground and official statements of progress.

And I can relate a few representative experiences, of the kind that I observed all over the country.

In January 2011, I made my first trip into the mountains of Kunar province near the Pakistan border to visit the troops of 1st Squadron, 32nd Cavalry. On a patrol to the northernmost U.S. position in eastern Afghanistan, we arrived at an Afghan National Police (ANP) station that had reported being attacked by the Taliban 2½ hours earlier.

Through the interpreter, I asked the police captain where the attack had originated, and he pointed to the side of a nearby mountain.

"What are your normal procedures in situations like these?" I asked. "Do you form up a squad and go after them? Do you periodically send out harassing patrols? What do you do?"

As the interpreter conveyed my questions, the captain's head wheeled around, looking first at the interpreter and turning to me with an incredulous expression. Then he laughed.

"No! We don't go after them," he said. "That would be dangerous!"

According to the cavalry troopers, the Afghan policemen rarely leave the cover of the checkpoints. In that part of the province, the Taliban literally run free.

In June, I was in the Zharay district of Kandahar province, returning to a base from a dismounted patrol. Gunshots were audible as the Taliban attacked a U.S. checkpoint about one mile away.

As I entered the unit's command post, the commander and his staff were watching a live video feed of the battle. Two ANP vehicles were blocking the main road leading to the site of the attack. The fire was coming from behind a haystack. We watched as two Afghan men emerged, mounted a motorcycle and began moving toward the Afghan policemen in their vehicles.

The U.S. commander turned around and told the Afghan radio operator to make sure the policemen halted the men. The radio operator shouted into the radio repeatedly, but got no answer.

On the screen, we watched as the two men slowly motored past the ANP vehicles. The policemen neither got out to stop the two men nor answered the radio—until the motorcycle was out of sight.

To a man, the U.S. officers in that unit told me they had nothing but contempt for the Afghan troops in their area—and that was before the above incident occurred.

In August, I went on a dismounted patrol with troops in the Panjwai district of Kandahar province. Several troops from the unit had recently been killed in action, one of whom was a very popular and experienced soldier. One of the unit's senior officers rhetorically asked me, "How do I look these men in the eye and ask them to go out day after day on these missions? What's harder: How do I look [my soldier's] wife in the eye when I get back and tell her that her husband died for something meaningful? How do I do that?"

One of the senior enlisted leaders added, "Guys are saying, 'I hope I live so I can at least get home to R&R leave before I get it,' or 'I hope I only lose a foot.' Sometimes they even say which limb it might be: 'Maybe it'll only be my left foot.' They don't have a lot of confidence that the leadership two levels up really understands what they're living here, what the situation really is."

Source: *www.armedforcesjournal. com/2012/02/8904030*

Background | Literature: Texts and Contexts—An Overview

This section of the course is meant to focus on how we come to construct and understand meaning in literary works. Though close reading and close awareness of the formal elements of literary works are still crucial components of this part of the course, this part focuses explicitly on how cultural elements of both the production and the reception affect how we "know" the meaning of a literary work. As the IB English A: language and literature subject guide notes: "Literary texts are not created in a vacuum but are influenced by social context, cultural heritage and historical change." And, again, these influences are in place when a literary work is originally written, when it is published or available for public consumption and when it is actually read. It is quite possible, even probable then, that the way we know or construct a meaning as a reader in one place and time is quite different from the way other readers, in other places or times, know the work or from the way an author could know, intend or even imagine.

One specific focus of this part of the course will be on works in translation. The intention of the use of works in translation is not simply to illustrate how different cultural contexts and heritages may lead to the development of unique kinds of literary works but also to allow us to become aware of our own knowledge, understanding or ways of knowing that may be influenced by our culture. One of the aims of this part of the course, then, is to know ourselves and our own culture as much as that of others.

An important aspect of the literature: texts and contexts section is to move beyond social and historical background as the only significant cultural elements. Though an author's life and times would certainly have an impact on what and how he or she writes, this course aims to greatly expand the myriad ways in which culture affects our understanding. Among the many possibilities of approach, you may be considering aspects as varied as:

- political, religious or social norms (for both production and reception)
- literary movements, formal elements or artistic intentions
- critical reception lenses (that a text may be approached from different foci leading to different readings)
- production elements.

Activity

Context can be transmitted, as suggested above, through a variety of means. Often, even the physical presentation of a literary work betrays a particular contextual viewpoint (whether historical, social or interpretive) or can have an impact on the attitudes and approaches we may have as readers. Consider the cover versions on the next page of the Albert Camus text *L´Étrange* (a popular work in translation chosen across IB schools).

- What different ideas are conveyed by the different translations of the titles (*The Outsider* versus *The Stranger*)?
- How do the different covers convey strangeness, difference or alienation? What attitudes might be further associated with these ideas, as evidenced by the covers?

- How might the covers suggest either the time and culture of the story itself or the time and culture of the publication of the novel?
- What basic ideas do you have regarding what the novel might be about based solely on the various covers?

 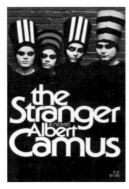 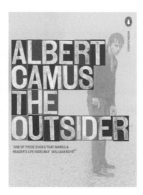

Assessments in literature: texts and contexts

As part of the study of literature: texts and contexts, you will be asked to complete the following for submission to the IB:

- paper 2 essay (a response to one of six questions that must be answered using two works from your part 3 study).

Most likely you will also be asked to do some of the following which may also be submitted to the IB:

- written task 1
- written task 2 (at higher level).

The skills and ideas you develop in this section will also be particularly relevant to:

- paper 1 textual analysis (standard level) and paper 1 comparative textual analysis (higher level)
- further oral activity.

Reception   Plot

Plot is, very simply, the "what happens" in a story. Generally, plot is a series of events that give a story meaning and effect, though the sequence of these events may or may not appear in chronological order. Events in a story very often occur in the form of conflict, either between a character and external factors (such as society, an evil villain or parents) or between a character and internal factors (such as conflicting desires, hubris or envy).

Though on some level every story has its own plot, students of literature may find it useful to identify general patterns that describe many works of fiction. With plot, the events of a story (regardless of where they fall within the narrative) generally fall within the bounds of Freytag's pyramid that identified:

- exposition: the basic setting, characters, background and description against which events will occur
- rising action: initial conflicts, complications or events that create tension in a story

- climax: the high point of a story where tension is greatest and towards which all events build
- falling action: events that occur as a result of the climax and leading towards resolution of conflict
- denouement: the conclusion of a story where conflicts are explained or understood, even if not entirely solved.

A consideration of plot can help us more deeply understand and appreciate meaning in a story and is a part of formal analysis involved in all close reading of works. The following example from a (very) short story by the writer Dave Eggers demonstrates an analysis of plot.

Activity

Read through the following short story by Dave Eggers. The comments on the side will draw your attention to some aspects of plot.

The Fighters

You all get out of your cars. You are alone in yours, and there are three teenagers in theirs. The accident was your fault and you walk over to tell them this. Walking over to their car, an old and restored Camaro which you have ruined, it occurs to you that if the three teenagers are angry teenagers, this encounter could be unpleasant. You pulled into an intersection, obstructing them, and their car hit yours. They have every right to be upset, or livid, or even violent. As you approach, you see that their driver's side door won't open. The driver pushes against it, and you are reminded of scenes where drivers are stuck in sub-merged cars. They all exit through the passenger side door and walk around the Camaro, inspecting the damage. "Just bought this today," the driver says. He is eighteen, blond, thin. "Today?" you ask. You are a bad person, you think. You also think: what an odd car for a teenager to buy in the twenty-first century. "Yeah, today," he says, then sighs. You tell him that you are sorry. That you are so, so sorry. That it was your fault and that you will cover all costs. You exchange insurance information, and you find yourself, minute by minute, ever-more thankful that none of these teenagers has punched you, or even made a remark about your being drunk, which you are not. You become more friendly with all of them, and you realize that you are much more connected to them, particularly to the driver, than possible in any other way. You have done him and his friends some psychic harm, and you jeopardized their health, and now you are so close you feel like you share a heart. He knows your name and you know his, and you almost killed him and because you got so close but didn't, you want to fall on him, weeping, because you are so lonely, so lonely always, and all contact is contact, and all contact makes us so grateful we want to cry and dance and cry and cry. In a moment of clarity you finally understand why boxers, who want so badly to hurt each other, can rest their chins on the other's shoulder, can lean against one another like tired lovers, so thankful for a moment of rest.

DAVE EGGARS

The scene is set with conflict immediately apparent.

Though no further conflict is yet evident, rising conflict is stated clearly as a possibility and tension is further conveyed.

The conflict shifts from that of the character and external forces to that of the character and internal elements.

The internal conflict reaches its climax even as the external conflict has fallen away.

Noticing the plot allows us to piece together events in ways that highlight tension and, thus, larger effect or meaning. Though the example above happens in a relatively straight forward manner, some works employ very complicated plots where causality can be difficult to discern. In all cases, however, an awareness of plot will help you to recognize and explain purpose and impact in works you read.

The resolution, though somewhat unspecified, helps further illuminate the nature of the internal conflicts in the story and helps a reader come to some understanding. Though many of the "events" in this story are not clearly stated, the plot allows for readers to imagine the protagonist's deep loneliness, isolation and pain more clearly.

Extension

Turn to page 204 and read the excerpt from Lorrie Moore's *How to Become a Writer*. Make note of the plot points in the work and how it develops and then answer the following questions.

- What is the central setting and how might this contribute to future conflict in the work?
- Where is the central tension or climax of the work?
- What seems to be the resolution?
- How is resolution connected to theme or larger impact in the work?

Reception   Setting

Setting is the background against which the action of a narrative takes place (most simply identified as time and place). Settings appear most obviously in the guise of physical locations or geographies but may also suggest particular historical, cultural, social, emotional, spiritual or economic environments. Setting is most commonly conveyed through geographical location—which may be a recognizable location or a more generic topography or scenery such as ocean, mountains, desert or space—but setting can also be conveyed through physical arrangements such as the use of windows, of dark and confined caves, the occupations, speech, clothing or daily mannerisms of characters in a narrative or the historical time or period in which the narrative takes place.

Different genres can convey setting uniquely. Generally speaking, dramatic performance makes significant use of stage props, placement and physical arrangement in ways that other forms of literature do not. In drama, setting can be very much a part of staging.

Most students of literature take setting somewhat for granted, associating it with the background of the plot rather than as a significant aspect.

Setting, however, can take on a dominant role in narrative as with "the period piece" in film (remakes of stories that lavish attention on exact details true to that historical era such as found in many of the Merchant and Ivory productions of popular films, for example *A Room With A View, Howard's End, The Remains of the Day* or *The Golden Bowl*). Literature, too, can focus exclusively on presenting the manners and customs of a particular location and is sometimes referred to as regionalism. However, whether to comment on a specific setting or location (in space or time) or to speak to more general or universal elements, setting plays a significant role in helping to convey and explain the actions of characters or events in narrative. Setting can be the most significant feature used to create mood, or the larger atmosphere of a work.

Setting is not limited to being only an aspect of literature. Many of the non-literary language works you study in the course will also make significant use of setting. This will range from literature-like setting issues found in film or television to highly stylized setting used in advertising and media to help convey particular attitudes towards a subject to implied cultural setting found in social networking sites and text messaging. Because we develop such strong associations and connotations—both social and emotional—with particular elements of setting, it becomes very useful to recognize elements in the analysis of many language works.

Activity

Consider the following two sentences from children's stories and the very different settings created. Make a note of how setting is conveyed and write down as many possible aspects of setting suggested through the brief descriptions as you can. What predictions might you make about the stories based on their apparent settings?

- "It was a dark and stormy night where not even the lowliest creature would dare step forward unaccompanied."
- "In the land of Vesulvius, filled with lush forests, broad fields, beautiful valleys and shimmering streams, there once lived a terrible creature."

Extension

Now turn to page 201 and read the excerpt from Thomas Hardy's *Tess of the D'Urbervilles*.

- How is the vale described and what is the impact on creating a mood or feeling?
- What predictions do you have based on the brief description of setting suggested here?

Literature is a term used to describe almost any written or spoken material. Broadly speaking, "literature" is used to describe anything from creative writing to more technical or scientific works including laboratory reports or scientific articles, but the term is most commonly used to refer to works of the creative imagination including works of poetry, drama, fiction and non-fiction. For the purposes of this course, literature can be defined as an intentional use of language in order to create effect and/or to provoke feelings rather than simply convey information.

Literature can be treated as both a formal style of communication (that can be further subdivided into distinct genre discourses) and as a part of a larger contextual history. The study of literature in this course is not about "knowing" a particular body of literary content or literary "answers", but is meant to build a set of skills with which to approach any literary work. Often, what distinguishes "literature" from other forms of language is the connection of content with form. This means, more simply, that literature tends not just to articulate an idea (content), but to highlight the unique ways (form) with which it articulates that idea (content). In other words, literature tends to emphasize both an idea and a unique way of expressing an idea.

Sometimes, it is the combination of content and form that can prove challenging for students. Literature is very rarely about communicating information but is about communicating experience. To focus, then, too much on the content (such as *the* answer or *the* right meaning) can take students too far away from significant and substantial literary elements. Literature is more appropriately considered for affect or as aesthetic experience than for a meaning: in other words, it is figurative. Such figurative language intends to disrupt the regular meaning, construction or syntax of language in order to increase the effect of expression, impact, visual effect or relationship between elements of the world (whether similar or dissimilar). Most often, such figurative language and, thereby, literature, either uses words in ways that change their traditional or familiar meanings or in ways that retain their traditional or familiar meanings but change their rhetorical effect. Though this may sound strange, most of us are familiar with literature and literary works even if we are not in the habit of clearly defining them. For the purposes of this course, however, it will be important to be cognizant of literature as a unique use of language and, in some ways, distinct from other communicative acts.

Activity

Read the two texts below, one literary and one not, and answer the following questions.

- What aspects are common between the two? What seems to be the subject?
- What are the major differences between them?
- How are the differences related to the apparent intention?
- What qualities distinguish the poem from the other work?

Text 1

All Day Long

All day long in fog and wind,
The waves have flung their beating crests
Against the palisades of adamant.
   My boy, he went to sea, long and long ago,
   Curls of brown were slipping underneath his cap,
   He looked at me from blue and steely eyes;
   Natty, straight and true, he stepped away,
   My boy, he went to sea.
All day long in fog and wind,
The waves have flung their beating crests
Against the palisades of adamant.

CARL SANDBURG

Text 2

Linear Theory of Ocean Surface Waves

Looking out to sea from the shore, we can see waves on the sea surface. Looking carefully, we notice the waves are undulations of the sea surface with a height of around a meter, where height is the vertical distance between the bottom of a trough and the top of a nearby crest. The wave length, which we might take to be the distance between prominent crests, is around 50m–100m. Watching the waves for a few minutes, we notice that wave height and wave length are not constant. The heights vary randomly in time and space, and the statistical properties of the waves, such as the mean height averaged for a few hundred waves, change from day to day. These prominent offshore waves are generated by wind. Sometimes the local wind generates the waves, other times distant storms generate waves which ultimately reach the coast. For example, waves breaking on the Southern California coast on a summer day may come from vast storms offshore of Antarctica 10,000km away.

If we watch closely for a long time, we notice that sea level changes from hour to hour. Over a period of a day, sea level increases and decreases relative to a point on the shore by about a meter. The slow rise and fall of sea level is due to the tides, another type of wave on the sea surface. Tides have wave lengths of thousands of kilometers, and they are generated by the slow, very small changes in gravity due to the motion of the sun and the moon relative to Earth.

In this chapter you will learn how to describe ocean-surface waves quantitatively. In the next chapter we will describe tides and waves along coasts.

Source: *http://oceanworld.tamu.edu/resources/ocng_textbook/ chapter16/chapter16_01.ht.*

Assessments in literature: critical study

As part of the study of literature: critical study, you will be asked to complete the following for submission to the IB:

■ individual oral commentary (an unseen passage commentary from one of the works studied in part 4 of the course, recorded and submitted to the IB for moderation).

Most likely you will also be asked to do some of the following which may also be submitted to the IB:

■ written task 1

■ written task 2 (at higher level).

The skills and ideas you develop in this section will also be particularly relevant to:

■ paper 1 textual analysis (standard level) and paper 1 comparative textual analysis (higher level)

■ further oral activity.

Many students come to my class with tremendous confusion over the nature of English. Perhaps it is the work they do in other subjects or just the nature of education for most young people in most places but students tend to think they will be made to read some books, I might give a quiz or two checking that they really do read, I will lecture where I reveal all that there is to know about the books and then I will ask them to complete an assessment task of some sort (an essay test, a commentary, an oral or a take-home essay) where they only need to follow a scripted template and fill in the responses they have already heard in class. In other words, they imagine that the class demands active work in absorbing explanation and "meaning" that I may have to offer but passive work in that it demands relatively little independent thinking.

While this description is somewhat exaggerated (but only somewhat), it does represent a core challenge for many students: understanding the degree of independent reading and thinking demanded by the subject. For some, this truly is the most frustrating component of this class. It can be very difficult to identify and define precisely what singular idea one has to convey or singular way to convey it. Like trying to define literature itself, the study of language and literature allows for many different kinds of approaches and many different kinds of responses or "answers". In fact, the true aims and objectives of this course are to show you just how varied the possible approaches can be and to develop both the competencies and confidence with which you will explore and develop your own approach.

After you develop these basic competencies and confidence, the real work of this course resides in the thinking and planning you do with a piece of literature. This work is hard and should not be minimized. But all thinking is hard that asks you to approach issues in novel ways and this is what the course asks of you. Too many students fail to internalize that the true demands are to engage independently with works—both literary texts and other language works—and that this is best accomplished through spending time alone with works thinking through various possibilities.

Elsewhere you have read about note taking and that process may prove useful as a model for spending time working through texts but a general approach might include the following.

- Take note of your initial impressions and reactions to a work. This is important information and even basic emotional responses such as "like", "intrigued", "amused", "confused" or "dislike" are useful as part of your thinking.

- Do not be discouraged if your first reading of a work does not "reveal all". It is challenging work that deserves concerted effort and such a reading is probably not possible.

- After your initial responses, begin to fall back on those basic competencies you have learned in class including features, form and purpose (or theme). This will not be a linear process but one that requires moving back and forth.

- Begin to imagine possibilities and patterns composed of the parts above. This need not be *the* answer but may consist of ambiguities or even just affective responses.

This time alone thinking is not completed until you plan out a response to a work. Once you have some ideas, you need to put them into a logical order that articulates an idea in a way that will make sense to a reader or audience (see more on this in the production section on body on page 159). What is important to remember is that even in formal examination conditions, you should build in time for thinking and planning; these are truly the essential skills and processes required for success.

Reception   Characterization

Characterization is the process by which authors develop characters—representations of humans—in their works. Character and characterization are frequently key elements of a story, with a deep awareness of the characters necessary for understanding. Generally, authors achieve characterization through three techniques with a direct connection to narrative point of view:

- direct characterization—overt presentation of characters and their traits, achieved as exposition from an omniscient point of view.
- character in action—showing a character engaged in activity, speech and reactions.
- internal characterization—a character's own thoughts or feelings, achieved through first person point of view, and without comment by the narrator.

Characters are also identified by their level of development and role within a story. Characters can be said to be flat or round and static or dynamic. A flat character is one-dimensional and often not central to the story while a round character is more complex, developed and likely to undergo change through the course of a story. Similarly, and sometimes used interchangeably, static characters tend to change little and often things happen *to* them rather than *within* them while dynamic characters change or are modified through their experience.

Some common significant characters encountered in story include:

- the protagonist—a story's main character
- the antagonist—the character most in conflict with the protagonist (this can be a person but may also be a social force, an environment, an historical era, a cultural norm or other factor)
- the foil—a character (or force as described for the antagonist above) who, through contrast, enhances the characteristics of another character.

Finally, the terms character or characterization may refer less to specific individual or individualized qualities than to a general quality, tradition or even stereotype of people or institutions (as in having "the character of a prison"). Character is this way may be a significant element of non-literary works as well as works of literature.

Activity

Looking at the images above of Oliver Twist (the protagonist in Charles Dickens' *Oliver Twist*), what different characteristics and types of character emerge from the images?

Students often fail fully to appreciate how significant finding an appropriate topic is for all essay and research work. In the IB Diploma Programme, in fact, the instructions to teachers in all subjects focus most heavily on assisting students' learning through help in selecting appropriate and viable topics and methods of approach. As teachers, our job is to help students find topics that meet the demands of the assessment task, provide opportunities for students to demonstrate independent and engaged work and yet remain manageable within the confines of the time, resources or other demands surrounding an idea. All of this is just to say that generating topics is a very important step with any assessment task, arguably even the single most important step.

It is likely that even in your own experience, when you are genuinely engaged and excited about a topic, the work goes both more quickly and more easily. One may find that the work almost "happens by itself" as, with careful topic selection, much of the work is already completed. This is certainly true for assessments such as the written task and the further oral activity in this class: a great majority of the intellectual work and rigour is in developing a topic. Once you have a good idea of topic and approach, the remainder of the work will probably feel very manageable.

If you have ever struggled with producing an essay or a paper of any sort, however, you are probably wondering exactly how one, then, does come to find this good idea of topic. In truth, because this is really the bulk of the intellectual work you will do in this course, this is a simple answer but no less challenging to accomplish. To generate good topics, you have to be engaged in the work of your study. This means reading carefully the material assigned or that you are asked to find; participating actively in class discussion in order to try out ideas, extend your thinking and develop new ideas with your peers and teacher; reflecting on your work (reading, discussion and any production); and genuine engagement with the material. Generating topics does not involve a trick or some more expedient process that will provide you with a guaranteed recipe for success. Instead, it is the result of careful and difficult labour at the core of the class. As the writer David Foster Wallace once noted, the work of an English course "gets very complicated and abstract and hard, which is one reason why entire college departments are devoted" to it. The implication is that it is through diligent and consistent attention to all of your work—in class and out—that interesting points, ideas and aspects that arouse your curiosity arise.

Here are some steps to consider.

- Read all material actively and carefully (including taking notes and rereading), participate actively in class discussions and think and actively apply yourself to all of your work. This may sound obvious, but this is the real labour of the course and is the single best approach to generating good-quality topics eventually.

- Think of what interests you about a topic, a text or an approach. Topics are much more successful when they are personally meaningful and of interest rather than assigned or otherwise passively received.

- Limit your topics based on the resources available (such as time, accessibility of materials, scope of assessment), including an emphasis on simplicity over unnecessary complexity.

- Work with your teacher. Your teacher's role, as mentioned above, is to assist and not to frustrate. Your teacher's experience, however, allows for greater awareness of viability. This does not mean you simply rely on your teacher to provide topics but do use your teacher as a primary resource.

- Be flexible. It is common to need to adjust or even entirely change topics as you proceed because you find there is too little to say, too much to say or even that you find the topic does not bear the fruit you originally expected. This is a normal phenomena and part of the difficulty Wallace refers to above. Relax, take a deep breath and continue; too rigid an approach, however, often leads to great difficulties.

- Manage your time effectively. For generating topics this means starting early (and, again, this means engaged work right from the start). Generating topics at the last minute only leads to frustration, compromise and frequently less good work in the end.

Though generating topics is only the first step in the final production of any assessment task, a good-quality topic will go a long way in smoothing the remainder of the process. Ultimately, the work here will be more than worth it.

Reception   Theme

Theme is considered the meaning or main idea you are left with after reading a work. In non-fiction work, theme may be considered the general topic of discussion, the subject or the thesis of the work. With some works, theme is straightforward or even obvious (consider fables that contain very clear morals). In other works, however, theme may be more elusive with multiple or even competing ideas or more general ambiguity.

While theme is often an important element of works, students can often get into trouble with too narrow a focus on finding "the meaning". Especially with works of literary fiction, the effort to exact a meaning can blind students to more emotional or affective impact, stylistic impact or effect or even a story's intentional ambiguity. Particularly with contemporary fiction, the function may be one of highlighting the very limitations of our processes for determining meaning and coherence and a fixed intention to locate a theme can actually take students far away from the works themselves. However, for most of the works you study in this course—whether literary or other works—theme will be an important aspect to consider as part of your reading and course discussion.

Activity

- Look at the excerpt from Andre Agassi's *Open* on page 202. Though this is a non-fiction work, this excerpt seems to focus on an element more specific than tennis itself. What theme or themes seem to run through this section of the work and what aspects of the excerpt suggest and support these?

- Now look at the poem *Recuerdo* by Edna St Vincent Millay on page 206. Are there any themes you are able to identify in this piece? If so, what leads you to such conclusions?

- In what ways do the two excerpts share elements that suggest themes in the respective works? In what ways do they differ substantially?

Extension

- What theme appears through the modified version of "Cinderella?"

- How is the new version achieved?

- Do you believe the theme is more overt in the original or in the "politically correct" version? Why or why not?

Reception   Symbol

Very simply, a symbol is something that is itself but also refers to or suggests something else. On some level, all language functions as symbol as it suggests both its physical form and some other component of tangible reality (just as the letters "c", "a" and "t" are combined to refer to the word "cat" as well as the small, domestic feline mammal) but in literature symbol can assume specific dimensions. It should be noted that there are several specific forms of symbol (or symbolism) such as metaphor or image which are treated separately. Note that, for our purposes, a symbol will be said to be any image, detail or name that refers to another object or idea that refers to still another level of meaning or association. Unlike metaphor or image, then, a symbol refers to an idea two degrees removed from itself (it refers to something that refers to something else) and ends in an idea or association rather than a physical object. Symbols may also be distinguished by the frequency, or centrality, of their use in works: where an image may be used just once, a symbol can be referred to repeatedly or becomes more essential in the meaning or effect of a work.

Symbols and symbolism occur often in literature but may be used just as frequently in other, non-literary language works. As in literature, however, what distinguishes a symbol from other images or metaphors is its more substantive role in helping to convey purpose. In either case, symbols occur in two broad types: the universal and the particular. "Universal" symbols are those used widely such as a long stretch of empty road suggesting perseverance or a voyage suggesting life, while the more "particular" are constructed within the context of the larger work rather than through more universal associations. While symbols obviously work most effectively through common understanding, different literary movements and writers have experimented with symbols as immediate, unique and personal response and association that communicate more privately than universally. These works experiment with indefiniteness as an expression of "true" experience and art and these writings seek constantly to remind us of the lack of stable knowledge and meaning, instead emphasizing the fleeting and incommunicable nature of our understanding.

Activity

Looking at the following list of abstractions and objects, create a list of symbols or meanings that a writer might associate with each.

Love	A wave
Desire	A lipstick print on a napkin
Hate	A kite
Hope	A field of fresh snow
Treachery	A guitar

Extension

Turn to Anne Bradstreet's poem *The Author to Her Book* on page 199. The poem employs the symbol of an illegitimate child, one who is dirty and unkempt. Note all the uses of this symbol alongside your ideas about how it is used to refer to a book, writing or artistic output more generally.

- How effective is the use of the symbol?

- What kind of tone or feeling does the use of this symbol create in your reading?

Reception · Style

Style, in literature, is about unique and recognizable uses of language. Style emerges through different dictions, or arrangements of words that may distinguish an individual writer (or voice) or a distinct approach to writing. What really makes style an interesting point of reception is how style implies both something extraordinarily unique and something more conventional or generic.

On the one hand, every writer arranges words and ideas in such ways that distinguish a unique style. No two styles can be the same with the individuality of a writer coming through in the always unique way one writer strives to convey one idea. In theory, one cannot say exactly the same idea in more than one singular, unique way, which leaves every writer with a style all their own. On the other hand, however, style refers to more general or conventional approaches to language that allow it to be categorized easily. In this way, we can recognize certain writing as, for example, journalistic versus literary, abstract versus concrete, sincere versus artificial, serious versus comic.

Paying attention to more generic stylistic conventions as well as the unique expression of a unique individual's unique ideas helps tremendously in recognizing ideas and how ideas are developed or expressed. Though style is something many students *feel*, it is an aspect that can be difficult to identify accurately and discuss with specificity. Again, practising with reading many different styles and working hard to break them down and discuss them in detail can pay off handsomely with your own study of language and literature.

Activity

Read through the following sentences and note the diction choices each author makes in conveying his or her unique ideas. Try to rewrite the same idea in your own words and note the different style you produce in the process.

- From *A Portrait of the Artist as a Young Man*
  Every part of his day, divided by what he regarded now as the duties of his station in life, circled about its own centre of spiritual energy. His life seemed to have drawn near to eternity; every thought, word and deed, every instance of consciousness could be made to reverberate radiantly in heaven: and at times his sense of such immediate repercussion was so lively that he seemed to feel his soul in devotion pressing like fingers the keyboard of a great cash register and to see the amount of his purchase start forth immediately in heaven, not as a number but as a frail column of incense or as a slender flower.
  JAMES JOYCE

- From *Heart of Darkness*
  She rang under my feet like an empty Huntley & Palmer biscuit-tin kicked along a gutter; she was nothing so solid in make, and rather less pretty in shape, but I had expended enough hard work on her to make me love her. No influential friend would have served me better. She had given me a chance to come out a bit—to find out what I could do.
  JOSEPH CONRAD

- From *Frankenstein*
  The appearance of Justine was calm. She was dressed in mourning, and her countenance, always engaging, was rendered, by the solemnity of her feelings, exquisitely beautiful. Yet she appeared confident in innocence and did not tremble, although gazed on and execrated by thousands, for all the kindness which her beauty might otherwise have excited was obliterated in the minds of the spectators by the imagination of the enormity she was supposed to have committed.
  MARY SHELLEY

- From *The Moor's Last Sigh*
  The woman who transformed, exalted and ruined my life entered it at Mahalaxmi racecourse forty-one days after Ina's death. It was a Sunday morning at the beginning of the late-year cool season, and according to ancient custom—'How ancient?' you ask, and I reply Bombay-fashion, "*Ancient*, men. From *ancient* time'—the city's finest citizens had risen early and taken the place of the highly strung, pedigreed local steeds, both in the paddock and on the track.
  SALMAN RUSHDIE

Extension

Turn to the excerpt from Andre Agassi's *Open* on page 202. What elements can you identify from the work that reveals that it is a work of non-fiction? What elements seem to convey a unique style or the voice of Andre Agassi? If writing about this work, what would you say about the style?

Now turn to page 200 and the excerpt from Raymond Carver's story *Preservation*. Repeat the exercise above noting the distinctions from the Agassi work. What elements in particular distinguish these works as emblems of non-fiction and fiction respectively? What elements in particular distinguish these works as entirely unique on their own?

Production   Writing Fiction and Pastiche

In the IB English A: language and literature course, there may are opportunities to produce some creative content with the written task 1 or the further oral activity. However, it should be clear that this is not a creative writing course and that the pure production of fiction is not an option for formal assessment tasks. The primary aim of the assessment tasks is to convey intellectual engagement with the texts and issues of language but there is an opportunity to convey these analyses in creative ways. One possible approach is through the use of creative fiction though, as must be emphasized again, to convey analysis rather than for the purely creative expressive reasons more traditionally associated with writing fiction.

The most likely opportunities to produce fiction formally include the following.

- **Pastiche**—the act of imitation of a particular style of a writer. Strong pastiche recognizes stylistic choices a writer makes, including an awareness of purpose or effect, and attempts to imitate these same choices to highlight understanding of a writer's work.

- **Remediation**—the reproduction of one work in a different medium, whether fiction into film, poetry into graphic novel, novel into drama or drama into poetry. Remediation is most successful when not haphazard but rather purposeful in order to highlight particular aspects and/or themes in a work. In other words, simply to rework a short story into a poem because one enjoys writing poetry should be avoided. But if a student were to read an author's style in producing a short story as one employing substantial visual imagery to create effect, there may be strong reasons to reproduce the work as a poem to highlight the use of the visual image. Remediation can be useful for highlighting very different textual elements from an original work but even in doing so seeks to capitalize on components that exist in the original.

- **Creative additions, diversions, beginning and endings**—many formal works of creative fiction in the course will involve creating additional elements such as alternative endings, or filling out details within works, for example developing a diary or series of letters between characters to explore motivations and the thoughts otherwise more subtly mentioned. In choosing to pursue such a task, it is important to do so with sufficient intention and forethought as such work should seek to highlight your intellectual engagement with material rather than simply being an exercise in creative writing (though creative writing is, by no means, a simple exercise).

Sample student work

The following samples are excerpts from longer works aimed simply at demonstrating a range of possible approaches. Some of the examiner comments should shed light on relative strengths and weaknesses but it is important to remember that these excerpts only show a part of the larger whole.

- (Referring to Ivan Turgenev's *Fathers and Sons*)

    … Pavel's sonnet reflects that he does not approve of Bazarov's views, but understands that Bazarov is an intelligent man. However, when he sees Bazarov kissing Fenechka, it is possible that he reflects upon his chase for a woman he could not have. He is also protective of his brother and wishes for Fenechka to stay true to Nikolai, which is why he interrupts and says, "You are here, I see." (147). Pavel's last line is the same as one of Bazarov's lines; this once again emphasizes the similarities shared between the two characters, especially in their love lives…

So sweet you are; yes, you're charming indeed,

I can be who I am, speak as I please,

Why dear Bazarov, you are such a tease,

It's this type of company that I heed

I appreciate that the intention is made clear by the candidate though I am still uncertain as to why the sonnet form was selected in particular.

Understanding would be more strongly demonstrated with fuller explanation of this quotation.

117

Come closer and I shall follow your lead,

My heart's locked up, but I'll give you the keys,

But we must be careful nobody sees,

Young, no care for status, you're what I need-

Back away! A kiss! You've gone much too far!

To Nikolai Petrovich, I belong,

I was wrong before, THIS is who you are

A monster, a devil, you are a scar,

I shan't be yours; my love for him's too strong,

Oh dear! Pavel's seen! In trouble we are!

- (Referring to *Lazarillo de Tormes,* an anonymous text)

  Dear diary,

  Several months ago, whilst residing at the Solana tavern in
  Tejares, I came upon a young boy by the name of Lazarillo. I
  asked his servant mother for him as a guide, but I actually saw
  him more as a son. The mother, though saddened by the thought
  of her son's departure, agreed; she could not afford to raise the
  child on her income. I told the mother that I would take care of
  Lazaro and treat him well. However, this must have meant two
  very different things for Lazaro's mother and me. I planned to
  teach the child life lessons that would help him in the world,
  even though some of these lessons may require some tough
  guidance on my part. After I spent a few days in Salamanca, I
  decided to leave the city as it was saturated with merchants who
  sucked the civilians' money like leeches. I felt it better I pursue
  other cities in order to make a living. In that regard, I am like
  a mosquito; I drink the wealth from one city, but when there is
  none left, I move on to another.

- (Referring to Thomas Mann's *Death in Venice*)

  …The next morning, the young boy noticed a familiar face that
  he couldn't quite identify. After staring at the figure for some
  time he finally realized it was the old man. Tadzio could hardly
  recognize him – his cheeks had become raspberry red, his grey
  hair suddenly black as it once might have been in his youth and
  his wrinkles buried beneath a cosmetic cream – Tadzio found
  him more repulsive than ever. Disgusted and ashamed at how
  foul the old man looked, he turned his back and joined his
  sisters at the beach. Tadzio watched as his admirer sat down on
  his chair and observed him, just as he always did but today the
  young boy didn't want the attention. He went on playing on the
  beach when he noticed a crowd around the old man. He chose
  to ignore it and accompanied his sisters back to their room. He
  never saw his admirer again.

There is basic awareness of this
moment though perhaps not quite
the turning point suggested here.
But this does work with Bazarov's
sonnet to convey the differing
perspectives.

This part of the diary simply retells
the content of the first chapter.
Unfortunately, this conveys little
larger understanding.

It is possible to pursue a line of
thinking where the blind man thinks
he is innocent as a result of larger
social corruption but this needs to
be expanded here.

This seems to "undo" the idea
above—is the blind man repentant,
impertinent or proud? I'm still not
quite sure where this is going and
what value producing a diary of the
blind man might offer.

This pastiche does capture the feel
of the original but with such similar
content, it is hard to distinguish
interpretation and ideas. Certainly
the language does reflect Mann in
this work and there seems to be a
point of the change of the old man
with a familiar use of the grotesque
that does show understanding of
the original.

Insight | Nerves for the Oral and Commentary Problems

Sometimes I see students who are bright, work hard, are well prepared and contribute with insight and fluency during class discussion but then flounder with performance on a more formal assessment task. Most typically (or, at least, stereotypically), performance jitters are a part of oral presentations, oral activities and oral commentaries though the stress involved in other kinds of formal assessments can have an impact on students as well.

Having a case of nerves during orals or being anxious about performance is actually not wholly bad. It is the students who have no worries at all who are of most concern as it suggests a general lack of care either about performance or the quality of the work. Generally speaking, it is natural to feel nervous when performing in any formal setting and particularly as the centre of attention in front of a group but suffering too much from nerves will get in the way and become detrimental. To minimize these nerves without removing them altogether, keep in mind the following ideas:

- Know the material you are presenting: be prepared. If you feel confident about your knowledge of the material you are presenting and sure about the points you are making, you will naturally feel less nervous about the process. Even if you lose some track of your plan, having the confidence that you can ad lib material based on your deep and thorough knowledge gives every speaker confidence.

- Practise in advance. Even with the formal oral commentary, you can practise the process in order to have a sense of the timings and the feel of speaking into a microphone but regardless of the assessment task, practice really does make perfect. Outside regular classroom discussions there are few places where oral presentations are truly impromptu so practising in advance not only helps to alleviate nerves, it is good practice to enhance performance.

- Relax. Though this may be easier said than done, you can rest assured that you know your audience (they are friends and peers and teachers) and that they want you to enjoy success. It can help to take steps such as a few deep breaths before presenting but key is remembering that this is an opportunity to showcase your knowledge and is not torture or a process to catch you out. Even when recording a commentary for a faceless examiner, know that all examiners are looking to reward students rather than penalize and we all want students to be successful.

The commentary, both the formal oral commentary and paper 1, can also present some challenges for students that are unique to the assessment task. With the formal oral commentary, keep in mind that though it is an unseen commentary, it is not from an unknown text. In other words, you can (and should) prepare by being as familiar as possible with all the works you might be given. This includes a thorough awareness of the texts but also preparing with a review of common themes, important episodes and significant features of all possible works you might receive during your preparation. Knowing that you are well prepared works well with all assessment tasks.

For an unseen written commentary, it is important to be confident in the skills that come with the preparation you do through your study. Be consistent and work hard and you will be prepared. Next is to know the assessment task by having practised with exact assessment times in order to know the *feel* of the work ahead as well as being thoroughly versed in what each of the commentaries specifically ask you to do (see the production sections on commentary on pages 155 and 171 for more information). Most important will be to take full advantage of the preparation time available.

Background | New Criticism

New Criticism, or The New Criticism as it was originally known, is quite simply a body of criticism that approaches a work of art (literature in this case) as an object in and of itself. This may seem simplistic but this represented a substantial shift in the view of literature at the time (through the 1930s and 1940s) and continues to have wide influence in the way we read literature today.

New Criticism largely developed as a critical response to mechanistic and positivist notions so closely associated with the modern world of that time. In this era between the two world wars, scientific determinism and a view that the world—including literature—could be known through fact and inference from facts prevailed. Because of this, literature was seen as differing only in style from journalism, scientific textbooks or even personal letters. It could speak to the human condition or other matters but could only communicate effectively through style rather than any inherent substance. This means literature was regarded as interesting, perhaps, but not at all essential or truly distinguished with any unique value.

As you might imagine, some writers and teachers of literature took umbrage with such a position. The New Critics argued—and sincerely believed—that literature is a truly unique and valid form of knowledge. Literature does not simply communicate the same ideas and truths of other language types (for example science or journalism) in a unique style but actually can convey ideas and meanings that those other language types are incapable of communicating. In this way, literature is a valuable phenomenon that communicates ideas that could not arise in any other way through means not found in any other language type.

For New Critics, this concept took the form of "objective correlative" which simply suggests larger experiential truths (the objective, or objective knowledge, truth) emerge from literature (correlate) in ways that cannot simply be described mechanistically. While journalism, for example, might describe an event, literature conveys ideas and truths that exceed the mere make-up of words.

As a potentially objective truth, the new critics also view literature and literary works as self-contained objective art forms on their own. This means that after creation, a literary work is an isolated object of study no longer influenced by the writer, the production, the times or any other contextual aspect. The "truth" of literary works exists solely between its covers and exists independently of writer, reader and external world. In fact, this is such a central tenet of New Criticism that New Critics developed the term "intentional fallacy" to describe the common error of attributing the meaning of a literary work to an author's experience or intention rather than as complete in itself.

Activity

Consider the following descriptions, one in a journalistic style and the other a very short story attributed to Ernest Hemingway in settlement of a bet. What seems to be in common across the two works? What emotions do each convey? How do they differ in conveying emotion or human response? Though they both consist of relatively few words, how does the Hemingway piece seem to convey ideas that exist beyond the words?

- At 9:30 a.m. in the southside of the city, paramedics were called to aid an infant in distress. In spite of all efforts, the child succumbed to their condition later that day.

- For sale: baby shoes, never worn.

While New Criticism speaks of higher truths communicated by literature, it also speaks to very precise methods for "unlocking" these truths and becoming the kind of sensitive and informed reader who can adequately understand meaning. Rather than experiencing a mystical event, readers can be trained to recognize literature's unique qualities in order to achieve a correct reading. The most central requirement is simply for very close reading of the words. In order to avoid the pitfall of intentional fallacy described above, readers must ignore all outside biographical or **paratextual** information and focus solely on the words contained in a text. New Critics are trained to focus on image, symbol, rhythm, allusion and meaning to unearth how the language exclusively is able to give rise to unique truth and meaning.

Though the ideas of New Criticism have lost favour over time—in particular, the idea that literature ennobles readers in ways no other discourse can provide—the ways of approaching texts and close reading continue to be important in studying literature today. More often than not, you are asked to approach your reading as a "practical" critic paying close attention to, for example, the words, titles, connotative suggestions, allusions, imagery and sound devices. Particularly with unseen works, we rely on these techniques and skills to come to an understanding of effect even if not outright meaning. Though many critical approaches have developed since the height of popularity for New Criticism, it remains a fundamental and useful approach to literary works.

Extension

Turn to Edna St Vincent Millay's poem *Recuerdo* on page 206 and consider the following questions.

- What is the rhyme scheme? How does the rhyme work with the structure of the poem to create a specific tone and what is this tone (happy, sad, stingy, giving…)?
- How does the use of "we" and "and" operate and to what effect? What is the purpose of the repetition of these words (anaphora)?
- How does the title work with the poem to help construct a holistic reading?
- What meaning can you ascribe to this poem?

Reception   Imagery

Imagery is quite a complex concept for its potential variety but at its simplest, imagery refers to the presentation of the physical world in language. As we, generally, perceive the physical world through the five senses, imagery can take the form of taste, touch, sound, sight or smell.

- Aural imagery uses images that evoke sound.
- Tactile imagery uses images that evoke physical touch.
- Visual imagery uses images that evoke sight.
- Olfactory imagery uses images that evoke smell.
- Gustatory imagery uses images that evoke taste.

Imagery can also occur in various forms. Most commonly, images appear as:

- tied—an image representation commonly associated with a real-world phenomenon such as "It was a dark and stormy night".

- free—an image representation that is unique and based on free association rather than a more common association such as "The cricket ball was hit and moved with a pace like a fiery meteor hurling through space".

- literal—"The flames rose as high as the adjacent skyscrapers".

- figurative—"The bull danced around the ring, moving as though a dandelion spread by a gentle, invisible yet deliberate and thoughtful wind".

Activity

Read through the following images noting what kind of image is evoked and how the language or structure reveals such an image.

The Open Boat

None of them knew the color of the sky. Their eyes glanced level, and were fastened upon the waves that swept toward them. These waves were of the hue of slate, save for the tops, which were of foaming white, and all of the men knew the colors of the sea. The horizon narrowed and widened, and dipped and rose, and at all times its edge was jagged with waves that seemed thrust up in points like rocks. Many a man ought to have a bath-tub larger than the boat which here rode upon the sea. These waves were most wrongfully and barbarously abrupt and tall, and each froth-top was a problem in small-boat navigation.

STEPHEN CRANE

The Fish

    wade
    through black jade.
        Of the crow-blue mussel-shells, one keeps
        adjusting the ash-heaps;
            opening and shutting itself like

an
injured fan.
    The barnacles which encrust the side
    of the wave, cannot hide
        there for the submerged shafts of the

sun,
split like spun
    glass, move themselves with spotlight swiftness
    into the crevices—
        in and out, illuminating

the
turquoise sea
    of bodies. The water drives a wedge
    of iron through the iron edge
        of the cliff; whereupon the stars,

pink
rice-grains, ink-
    bespattered jelly fish, crabs like green
    lilies, and submarine
        toadstools, slide each on the other.

All
external
    marks of abuse are present on this
    defiant edifice—
        all the physical features of

ac-
cident—lack
    of cornice, dynamite grooves, burns, and
    hatchet strokes, these things stand
        out on it; the chasm-side is

dead.
Repeated
    evidence has proved that it can live
    on what can not revive
        its youth. The sea grows old in it.

MARIANNE MOORE

Imagery, however, tends to serve a purpose in literature beyond merely representing the physical universe or physical phenomena. Though it may well be that imagery does describe the physical world, it is likely that there will be an attendant intention. Among the most common are:

- conveying a rhetorical pattern that appears repeatedly in a work
- conveying a psychological or reality in which the work is either produced and/or narrated and indicating a deeper, figurative meaning (often as levels of allegory)
- reinforcing or contradicting that apparent meaning of a work, often creating a sense of irony, humour or farce
- producing emotive power with the use of familiar, sacred or confrontational images.

Imagery of some sort is found in virtually all, if not all, literary works. Partially due to its ubiquitous nature, imagery can be challenging to define precisely but it is always an effective device to consider when approaching literary works.

Extension

Turn to page 207 and note the imagery used in the excerpt from Folman and Polonsky's *Waltz With Bashir*. What are the physical images created and how is this done in the work? What larger psychological associations or meaning do we take from this imagery in order to develop a larger meaning?

Production   Individual Oral Commentary

The individual oral commentary is a highly formal assessment task allowing students to showcase sophisticated and detailed understanding and interpretation of a literary work. Your teachers will select short excerpts from works you have read and studied as part of part 4 of the course (literature: critical study). Generally, these excerpts will be approximately 40 lines in length though with poetry the commentary should use the entire poem when practical. The selection of excerpt will remain unknown until the formal commentary allotted time when you will receive the selected passage as part of your 20-minute preparation time.

The process for the individual oral commentary is as follows.

- Students enter a supervised preparation room where they receive their randomly selected passage.
- You have 20 minutes to prepare your commentary including reading through the passages, marking the text, making notes and developing an organization for the presentation of the commentary.
- Passages will be accompanied by guiding questions. Guiding questions will draw your attention to significant aspects or thematic elements of the text. Guiding questions should be seen as helpful anchor points from which to develop larger literary readings rather than questions that are meant to guide the totality of the response. Responding only to the content of guiding questions will not demonstrate the significant and comprehensive knowledge asked for by the assessment task.
- Students will then move to a recording room. (You may not physically change locations depending on your school's set-up but there are generally two rooms: one for preparation and one for presentation.)

- You will speak your commentary for 10–12 minutes followed by any further questions asked by your teacher. These follow-up questions are intended to allow you to further clarify interesting ideas, draw your attention to elements that may demand your attention or extend your analysis to show superior analysis. Commentaries and follow-up questions are recorded as audio files for possible submission for external moderation.

Perhaps the greatest challenge for students with the individual oral commentary is to understand the balance between receiving an unknown specific passage with 20 minutes preparation time and recognizing that the same unknown passage will come from a text you have formally studied as a class; in other words, recognizing how the individual oral commentary differs from the unseen commentary encountered in paper 1.

While it is not expected that students memorize entire texts in part 4 of the course (or in any part for that matter), it is expected that you will walk into individual oral commentary preparation with an arsenal of knowledge already at your fingertips as a result of your classroom study. You should be familiar enough with the larger work (or body of work in the case of short pieces such as poems or letters) that you will be familiar with stylistic trends, themes and effects and anticipate what you might find. You should be able to place the extract in context in the larger work or body of work and not find it too difficult to make meaningful points about the work.

Ultimately, if you "know" the works of your study, the individual oral commentary is an opportunity to showcase this knowledge. Do remember that the individual oral commentary is not an impromptu exercise and you can prepare, whether through reviewing the works of your part 4 study or practising for the commentary (both are encouraged). This assessment task is similar to all others in its demand for a demonstration of understanding of the work, interesting analytical ideas, an awareness of some literary features, careful and pre-planned organization and the use of accurate language. With good study habits, consistent preparation and participation in class, an awareness of the demands of the rubrics for the assessment task and some pre-commentary preparation, the individual oral commentary should be a place to shine.

Activity

- Read through the excerpt from a transcript of a student's work alongside the examiner comments. The commentary is based on Edna St Vincent Millay's poem *Recuerdo* (see page 206), but note that she is not an author featured on the prescribed list of authors and this could not be the basis of a commentary for an authentic individual oral commentary.

Sample student work

Edna St Vincent Millay's poem "Recuerdo" is, a note tells us, about a memory or a recollection. The memory in this case is about a happy moment shared by two lovers who seem to be in the height of their courtship. Really, it is a simple poem on the surface but maybe because love can never really be simple, this is slightly… um… misleading but on purpose. Actually, this is part of the most interesting part of the poem which is the use of so many contrasting elements. It's the complexity of love that leads to the simplicity of feeling and emotion and this is supported by internal contrasts of pain and pleasure or challenges and happiness. Millay uses the structure and these contrasts to create an unexpected harmony and create a simple love poem that is actually more complex underneath.

This an interesting approach that demonstrates extended thinking and analysis.

There is a clear structure here as the poem consists of three stanzas, each six lines long. The lines are further divided into couplets giving each stanza a rhyme scheme of aa bb cc. There's also a regular meter to the poems and all of these elements create a soothing, happy quality rather than anything jarring or bitter. It isn't quite a lullaby but the consistent pattern and meter does give it a simplistic quality that probably hides some of the complexity of the meaning. Also, the couplet often speaks about a meaningful or powerful point but the combinations of couplets here don't emphasize with authority but instead just help give the poem a sing-song quality. Finally, each line usually consists of two clauses. These clauses create a kind of back-and-forth give-and-take that creates some of the contrast. So the structure itself seems simple and soothing but also has contrasting elements and juxtaposed elements that can actually suggest more complexity than might be visible on the surface.

Recognizes features but also tries to demonstrate effect.

I'm a little unclear about authority and the couplet.

The first stanza starts with a couplet that is repeated throughout the poem. Actually, each stanza ends this couplet with a different punctuation but it still works as a kind of refrain. Even this repetition creates simplicity but the content is also reinforced to remind us of the subject of the poem. The use of anaphora with "we" is important because it immediately highlights that this is a poem about more than an individual and we learn that it is two lovers. And the emphasis is about the shared experience. Maybe, again, the contrast here is that it might not really be a shared memory but only one person's. We can't really know for sure if it is first-person plural or just a single narrator that recalls on behalf of both the parties. The rest of the two lines also set up contrast: first, they are described as "very tired" and "very merry". There's an opposition here between "tired" and "merry" but the opposition doesn't disrupt the poem, again because the structure contains this contrast so well. The second line says "We had gone back and forth all night on the ferry." There isn't a contrast here but the "back and forth" of the ferry and their ride mimics the movement between contrasting poles like "tired" and "merry". So this very first couplet actually sets up what is to come throughout the poem: there is a shifting between contrasting elements—"tired" and "merry", "back and forth", the "we" of the plural or the "we" as remembered by one

OK.

Great point to notice. A good job of really engaging the poem and digging into possibilities.

Yes.

person, and a couplet that is sing-song and soothing and sweet, even too sweet. But these all work together in a way that makes it read easily and all suggest something deeper underneath.

The next couplet just continues the contrast and mimics the rocking back and forth of the ferry: "bare *and* bright" *and* "smelled like a stable," so there is some that seems positive and some that maybe is not so great or just ordinary and not associated with a love poem and the next line seems like a contrast to line three with the word "But" and then again there is the rocking between this-and-that or, in this case, "looked into the fire" and "leaned across the table." There's some internal anaphora with "we" again so there's a connection and bringing together of these different things so it's like you move back and forth but it's all contained within a common experience or memory. That reconciles the movements and makes it seem more constant, like a couplet, even though the internal parts might be a little… um… disjointed or broken.

Then the last couplet starts with the "We" and continues the anaphora and then back to the contrasts: they are "on" a hill but "*under* the moon" and in the sixth line there is the contrast, sort of, between whistles blowing, which might be harsh but then there is the new day or "dawn" that will soon come. So the contrasting elements are always there but these contrasts achieve a harmony because the structure is easy and pleasant and this is maybe like love. It's even a kind of paradox because it is through the differences you know it is two different people and there are differences, but these different pieces can come together when you don't expect it and make a harmonious whole. Even though the stanza is in the past tense—actually the whole poem is—and we still have to question the memory, if it's shared or one-sided, that might be part of the paradox of love. You have to believe in it or think of it like Millay does, with this kind of structure, so that it can have this effect and be realized…

OK. Good.

Yes. Good points. Good attempt at extending and explaining your analysis.

Very interesting approach that shows sophisticated reading.

Reception | Metaphor and Allegory

Metaphor

Metaphor is an analogy that identifies one object or idea with another. Through an imaginative process, the qualities of the second object or idea are ascribed to the first. It may seem strange to communicate—either in literature or through another use of language—indirectly through metaphorical comparison, but metaphor is used extensively in the English language. In fact, much of the language we use in everyday situations is filled with metaphor even when we do not fully realize it. Whether we use a phrase such as "Don't put all your eggs in one basket" or even single words like "transgress" ("trans" and "gress" used to literally mean "cross line" that was used as a metaphor for doing something wrong but now refers to the metaphorical association exclusively), so much of our everyday language employs metaphor that we are often not even aware of it.

Metaphor in literature tends to be colourful and creative to create heightened effect even if the process is similar to the above. In literature we frequently encounter metaphor and simile (the former equates object or idea one with object or idea two; the latter makes them similar, often using "like" or "as is") and even allegory. Metaphor is technically broken into two parts: the tenor and the vehicle. The tenor is the idea expressed while the vehicle is the image through which the idea is conveyed. For example, a common metaphor for death or dying occurs through the use of the season of winter. The association of a barren landscape, lengthy hibernation and inhospitable weather may be used to refer to the conclusion of life itself. In such a case, the tenor is death or dying while the season becomes the vehicle for expressing this idea. Finally, in literature one finds both simple and complex, or extended, metaphor. Simple metaphor is isolated and a singular event while extended metaphor occurs repeatedly throughout a work in different forms. It is these extended metaphors that can give rise to allegory.

The very prevalence of metaphor makes it a challenging aspect to treat with sophistication. Because it can be so frequently used, it can be difficult to "pull back" and gain perspective with which to make sophisticated analyses. As with all aspects of this course, the key to success is continued practice, for it is almost certain that metaphor will be a key component of the texts you will study.

Allegory

Allegory is really a form of extended metaphor, or the cumulative effect of a series or collection of all or several metaphors across a work. It is a collection of symbols, character and events that come together to represent a different metaphysical, political or social situation than what appears on the surface and, most often, extrinsic to the work itself. In other words, it is the total range of metaphorical images within a work to stand for a different idea or concept outside the work. In its most effective use, allegory evokes two different foci and interests simultaneously: one on the characters, images, aspects and events within a work and one on the ideas or significance these collectively intend to convey that exist outside the work.

Traditionally, if such can be said, allegory has been associated with religious and moral ideas. In Western literature, Christian themes have been prominent allegorical motifs but so too have typical mythical trends that tend to cross cultural boundaries more effectively (ideas such as a hero's journey or outsmarting the powerful but evil overseer). More recent works make wider use of political, social and satirical allegories as well and allegory is now truly established as a literary aspect. One must, however, avoid looking for allegory in all works of literature above all else: a common error for students of literature is to work so hard to find allegorical meaning that they overlook more likely literary effect and tend to totalize literature where such an outcome is neither guaranteed nor required. Many works of literature have "meaning"; many more, in fact most, employ effect; and only some endeavour to convey allegorical meaning.

- Using the list of ideas and objects below, create your own metaphors. Extend yourself to produce interesting ideas but viable for expressing larger ideas. Try and create a mix of metaphors and similes.

Love	Balloon	Salt
Carpet	Mistrust	Orange
Delivery	Shell	Disbelief
Barrier	Long pants	Glacier
Soar	Machine	Juice

- Read through the following paragraph from the beginning of George Orwell's *Animal Farm*. Though this only represents a fraction of the work, what kinds of allegory can you detect arising and what aspects in particular seem to suggest this?

From *Animal Farm*

At one end of the big barn, on a sort of raised platform, Major was already ensconced on his bed of straw, under a lantern which hung from a beam. He was twelve years old and had lately grown rather stout, but he was still a majestic-looking pig, with a wise and benevolent appearance in spite of the fact that his tushes had never been cut. Before long the other animals began to arrive and make themselves comfortable after their different fashions. First came the three dogs, Bluebell, Jessie, and Pincher, and then the pigs, who settled down in the straw immediately in front of the platform. The hens perched themselves on the window-sills, the pigeons fluttered up to the rafters, the sheep and cows lay down behind the pigs and began to chew the cud. The two cart-horses, Boxer and Clover, came in together, walking very slowly and setting down their vast hairy hoofs with great care lest there should be some small animal concealed in the straw. Clover was a stout motherly mare approaching middle life, who had never quite got her figure back after her fourth foal. Boxer was an enormous beast, nearly eighteen hands high, and as strong as any two ordinary horses put together. A white stripe down his nose gave him a somewhat stupid appearance, and in fact he was not of first-rate intelligence, but he was universally respected for his steadiness of character and tremendous powers of work. After the horses came Muriel, the white goat, and Benjamin, the donkey. Benjamin was the oldest animal on the farm, and the worst tempered. He seldom talked, and when he did, it was usually to make some cynical remark—for instance, he would say that God had given him a tail to keep the flies off, but that he would sooner have had no tail and no flies. Alone among the animals on the farm he never laughed. If asked why, he would say that he saw nothing to laugh at. Nevertheless, without openly admitting it, he was devoted to Boxer; the two of them usually spent their Sundays together in the small paddock beyond the orchard, grazing side by side and never speaking.

GEORGE ORWELL

Extension

- Read any editorial or political column in your local newspaper. Note all the metaphors used, in addition to the tenor and the vehicle that make up each and the intended effect.

Production   Literary Research

Literary research is, as the name implies, research but focusing on literary aspects. It is likely that you are already familiar with research though frequently you have done research papers on a wider array of topics (the extended essay is a research project; one option involves literary research though the majority involve something more akin to social science or scientific research). Literary research involves common components of research including finding a topic, performing research, narrowing a topic, organizing research, developing a thesis, organizing and writing results and citation.

Selecting a topic is one area that may be unique to literary research. With the array of literatures, writers and eras, simply selecting a topic at random becomes impossible. While exposure to a writer or a work that is completely unknown to you can open your eyes to new favourites, literary research is much more likely to arise, and be successful, when based on something with which you are already familiar and in which you have some interest. Literary research, then, should arise out of something you have found interesting along the route of your class study and may range from an author's work, a genre you would like to explore further, a style of writing, a particular historical period or author's biographical information, an artistic era or any other particular contextual issue involved in the reception or production of literature (for example psychoanalytic criticism as a way to analyse texts or the influence of modernist painting on poetry).

Literary research also differs from other research styles in that the results of your research are intended to help further inform your own readings and analyses rather than stand alone as a body of knowledge you are investigating. This means that rather than research a topic in order to confirm or challenge a hypothesis, literary research is "reinserted" back into your own readings: you will take your research findings and apply or discard ideas (including challenging ideas) as you see fit to create your own independent analyses. Typically, then, literary research does not involve a research question, per se. Literary research is not about exploring an answer to a question but rather investigating the presence, absence and effect of aspects (either literary aspects operating internally in a work or contextual aspects operating externally around a work). With all literary research projects, the result should still be independent analysis of a work or works. With literature, while outside information and aid can be an asset, the final product should always emphasize your own singular reading and ideas. One unique element of literature as an academic discipline is the belief that all readers can have meaningful and interesting interpretations and, with literary research, it is sharing these interpretations—even when informed by the ideas of others—that is valued most highly.

If you are exploring contextual matters, including an author's biographical data or the historical context influencing a writer or important in a work, it is likely your research will proceed in a familiar pattern with Google searches, making use of the library and an array of digital and print sources. But more specific literary aspects are often treated more explicitly within a range of reference texts devoted to literary criticism. Your library may own sets of reference works devoted to literary criticism (such as the Gayle group collections on contemporary criticism) in either print or digital form but many of these references are usually in the form of academic journals that your school library is unlikely to possess. However, it may be that you have access to many of these sources online via the use of popular online databases such as JSTOR or Project Muse. These are excellent resources but a warning before you approach them: they contain academic papers written for a very specialized and learned audience and many of the works can be difficult to read and understand. This should not, however, put you off. Spend time reading the abstracts to glean whether a paper truly addresses a topic you are thinking of exploring. If you believe you have a paper worth reading, skim the article looking for material pertinent to your subject. Finally, be patient and read carefully—ideas will become clear. Literature is a demanding subject that deals with complex material: the existence of university departments devoted to its study and equally complex, even esoteric, language when analysing literary works only further attests to this complexity. But the personal reward for managing such complexity and developing a cohesive reading of your own is well worth the effort and brings its own reward.

Literary research would most likely be formally a part of an **extended essay** in group 1, a **further oral activity** or, possibly, a **written task 2** (for higher level only). With all of these assessment tasks, you will want to work with your teacher (or adviser in the case of an extended essay) to develop topics and discuss avenues for further research.

Sample student work

Read through the following example paragraphs that have made use of some external literary research. These samples do not necessarily represent exemplars of exactly what students must do but they demonstrate a little variety with varying degrees of success. The examiner comments may help note the different strengths of each approach.

1. In *Unnatural Voices* by Brian Richardson, the implied author is defined as such: "…the figure constructed by the reader of the person who produced the narrative, and who may differ significantly from the actual flesh-and-blood author." In the case of *Freedom*, the implied author—Patty—differs significantly from Franzen; both are opposites in terms of gender and the married lives they lead. In *Notable American Women* however, the implied author is fused with the real author; both share the same name, the same birthplace and the same physical appearances. The point where the implied author diverges from the real author is the anti-mimetic construct in which the novel is set. This is in contrast to *Freedom*, where Patty's life intersects with Franzen's only in terms of the location of her childhood home and the time period of her life. Patty's use of third person pronoun in her memoir adds a further layer to the narrative framework, and further substantiates the separation of the author from the narrator; Patty's irreconcilable use of "I" with herself shows the distinct difference with which she views herself and her written self. Hence, while Franzen signifies the "death of the author", Marcus raises the issue of the influence that the author has on the text, and vice versa.

    Much like in "The Tell-Tale Heart," Marcus differentiates between the implied reader and the real reader through the varying context in which the second person pronoun is used. Although the use of "you" engages the reader, the "you" in Poe's short story overlaps with the real reader in the sense that the protagonist

The use of this source is to define a point against which the texts will be measured. Immediately after citing the definition, each text is positioned in relation to the definition and to one another.

It could be helpful here for the candidate to reword the critic's definition on his or her own and to extend into a succinct main idea.

In this case, it is clear that the outside research has provided an interesting starting point from which the candidate develops his or her own analysis.

already deems the listeners as outsiders and being contrary to his opinion of himself, which are also true for the real reader. The "you" in Marcus, however, alters the tone and context of the moment of narration; the mother's accusatory "you" in her letter makes the reader sympathize with the father, much like how the "you" in the father's direct address to Ben disengages the reader from a passive role and enables the reader to see the relationship between characters on a more personal level.

Franzen, in comparison, does not address the reader directly. Patty makes certain presumptions on the part of her reader: "The autobiographer, mindful of her reader and the loss he suffered… The reader has no doubt heard about…" Patty's use of third-person pronoun, combined with the indirect address to the presumed reader, Walter, makes the narrative layer distinct to the real reader. This ties in with the heteroglossia present in the novel, which make the reader omniscient and hence brings about the relativity of fictional reality.

2. It is important to note in Pinter's play that both of the characters in the principal relationship are cheating on their husbands or wives; however, the audience is likely to form a strong opinion only on Emma's affair as we meet her husband, whereas Jerry's wife Judith remains in the dark. Emma's betrayal of Robert is a lot more striking and real for the audience because Jerry and Robert are best friends, as Jerry states when their affair has begun to disintegrate, "I might remind you that your husband is my oldest friend" (p 52). Furthermore, the audience is made aware of the nature of Emma and Robert's relationship, for example when Robert discovers the affair he comments to Emma that, "To be honest, I've always liked [Jerry] rather more than I've liked you" (p 87). Here it is interesting to note that this exchange occurs in Torcello, which is, as Linda Wells writes, the place where Robert and Emma came on their wedding trip at the start of their romance and is now the place where their romance ends (Wells, 1983). As the play progresses, the audience becomes increasingly aware that the relationship between Robert and Emma may not have been a happy one, thus enabling them to possibly begin to forgive Emma for engaging in an adulterous relationship in the first place. By contrast, the audience is unlikely to feel much emotion towards Jerry and Judith as Jerry's infidelity is not placed in context like Emma's.

Reference: Wells, Linda S. (1983) A Discourse on Failed Love: Harold Pinter's "Betrayal" *Modern Language Studies*. Vol. 13, No. 1 (Winter). Pp. 22–30. Modern Language Studies Article Stable. www.jstor.org/stable/3194315.

3. In common with other genres, Southern Gothic literature comments on reality blending realism and grotesqueness to result in a gloomy version thereof (Boyd, Burns, Gleeson). The latter is highlighted through common themes such as miscegenation, sexual deviance and violence (Gleeson). Even though it is shocking and unsettling, it is usually masked or softened by adding some element of humor or irony into the story (Burns, Boyd). What makes Southern Gothic literature so appealing is its ability to shock readers, thereby holding their interest. The colorful, abnormal characters, combined with extraordinarily strange plots and an element of humor is what makes this genre fascinating. The morbidity and grotesqueness excite and allow for a good story.

This works to extend the contrast by providing more detail, which is a good approach though even a little further explanation would be helpful with this topic. There is some confusing use, or rather mixed use, of the names of authors and of texts. Applying a more consistent approach can be helpful for a reader and avoid the slightly awkward mixing of title and author through these paragraphs.

This quote does not quite work as self-evident and requires a little further explanation.

This idea needs to be explained a bit further.

With such a complex set of "affairs," this deserves a little more space to make the point clearer.

The idea that different contexts are created in these relationships and that an audience will react differently to these differing contexts is interesting. This seems as though it may be the primary point but would be much more effective coming earlier to help the reader follow the support used above.

Why would you link the grotesque, common themes and miscegenation, sexual deviance and violence?

This is a reasonable interpretation of these critical definitions and represents good work at consolidating the critical work of others.

Irony is quite a broad term used to suggest any verbal, gesture or image play where reality (or real intent) is different from the masking appearance. It works effectively as we expect one outcome but find that something quite different actually occurs. At its simplest, an ironic expression (again, in words, gesture or image) is used to convey its opposite meaning (as when, for example, someone makes an expression of horror or great fear when trying to indicate something small and not at all scary) but irony can also be used much more subtly. In fact, irony is much easier to detect in image, speech or gesture than in written words, perhaps because of other sensory clues conveyed through non-verbal exchanges.

Irony is often confused with sarcasm, though sarcasm usually implies something more obvious and more harsh or hurtful than irony. Irony is much more often used for humorous intent and it can be helpful to understand the difference between facetiousness, irony, innuendo and sarcasm as on a spectrum (from most playful to most bitter). Irony is considered the most sophisticated of these usages as it involves an emotional detachment and often conveys a grim humour. It is most associated with critique but can also be used to praise through clever manipulation of understatement. Beyond verbal statement, irony can occur in event, setting, structure and situation as in the scenarios of:

- an assembly of mourning during a birth
- an isolated and lonely individual amidst a celebrating crowd
- an ode to distrust or sadness
- a sudden and violent storm during a wedding.

Finally, in drama irony operates in a unique fashion. Because drama relies on performance and audience, it is able to make use of these structures to create irony in what you could argue is more "three-dimension-like". Dramatic irony involves turns of speech that mean more than they seem because of other contextual information not available to all characters. In this way, some characters—and the audience—know and can predict events to come while other characters—usually the victims—move forward unknowing and in ignorance. Most often, such ends are tragic, at least temporarily.

Activity

Irony can make for interesting humour or make a poignant point, especially as **situational irony** (a situation that includes sharp contradictions or sharp contrasts). Look at the following image and analyse the irony and how it is used.

Background | **Structuralism and Post-Structuralism**

Structuralism

Structuralism is primarily a linguistic theory that seeks to make sense of language systems. On the one hand, structuralism posited the notion that language is not mimetic. This means that words in any language do not replicate the thing they name but are merely arbitrary signs standing in for them (for instance "cat" does not inherently mean the feline creature but does so by social association; "drat" might just as easily been developed as the English noun to represent this object). On the other hand, however, structuralism posited that there is a system that is organized, not arbitrary, fixed for all languages and that we can use this system to make sense of any language system.

Structuralism focuses on two distinct components: the *langue* and the *parole*. The *parole* suggests the actual speech or language used to make sense within any language system while the *langue* suggests an underlying grammar that governs the language system. Though we could use many—perhaps infinite—combinations of *parole*, or actual words, the thinking with structuralism is that all groups of words must adhere to a finite, or set, number or grammatical permutations (the *langue*). In other words, structuralism posits that there is a governing system to language and though very likely a complex system, a system nonetheless that includes rules, operations and procedures that can be studied, understood and predicted (hence, a grammar).

Structuralism is most recently and most pragmatically recognized as a system of mythemes that help govern the uses of the English language. This means, most simply, that all uses of language adhere to a governing system of "mythic" realities that must be conveyed via literary language. In this case, though we may employ any number of a variety of *paroles* that suggest the colour black, for example, the underlying *langue* that governs our use of language associates black with evil and so every instance of the use of "black" in one form or another (regardless of how overt) would suggest an underlying meaning of evil, bad, or malfeasance.

Post-structuralism

Post-structuralism built upon looking for semiotic meaning (looking for systems or identifying or understanding signs) that came through the idea of the *langue* in structuralism, but wholeheartedly rejected the idea of a universal system for understanding semiotics. Instead, post-structuralists focused on how the signs of language inevitably gave rise to irreconcilable and contradictory readings rather than more unified whole. Post-structuralists ultimately focused on the undecideability of literature (and other works) and the *play* that such undecideability allows.

Central to post-structuralist thought is the notion, or lack thereof, of a *transcendental signified*. This term refers to a singular word that is absolute and known to all simultaneously. Since all language is arbitrary, as the structuralists established via the notion of the *parole*, all meaning is arbitrary. But the post-structuralists also believed that there was not an absolute governing grammar system (a *langue*) underneath and that this underlying system could be as arbitrary as the language, or *parole*, system on top. In this way, not only could "drat" have ultimately meant the feline, domestic animal (rather than "cat") but "black" could be easily associated with right, purity, goodness and fairness.

Post-structuralists seek to challenge works and readings of works by asking that we revisit our assumptions, either with *parole* or with *langue*. In other words, what differences occur if the word "cool" means "not warm", or "hep", or if that term suggests being a part of the popular or "in-crowd," or if it refers to being a part of the majority that is truly ignorant, misguided and problematic? Post-structuralists look to play with the variety of possibilities because of the recognition that determining any certainty between the poles is, without a universal signified, impossible.

Reception   Point of View and the Narrator

Point of view refers to the narrative "voice" whether it take the form of an external narrator or through the perspective of a character or characters. Point of view, then, is the source and scope of the narrative voice. An author's choice of point of view has significant effect on a story's voice and the type of information available to receive as a reader which can have an impact even on the way you read a work. If you are presented with the materials of a story from one vantage point versus another, the same story may look and read very differently.

Point of view may take the form of one of the following:

- First person—the use of "I"—presents a story through the viewpoint of a single character. This point of view necessarily limits perspective and asks the reader to consider reliability, though you may receive significant knowledge of this character's thoughts and motivations.

- Second person—the use of "you"—is a rare use of point of view. The strangeness of a narrative voice focalized through the reader as a kind of character in a story is used only for very specific effect.

- Third person omniscient—the use of "he", "she", "they"—offers an unlimited perspective all-knowing with regard to the thoughts and motivations of all characters, action, setting, and so on.

- Third person limited—again the use of "he", "she", "they"—offers the perspective of some of the characters (often just one character) in a story but not all-knowing to all characters, action, setting, and so on.

- Third person objective—again the use of "he", "she", "they" —offers only a expository summary of events as experienced by the character or characters, presenting what may be variously called an objective or scenic or panoramic perspective of what is, without comment on interior motivations and thoughts.

Many works of fiction employ a single point of view but there are many others, particularly among contemporary fiction, that employ multiple and shifting points of view in a single work. Paying attention to point of view and even considering points of view not available from the author can be a useful tool in helping tease out the meaning or effect of works.

The narrator is the teller of a story and exists in some form regardless of point of view. After determining point of view, it becomes important to question the narrator's reliability: a reader accepts a reliable narrator without serious question of the narrator's judgment while a reader must question both statements of fact and the judgment of an unreliable narrator.

Activity

A consideration of point of view can be a critical lens with which to view cultural context in literary works. Even playful versions such as *Politically Correct Bedtime Stories* that present common fairy tales through the perspective of different characters offer a lucid and insightful feminist critique of a clearly male-dominated world in which women are to be rescued and find "true love" as their *raison d'être*. Pick a character (either one of the goats or the troll) from the following excerpt and rewrite the work from that character's perspective to highlight a contextual issue. This kind of critical activity could be an approach to a written task as you work through the course.

The Billy-Goats Gruff

Once upon a time there were three billy-goats, and the name of all three was Gruff. One day the three Billy-goats Gruff set off to the hills where the sweet grass grew. There they would eat and eat until they were fat.

On the way was a bridge over a stream, and under this bridge there lived a troll. His eyes were round as saucers, and his nose was long as a poker.

First of all came the youngest Billy-goat Gruff to cross the bridge.

"Trip trap! Trip trap. Trip trap! Trip trap!" went the bridge.

"Who's that tripping over my bridge?" roared the Troll.

"Oh, it's only me, the littlest Billy-goat Gruff and I'm going off to the hills to make myself fat," said the littlest Billy-goat Gruff, in such a tiny voice.

"Now I'm coming to gobble you up!" said the Troll.

"Oh no, please don't take me. I'm far too little," said the billy-goat. "Wait until the second billy-goat comes—he's much bigger."

"Very well—be off with you," said the Troll.

"TRIP TRAP! TRIP TRAP! TRIP TRAP! TRIP TRAP!" went the bridge.

"Who's that tripping over my bridge?" roared the Troll.

"Oh, it's only the second Billy-goat Gruff, and I'm going off to the hills to make myself fat," said the second Billy-goat Gruff, who hadn't such a small voice.

"Now I'm coming to gobble you up!" said the Troll.

"Oh no, please don't do that. Wait until the big billy-goat comes—he's much bigger."

"Very well, be off with you," said the Troll.

Just then along came the big Billy-goat Gruff.

"TRIP TRAP! TRIP TRAP! TRIP TRAP! TRIP TRAP!" went the bridge, for the billy-goat was so heavy that the bridge groaned and creaked beneath him.

"Who's that trapping over my bridge?" roared the Troll.

"IT'S ME! THE BIG BILLY-GOAT GRUFF!" said the billy goat, who had a great hoarse voice of his own.

"Now I'm coming to gobble you up!" roared the Troll.

"Well come along, I'm ready for you!" said the big Billy-goat Gruff. Up climbed the Troll, and the big Billy-goat Gruff put down his horns, and tossed the Troll off the bridge into the stream. SPLASH! Then the big Billy-goat Gruff crossed the bridge and went up to the hills.

There the three Billy-goats Gruff got so fat that they were barely able to walk home again.

SIR GEORGE WEBBE DASENT

The Romantic period, or Romanticism, was both a philosophical and an artistic era that most flourished in the early 19th century, though it began in the late 18th century. As is always the case when trying to define an era or a philosophical or artistic movement, finding singular or totalizing descriptions is exceptionally problematic and one will always find challenges to any asserted tenet. However, if for no other reason than the purely pragmatic, it can be useful to understand some of the trends and, in particular, how Romanticism differs from movements that both preceded it and followed it.

Preceding Romanticism was the age of Classicism (or Neoclassicism) that valued order, reason and governing laws. Such values even influenced art and literature where the heroic couplet celebrating ordered greatness was most favoured. The Romantics reacted against the idea that all beauty, experience and humanity could be neatly contained, described and understood and believed instead that they extended beyond the domain of formal logic and ordered description. Imagination over reason and rules, then, came into favour. Some people attribute part of this change to psychological need to escape some grim realities in many of the quickly industrializing Western countries where a utilitarian worldview was reducing many to feel they were nothing more than pieces functioning in an unfeeling machine. The late 19th century brought movements towards realism and naturalism that rejected the Romantics' notions of transcendent imagination and idealism towards the actual and natural scientific laws as uncovered by discoveries from psychology to biology. It is the significant distinctions between Classicism before and Realism after that can usefully identify romanticism.

Here, in the form of a very brief list, are some of the more common associations with Romanticism as a unique period in literature.

- The individual is the centre of life and experience.
- Art and literature are unique expressions of unique feelings and attitudes; these may be fragmentary, incomplete or singular rather than complete, unified and universally transferable.
- Creativity and imagination are most highly valued and more noble than fact, reason and logic.
- "Truth" is known only through individual imaginative experience and not through fact, reason and logic.
- Nature, not as precise and ordered but as messy, gothic and untended or unfettered, is valued over the man-made and precise.
- Romanticism seeks the "ideal" that transcends the actual and is beyond the base worldly concerns of politics, law, education and society.
- Romanticism focuses on the simple, commonplace and natural.
- Romanticism celebrates the ordinary person and basic humanity.

Production Close Reading and Commentary

In an earlier background section on New Criticism you read of the focus on close textual reading and careful attention to literary features in a work (in fact with New Criticism, a better reading is one that looks exclusively at how the literary features within a work operate). This remains one of the essential skills of this course as the ability to read closely and critically is not only crucial for a full appreciation of literature but necessary to be a truly informed consumer of all language texts you will encounter in life.

Close reading is actually assessed throughout the course as a primary skill. Close reading, however, is quite formally assessed in both the individual oral commentary (see the production section on page 123 for further details) and in paper 1, the comparative textual analysis for higher level or textual analysis for standard level (though this may not be of literary works at higher level and will not be of literary works at standard level). The unseen written commentary can be a daunting task—you are asked to approach an unfamiliar work, often only an excerpt, and develop a textually supported reading with no outside assistance and within a limited period of time. It can be argued, though, that this is truly the most authentic assessment that gauges the most fundamental skills demanded of the course. It can be useful to think of the demands of the unseen written commentary as follows: what meaning or effect does the text convey and how does the language operate in ways that give rise to this meaning or effect?

While it is close reading (of works of literature, works of non-fiction and even image) that is the central skill involved in paper 1, this assessment task also asks you to communicate about your reading effectively. Specifically, you are asked to produce a coherent and well-organized essay that contains a clear logic and structure as well as the familiar range of required formal elements (such as an introduction and conclusion, transitions and formal use of language). What this suggests is that paper 1 necessarily involves significant planning and forethought—if you walk into your paper 1 examination and begin writing out your response immediately (after, say, reading through the texts once only), it is highly likely that you will not be producing a good-quality and well-organized piece. In general, you can safely spend 15–20 minutes reading and thinking, taking notes and planning your work. For more useful information on paper 1, turn to the production section on analysis and comparative analysis on page 27.

In this section, we are focusing on commentary on unseen pieces of literature and approaching an unknown literary work. Though this is not truly a unique skill performed any differently from close reading of any language work, it can be helpful to consider the following with an unknown prose excerpt or poem.

- Your goal in close reading and commentary is to formulate a reading that is an argument about the fundamental effect or purpose of the text. Simply listing ideas or literary features is not sufficient.

- Read with an open mind. Be open to what the text will offer. Read slowly and carefully. Your first reading should be uninterrupted.

- Take notes on your second and further readings noting interesting ideas (see the production section on page 12 for ideas on note taking). Here, you are gathering data with which to formulate your argument.

- Ask questions such as these to develop a larger reading:
  - Who is the speaker as suggested by particular uses of diction, setting, motives, emotions or other features?
  - Who is the intended audience? Is there anything that suggests intent to persuade or share intimate knowledge?
  - What seems to be the subject of the text? Is there a primary issue, situation, problem, feeling or memory that recurs? Are there significant gaps in the work that disrupt treatment of a subject?
  - How is the form significant? If the text is a poem, is form or meter important? If prose, what is the point of view? Is dialogue used? Can the text be clearly understood as sections or does it flow as a unified whole?
  - What significant literary features stand out? (Do not look for literary features in isolation; these should only be mentioned if significant in helping you to understand the text and develop a larger reading. If you note a literary feature, or possible literary feature, but it does not fit into your larger understanding, it is not significant enough to mention in your commentary.)
- Ask final questions such as these to develop an argument.
  - Is there significant change by the end of the text?
  - Are there inherent contradictions or ambiguities in the text?
  - Does the form have a direct impact on meaning?
  - How might the title be significant?

After going through the text with an eye towards some of the features mentioned above (which are, by no means, exhaustive), you should now be in a position to formulate an argument that conveys your experience of the work. Avoid self-evident points or simple paraphrase (it is especially common with poetry that students basically "translate" the poem into prose format—this is not sufficient). Your argument need not be *the meaning* of a work but rather should reveal something of the experience of engaging with this work and its apparent effect or purpose. This must go beyond basic points such as "makes a reader want to read more" (presumably, all writers hope readers will read more), but to argue that it "generates excitement and enthusiasm in a reader" is perfectly appropriate.

Sample student work

Read through the following excerpts of sample student work and examiner comments. These samples include body paragraphs only that focus on analysing a literary work though this mirrors the actual skills required of all paper 1 analyses.

1. Based on Walt Whitman's *Song of Myself*, part 13.

Whitman begins the poem with a description of the subtle beauty of an African-American laborer. He draws focus to the worker with the use of anaphora. He repeatedly uses the word "negro" and "his" in the first stanza, thus establishing that it is the laborer he is describing. Next, at the end of the first stanza, Whitman describes the beauty of the "negro" in an almost erotic manner: "The sun falls on his crispy hair and mustache, falls on the black of his polish'd and perfect limbs". It is apparent that Whitman is celebrating the worker's physical form by describing his "hair and mustache" and "perfect limbs". However Whitman's use of the adjectives "crispy" and "polish'd" seem rather out of place. They make the description almost erotic. In the next verse Whitman further adds to the erotic image of the "negro" by writing, "I behold the picturesque giant and love him". It is unclear what Whitman intends to mean when he says "love him". However, an interpretation many would draw is that Whitman is speaking of a physical, sexual love. For this would add to the already established erotic image of the laborer. Regardless of whether Whitman is indeed speaking of a sexual "love", what is apparent in these two stanzas is that Whitman is celebrating the body of the African-American.

In the following stanza, Whitman digresses in the sense that he seizes to celebrate for an instance. Instead he alludes to poem 1 from *Song of Myself*. He describes the harmony of the effect life has on him. He emphasizes that what he is experiencing is harmonious by using rhyme in two of the lines of this third stanza. The reason why Whitman's use of rhyme stands out here is because he does not usually use rhyme. Whitman writes in free verse. In the first line of the stanza Whitman rhymes the word "moving", from the middle of the line, with the word "sluing", from the end of the line. In the next line Whitman uses a slant rhyme – he rhymes the words "bending", again from the middle of the line, and "missing", from the end of the line. Whitman then makes it apparent that this stanza is meant to refer to poem 1 from *Song of Myself* by writing, "Absorbing all to myself and for this song". This line is remarkably similar to the first line of poem 1: "I celebrate myself, and sing myself".

2. Based on Salman Rushdie's *The Moor's Last Sigh*.

Moor states that he himself would find himself trapped in this "war of the worlds" between Mainduck and Abraham "like dust between coats of paint" (p 318). The fact that Moor describes himself, "Bombay, and even India itself" (p 318) as dust instead of one layer of paint or the other suggests that Moor does not identify himself as a part of either his father or Mainduck's side of the "war", but that he is unsure of where he belongs, similar to how in Bombay and India, it is uncertain which side it will end up taking politically and religiously. This is also demonstrated when Moor describes Mainduck as "unleashing a mad tirade about anti-Hindu robots and what-not" (p 318). The tone in this statement is one of tiresomeness and sarcasm, clearly indicating that Moor does not take Mainduck's beliefs seriously. Moreover, earlier in the novel Abraham indicated his disinterest in the family business, suggesting that he does not identify himself with either side.

Through comparing the two sides in the 'war of the worlds' as two layers of paint, or as a palimpsest, brings the theme of 'what lies underneath' to the forefront. This palimpsest imagery works as a metaphor for indicating that India in all its plurality and complexity is being covered, hidden, and ignored by political forces such as that of Abraham and Mainduck. It suggests that through trying to

---

Reasonable explanation.

Explain how exactly.

In the start of this paragraph, you argue for subtle beauty—do you ultimately find the stanza subtle or not and what difference might this make?

This certainly shows an awareness of some features of the poem. But for what larger point is this digression of form employed? How does this work in contrast to the other stanzas?

Good point.

Yes... and so? Push a discussion of significance. Nice use of language.

Reasonable larger point.

paint their own reality of India, they are covering 'what lies beneath' or the true nature of India as it is. In addition, the palimpsest functions as a metaphor to Abraham himself, raising the question as to what his true identity is.

3. Based on Emily Dickinson's "These are the Days".

The fifth and sixth stanzas are significant because the anaphora used – the word "Oh" – begins to shift the tone once again to that of a musical plea, or perhaps a hymn. These final stanzas are a plea to the summer days to "permit a child to join". The child seems to be the sudden summer day, while Dickinson asks if *true* summer would accept these days as one of them, permit them to call themselves "summer" or be looked upon the same way as true summer. Not only is this a somewhat childish view on the summer days (it is almost as if Dickinson is saying "you're not summer— you're a fraud! Let summer accept you as one of its own; I will then believe you") but it also gives these days a sacred feeling. It makes the summer —both real and fraud—seem like the work and mischief of God.

The rhyme scheme throughout the poem is varied in accordance with the changes in tone and rhythm. The first stanza does not rhyme apart from the line "A very few—a Bird or two"— which shows internal rhyme. The second stanza, however, progresses to a near but not exact rhyme—with "resume" and "June". The third, fourth, and fifth stanzas all have perfect rhymes, and the final stanza, instead of rhyming, uses the same word ending ("partake" and "take"). As for the rhythm, the entire poem has a slow, relaxed rhythm to it, which changes only slightly—once in the third stanza where these days are accused of fraud, and near the end of the poem, where, as mentioned, a hymn-like tone and the accompanying slowed pace are created.

This work is effectively developing points with a clear sense of organization and purpose as well as indicating strong understanding and analysis.

An interesting interpretation but it breezes a bit too quickly over the stanzas. It is a bit unclear what Dickinson is literally saying here.

OK, but it would be better to integrate this with the rest of the discussion. And what is the effect of all this?

> **Activity**
>
> Read through the excerpt from Emily Bronte's *Wuthering Heights* on page 202. How does the short section reveal action, conflict, revelation and voice?

Background Reader Response

Reader Response is both a general term that can be used to imply a number of popular critical approaches to reading and interpreting literature that arose after New Criticism and a specific early theory and approach as a fundamental shift from New Criticism. As the name implies, Reader Response turns its focus from the work of literature to the work of the reader.

You may recall that New Criticism believed in the objective truth of the literary text as a self-contained artefact with all of its meaning contained within the confines of the work. A reader's work was to uncover and recognize all of the allusions, images, allegories and other employed devices that conveyed the inherent meaning within a text. Though this type of close reading is by no means a simple feat, there is an element of passivity on the part of the reader under New Criticism in that a reader plays no role in the production of meaning but merely follows clues left by a text towards a meaning pre-determined within that text.

Some early critics took exception with this approach, arguing that readers must be actively involved in the production of meaning. At its simplest, there is the basic transactional requirement for a reader in order for a text to have meaning at all; after all, if nobody is there to read a book, can its meaning be said to truly exist? But, of course, early reader response theory was much more subtle with critics such as Louise Rosenblatt arguing that a work is "what the reader lives through under the guidance of the text and experiences as relevant to the text". This implies a much more cooperative effort between reader and text to manufacture a meaning that would always be greater than a text in isolation could be (that is, without a reader).A reader response approach is obviously more affective than the objective approach of New Criticism. Rather than a text containing all of the answers, reader response theorists argued for gaps in works that required readers and their unique experiences to complete. Such aspects, then, do not exist within works but are instead inspired through the reading of works. It is possible, then, that a single text could evoke multiple interpretations based on the variety of experiences different readers will bring to a text. In fact, this suggests that even individual readers could have multiple and different experiences with a text. It is likely, for instance, that your reading of a literary work at age 17 will be very different from your reading of that same work at age 37 and informed by an additional two decades of reading and life experience.

Reader Response theory has continued to grow and change into more specific literary approaches (see the sections on feminism, Marxism and post-colonial criticism or New Historicism for some examples) over time. Even the term "reader response" is now sometimes referred to as "reader-oriented theories" to reflect the larger range of approaches associated with reader response. However, students do need to understand that reader response theory does not allow for a "free-for-all" approach to reading and that, especially for the demands of this course, students are expected to support assertions with logical textual analysis. Students often go astray with analysis that is based so purely on private association that it fails effectively to demonstrate close reading. An example would be a fan of science fiction work who reads the word "portal" and, based on this association, constructs a new text of space travel, when the text's use of "portal" more likely implies a window. In our classes, we the authors say—only slightly jesting—that there is no single right answer to a reading but that there are wrong answers. In general, and combining the close reading skills promoted by New Criticism with the active engagement promoted by reader response, you are asked to base your interpretations and readings not only on single or isolated elements within a work. Instead, your interpretations and readings will treat the text as a whole (rather than simply focusing on a word, phrase or line) and therefore your interpretations will logically hold true for the entire work.

Because we know literature is created to have an effect, we also read with this knowledge and know, based on clues as well as our understanding of what literature is, to read it looking to create and find meaning or effect. We understand that we read as what the literary critic Wayne Booth called "implied readers". We (the authors) don't, for instance, pick up a poem and read it as Rob Allison and Brian Chanen the actual people but as Rob Allison and Brian Chanen, readers of literature. Because we know we are reading literature, we shift our thinking and open up to what we know to be literary possibilities and operations within a work and perform a kind of process of give and take: we look for what we think or expect a text to do (as literature) and bring to this work our own experiences, understandings and backgrounds. In taking these together and balancing our own readings with what we know to be happening within a work as literature, we are that much more likely to develop rich and viable interpretations of literary works.

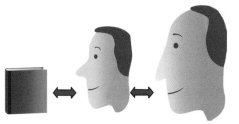

Text   Implied reader   "Real" reader

In the illustration the text exists but not independently. The "real" reader—you in your "real" life—exists on the far right and engages the text. But you do not actually read as though it is the "real" you expressing surprise at some of the features or story lines you come across in a work. Instead, based on all you know and have learned about literature and reading literary works, you become the middle "implied reader". If literature does function with a set of tropes, or traits, that allow us to see a resemblance to reality yet also understand that it remains fiction, then the "implied reader" is the persona we adopt as a kind of medium through which to read. It is when students fail to recognize their work as "implied readers" and approach only as "real" readers that serious problems with analysis arise.

Production   Responding to Essay Prompts

Paper 2 in the IB English A: language and literature course is an essay written in response one of six self-selected prompts (that is, you will have a choice of six prompts and are required to write an essay in response to one only). The prompts are the same for both higher level and standard level, though the length of the examination differs (two hours for higher level and an hour and a half for standard level) as do the marking criteria (which are more demanding for higher level). The approach to responding to essay prompts, however, remains the same.

Paper 2 is, as the name implies, an essay. This essay should include all of the elements of a formal essay including careful planning, an introduction and conclusion, a clear and logical organization and the attendant attributes of any formal writing assignment (such as formal language and transitions). As paper 2 does not allow for the use of texts, you are not required to memorize quotes for use but you should be familiar enough with the works in your study that you can refer to specific episodes or elements of the works through anecdotal reference. It is likely, however, that if you do read works closely (including rereading) and prepare fully for the examination, you will find repeated refrains or memorable lines that you can cite directly.

As mentioned above, approaching the essay prompts begins with careful preparation before entering the examination. This starts with very careful and close reading, active engagement in class discussion and pre-examination preparation including practising the examination. (It is best to practise in conditions as close to those in the examination as possible but especially with no reference materials, with accurate time limits and good essay prompts). It may be helpful to further break examination conditions into parts in order to practise components (for example, practise only the reading, thinking, note taking and preparation component of the examination of about 15–20 minutes for higher level and about 15 minutes for standard level or just this early part of the examination process along with writing an introduction). You really would do well, however, to practise a "full" examination in advance at least once. Part of your preparation might also include sets of notes that list distinguishing elements, themes, common devices and contextual issues used in the texts in your study in order to see common or contrasting components across the works. Remember that a "work" will involve multiple texts if the work in your study consists of shorter writings such as poems, letters or short stories.

After all of the preparation mentioned above, you will be ready to approach the examination. The first step will be to read through the six available prompts, select the one about which you feel best and plan your response. But there are some helpful hints for selecting the best prompt.

- Read through all six options even if you feel as if you can respond to one of the first options you see. You need to consider carefully the prompt you choose so it is worth resisting an impulse decision.

- Work hard to understand what the prompt is really asking. This can be accomplished through rewriting the prompts in your own words to understand fully the gist of the prompts. One of the biggest hurdles for students in paper 2 is actually to respond to the question; in an effort to rush through and get down what they have learned about a text, students fail to appreciate fully the demands of the prompt. This leads to a reduction in marks.

- Recognize and understand that you must address context in your responses. Whether or not a prompt specifically refers to context, contextual issues absolutely must be addressed. This will be included in your study for this part of the course but you will have to bear it in mind with the above bullet point emphasizing the need for strong understanding of the prompt. Remember that contextual issues may involve the production of works, the reception of works or contextual themes.

- Plan your response carefully, including noting what main ideas you will make and what support you will use to illustrate your points. If you are working at higher level, think carefully about which two texts are most suitable to address the prompt.

- Express what you know about works in your study. This does not mean that you may disregard the intent of the prompts but you do want to select prompts that allow you to demonstrate your knowledge most fully.

- It may be helpful to consider questions like the following when approaching prompts. What contextual issues does the prompt imply? How are these contextual issues conveyed in the works you have studied? What literary features or uses of language in the works help convey these contextual issues?

- Finally, it is worth noting what is not helpful in paper 2. Simply memorizing a reading that you reproduce during the examination will not be helpful. Paper 2 asks students to demonstrate their understanding of works in unique and agile ways and not simply to reproduce the "right" answer or the answer they have passively received in class. Students who produce "stock" answers do not adequately convey an ability to engage with works independently and critically.

Activity

Practise reading the following prompts and identifying exactly what is being asked in each. Plan how you would respond using two of the works you have studied.

1. Analyse how justice is represented and understood in **at least two** works you have studied.

2. In order to explore cultural or social values, writers often use a character who is alienated from his or her culture or society. Examine this idea with reference to **at least two** works you have studied.

3. Literature is often said to be timeless. To what extent is this true of **at least two** works you have studied?

4. Focusing on **at least two** works studied, show that more than one interpretation could be made of those works.

Sample student work

"In drama there are more interesting roles for men than women."
Discuss to what extent you agree with this statement and what is it
that makes a role interesting.

The statement above, "In drama there are more interesting roles for
men than women" holds some truth with regards to Shakespeare's
Much Ado About Nothing. At a glance, one might be tempted to
agree with it— there are at least four main male characters that have
a lot of stage time and a lot of dialogue. Their actions also do spark
a lot of conflict in the play. However, upon closer scrutiny, one
comes to realize that although the women in the play may not speak
as much as the men, their actions as well as the impressions they
make on the men fuel a lot of the men's actions and therefore the
action of the play. This essay will analyse the principal (and some
of the secondary) characters in this play, with the hopes of showing
that Shakespeare, in this play, provides interesting roles for both
male and female characters.

One of the things that make characters interesting is their past
actions and their back-story. For instance, Don Pedro (just before
the play begins) has defeated his brother, Don John, in battle
and has forced Don John to stay with him and remain in his
submissive circle of friends. Don John is infuriated by this and,
in retaliation, creates much of the mischief that brings about the
final conflict—the fight between Hero and Claudio on what was
to be their wedding day. The audience going into the play know
that the characters past encounters with one another will influence
the course of the play, and the hint of a conflict between the two
in the very first scene of the play allows the audience to know that
these two characters are going to be engaged in some kind of a
conflict during the play—the audience's interest is immediately
piqued, they know that these two characters are going to be ones
to watch. Another instance would be the past relationship between
Benedick and Beatrice; from the very first scene Beatrice begins to
insult Benedick, despite the fact that he has not been introduced
to the audience yet. This immediately makes the audience wonder
what had happened between the two for Beatrice to form such a
strong and bitter opinion of a man who the messenger spoke so
highly of. Leonato stating that there is a "merry war" between the
two, and Beatrice saying in her aside that she "knows [Benedick]
of old" serve as foreshadowing of what is to come—the audience is
hooked onto this clever couple who seem to be constantly at war,
they want to see what will come of it. What makes a character's past
so interesting is the fact that the audience knows close to nothing
about it: they want to see how things progress and find out more
about the character's past, giving them a chance to be involved in
the play and connecting the dots rather than being mere observers.

It would not be a stretch to say that most conflict in *Much Ado
About Nothing* is retaliation against some prior conflict. The
characters causing the conflict in this play are primarily Don

This is a clear thesis statement.

Good start overall—quite clear.

Quite true—does this make enough
overt connection to the question of
the difference between gender roles?

OK—a reasonable and interesting
argument—but would be better if
we had it related to women. I'm
also not sure this is enough in
terms of a definition (would an
interesting background story make
a part interesting to perform?)
Good use of language and voice.

John (though he is helped by Comrade and Brachia) and Claudio. Don John is bitter towards his brother for defeating him, and also Claudio as he played an instrumental part in that defeat. So, he decides to spin a web of deception that will trouble the two. Don John himself admits that he is "villainous" and that he cannot do anything about it, it is in his nature. The fact that Don John has such an extreme character is interesting to the audience, because they want to try and understand the motives behind his actions. The very shock that the audience receives when he discusses the fact that he does evil because he enjoys the feeling he gets piques the audience's interest. Claudio, on the other hand, is a character that the audience can relate to—he is very likeable, albeit slightly gullible. He causes the conflict during his wedding with Hero because he has been led to believe that she has been unfaithful. His actions, though a result of Don John's cunning, are in reaction to what he thinks Hero has done—he wants to humiliate her as much as she humiliated him. The audience can understand this urge, even though they know he has been misled, and they are therefore more likely to sympathize with him, and wonder how all this will turn out in the end. Thus, it can be said that a character's nature plays quite a large role in how interesting they are—the audience is hooked if they are either shocked, or if they can sympathize.

Ah yes—and what about the women? Good knowledge and understanding here but not so great in terms of the question—the focus on men seems to take you a little off-track.

Reception Sound Devices

One distinct feature of literature is the use of sound devices. The sometimes playful, sometimes serious, interplay of the connotations or denotations of words with their sounds can give rise to powerful effect in all language works but finds more common use in specifically literary works and, especially, with poetry. Some people refer to sound devices as musical devices suggesting their most obvious effect but the various sound devices can accentuate the tone and mood of texts or work in contrast to help convey larger effect or purpose. The primary sound devices are rhyme, alliteration, assonance, consonance and onomatopoeia though meter and anaphora can work to help with sound as well.

Rhyme

Rhyme is a correspondence of sounds between words. Technically, a true rhyme must include common vowels and succeeding consonants on the accented syllables preceded by different consonants, such as "cat" and "bat". While this is how we understand the use of rhyme at its most basic, rhyme is used much more liberally in literature. Generally, rhyme is a more significant literary feature in poetry than in prose so the rhymes described below are based on poetry; however, rhyme can be used in all forms of literature or language works so any of the types of rhyme described below could be found in anything from a political speech to an advertisement. The following are among the more likely uses of rhyme you will find.

- **Masculine rhyme**, which is sometimes called a full rhyme or perfect rhyme, is a rhyme where the correspondence of sound is restricted to the final accented syllable of words ("fish" and "dish"). The rhyme falls, technically, at the end of a line of poetry. This is what distinguishes a "masculine" rhyme from a "perfect" or "full" rhyme that can exist anywhere, including beyond merely the genre of poetry—obviously, perfect rhymes exist beyond poetry and may be used effectively in everything from political speech to advertisement.

- **Feminine rhyme** is sometimes called a double rhyme, a rhyme where the correspondence of sound is in two consecutive syllables such as in "lighting" and "fighting".

- **Half rhyme** can be referred to as a slant rhyme or an off-rhyme, a rhyme where either a consonant or a vowel sound rhymes but not both. This can sometimes be a visual rhyme (eye rhyme) as well. Examples include: "smiling" and "falling"; "death" and "earth"; "erasing" and "learning"; "cough" and "dough".

- **End rhyme** occurs at the end of lines of poetry.

- **Internal rhyme** occurs within lines of poetry rather than at the end.

Rhymes are frequently used in poetry not just singly but as part of a larger pattern within a poem. Because of this, an understanding of **rhyme scheme** may be useful. Rhyme scheme is simply a system of notation that notes the sequence of rhymes to occur; each rhyme within a stanza is marked by a common letter. The first line of a stanza is marked "a" as are all subsequent lines that rhyme. The next line of a stanza that does not rhyme with "a" is labelled "b" and the process is repeated. For example, here is the rhyme scheme for the final stanza of Shakespeare's "Rape of Lucrece":

When they had sworn to this advised doom,	a
They did conclude to bear dead Lucrece thence;	b
To show her bleeding body thorough Rome,	a
And so to publish Tarquin's foul offence:	b
Which being done with speedy diligence,	b
The Romans plausibly did give consent	c
To Tarquin's everlasting banishment.	c

Some common rhymes, by rhyme scheme, include:

- couplet—a pairing of rhymed lines (aa bb cc…)
- tercet—a trio of rhymed lines (aaa…)
- terza rima—interlocking trios of rhymes (aba bcb cdc…).
- quatrain—a stanza of four lines rhymed in various ways (abcb or abac…)

Anaphora

Anaphora is the repetition of an initial word or phrase in successive lines (or clauses as may be the case in prose). Anaphora has a connection to rhyme but because it is a repetition of the same word or phrase, its effect as a sound device is more obvious. Edna St Vincent Millay's poem *Recuerdo* on page 206 employs both "We" and "And" as anaphora as an example.

Assonance, consonance and alliteration

Other common devices include assonance, consonance and alliteration.

- **Assonance** is the repetition of vowel sounds through a small section of text (a line, a stanza, a paragraph.). Though not exactly a component of rhyme, assonance can feel "rhyme-like" and create euphony.

- **Consonance** is the repetition of consonant sounds with differing vowel sounds preceding. Technically, there should be a repetition of consonant sounds both before and after a different vowel, such as "black" and "block", but consonance is frequently associated with only the end consonant in words such as "bell" and "tall" or "pass" and "elopes". Consonance clearly also has a relationship to half rhyme and eye rhyme.

- **Alliteration** is the repetition of consonant sounds, most frequently the initial consonant sounds of words as in "broken battered bush" or "elongated alliterative allegory".

Onomatopoeia

Onomatopoeia is the formation and use of words to imitate the sounds they are meant to describe, such as "bang," "moo" or "whoosh".

Meter was mentioned above as having some significance as a sound device. For more on meter, turn to the production section on page 190. Arguably, all of the above sound devices are used to create a positive and intentional structural or auditory experience. But some authors may intentionally disrupt such harmony of sound (euphony) by working to create **dissonance**. Dissonance is not haphazard but rather the intentional arrangement of cacophonous sounds, whether through diction or pattern. Unintentional dissonance is… well… a mark of poor writing overall.

Background   Feminism

"Feminism", or "feminist criticism", is a general term that actually encompasses a wide variety of critical approaches. However, we may commonly use the term "feminism" to refer to critical study that seeks to describe and interpret women's experience in literature and in the world. Feminist criticism begins from a position that critiques a patriarchal system that equates male experience as human experience. By arguing that most popular writing (accepted by critics as well as a general public) is produced by men, focusing on male experience and forwarding patriarchal values as the dominant, long-standing and even "right" worldview, feminist critics seek to re-approach the field of literature with an eye towards women's experience as valuable and unique.

Feminism as a critical approach tends to take one of two routes: one school of feminism approaches the existing cannon with a sharp eye on the treatment of women in texts and how this either reinforces a prevailing patriarchal view or challenges or even undermines it. Feminist critics would note the treatment of female characters—including their outright absence—in addition to critiquing male characters and the representation of their attitudes. This critical approach is not limited to male authors as female writers could, wittingly or not, also fall into reproducing patriarchal norms. A second school of feminism sought out works specifically written by women and possibly overlooked or ignored. Sometimes called "gynocriticism", this approach seeks to understand women's experience and how women view the world uniquely from men.

Today, feminism is an exceptionally broad topic and there is much debate over the merits of a singular, female experience. Instead, contemporary feminism consists of many parts rather than a monolithic whole and you are likely to find critics focusing on a wide range of differing social concerns. These may include, for example, women of colour, post-colonial women, lesbian feminism and gender criticism. If, however, we seek to conceptualize feminism as a whole, the following would make a general list of the work of feminism.

- Feminism revalues women's experience.
- It examines and challenges representations of women and men in literature.
- It examines power relations between men and women in literature and in life and challenges patriarchy that values men above women.
- It recognizes the role of language in making what is socially constructed appear "natural".
- It explores the possibility of a unique feminine language and understanding.
- It re-examines the existing literary canon, discovering and rediscovering alternative female voices.

Reception   Meter and Rhythm

Meter

Meter refers to the pattern of regular, or almost regular, stressed and unstressed syllables in poetry. The most basic unit of meter is called a **foot** but there are varying orientations of stressed and unstressed syllables that result in the following types of feet:

- iambic—two syllables; unstressed, stressed ⌣ /
- trochaic—two syllables; stressed, unstressed / ⌣
- anapestic—three syllables; unstressed, unstressed, stressed ⌣ ⌣ /
- dactylic—three syllables; stressed, stressed, unstressed / / ⌣
- amphibrachic—three syllables; unstressed, stressed, unstressed ⌣ / ⌣
- spondeic—two syllables; stressed, stressed / /
- pyrrhic—two syllables; unstressed, unstressed. ⌣ ⌣

A line of poetry consists of varying numbers of feet, categorized by the following common forms:

- dimeter—two feet
- trimeter—three feet
- tetrameter—four feet
- pentameter—five feet
- hexameter—six feet

- heptameter—seven feet
- octameter—eight feet.

Finally, there are some common types of meter that employ specific combinations of types of feet and the number of feet per line. Some of the most common include:

- iambic pentameter—five iambs per line
- blank verse—unrhymed iambic pentameter
- free verse—poetry without any fixed meter or rhyme.

Rhythm

Rhythm is closely associated with meter as it is defined as either the recurrence of patterns of stressed and unstressed syllables or the recurrence of sounds and sound patterns (largely created through stressed and unstressed syllables). When these patterns become regular, readers often enjoy heightened emotional response and writers use rhythm—or its lack—to achieve particular effects. While meter is most associated with poetry, rhythm appears in prose as well (sometimes referred to as cadence). Though it may lack some of the regular patterning that arises from poetic meter, prose—both fiction and non-fiction—can made great use of rhythm.

Activity

Compare the meter and/or rhythm employed in the following texts. Identify any meter that is used; identify a rhythm that occurs; in the case of prose works, consider what gives these texts this rhythm; note the effect, impact or apparent purpose with the use of meter and/or rhythm:

- page 206, Edna St Vincent Millay's *Recuerdo*
- page 202, the excerpt from Andre Agassi's *Open*
- page 199, Elizabeth Barrett Browning's *Grief*.

Production | Introduction

The introduction of any work has an important function. Not only does the introduction alert the audience to topic and focus but it also sets the tone, mood and language for the entire work, preparing an audience to adopt a particular perspective. Employing a silly comic-strip format to introduce a serious discussion of genocide in an armed conflict would be inappropriate but would also put an audience into such a different "mind set" that communicating the serious information would become that much more difficult. Producing, then, a solid introduction is more than just dressing a presentation, essay or commentary but prepares an audience to appreciate your work that much more.

Beyond this "setting of the scene" effect described above, an introduction really only seeks to complete two objectives:

- Get the reader's attention.
- Identify the focus and convey the main argument or idea (thesis).

As long as your introduction communicates these points effectively, you will have produced at least a functional introduction. However, some additional elements may be included that might enhance an introduction—for the reader's benefit and for your own as the writer—or expand it with slightly more variety. Examples are as follows:

- Point your way into a topic.
- Establish the language.
- Establish a framework, blueprint or road map for the rest of the work, including touching on main points to be covered or even hints of the conclusion.

While you may find these additions helpful, again, it is the first two bullet points that must be emphasized.

After understanding what is required of an introduction, the next step is to actually produce one. We must emphasize that there is no set format for an effective introduction and that there are variety of approaches. It is appropriate to get the reader's attention *before* conveying the thesis, but beyond this order of "events" there are a variety of possibilities. Some like to think of an introduction as an inverted pyramid where you begin with general (larger) statements to get a reader's attention and then gradually move to the most specific information by the end. While this is a perfectly acceptable framework that may be useful to you, it is by no means the only approach.

Most students have a sense of what they want to say (that is, their thesis) before writing an introduction but struggle with the first sentence: the opener or statement to get a reader's attention. What follows is merely a list of possible approaches you could employ.

- Briefly summarize the work you are analysing.
- Make general statements about the genre or text type and how your topic supports or undermines these typical trends.
- Include an anecdote from the "real" world.
- Ask a rhetorical question.
- Provide a quote from the text that highlights an element you will emphasize.
- Give a "hint" of your conclusion.
- Give a definition of a related term, feature or aspect and how your topic supports or undermines this definition.
- Make an unusual point about the topic or text.
- Give a straightforward account of your main points and thesis.

Again, there is no "correct" approach. You should experiment with different kinds of introductions to see what works best for you and understand that different introductions may suit different assessment tasks or topics best. As you practise, you will feel both more comfortable about and more competent in producing a quality introduction. As a final point, it is worth noting that while an introduction can serve as a blueprint for the remainder of your work, with prepared written work it is always necessary to go back and review your introduction at the conclusion. It is possible, and even likely, that through the course of your writing some change has occurred and you may want to have this reflected in the introduction.

Sample student work

Read through the sample introductions from the commentary below along with the examiner comments. Try your hand at writing an introduction of your choice making use of the ideas above as well as comments below.

1. Moreas Zogoiby, the narrator of *The Moor's Last Sigh* by Salman Rushdie, in many ways embodies the ideals of the book's genre: magic realism. Moreas finds himself aging at an accelerated rate, yet aside from his visionary "differentness", he continues to strife for normality. Similarly, in magic realism the magical and unrealistic blends into a realistic background. This passage covers an important development in Moreas' struggle with himself and provides some insight on the motives behind his writing. Rushdie

1. "strive" not "strife"

Are these ideals of the genre?

Perhaps "similarly" is not quite the right word here.

Whose writing? Zogoiby's or Rushdie's?

emphasizes the sincerity of the narrator's revelations through the simple, very controlled sentence structure. Nevertheless, the flow of the writing is not disturbed since ideas are continuously picked up again. Moreas' situation is made clear by means of a comparison to another character in the book and the use of metaphor and allusion.

2. The passage I have chosen starts from the last paragraph of page 311 of *The Moor's Last Sigh* by Salman Rushdie. Written straight after describing Nadia Wadia and Fielding fancying her, this passage speaks of a variety of things including his recent disinterest in women, his satisfaction of working for Raman Fielding, his aging body and its effect on his work. Throughout the passage there seems to be a great sense of sophistication deriving from his use of imageries and diction which also increases the effectiveness of the impact towards the readers. Despite being seemingly straight forward in each sentence of the passage, I believe that within Rushdie's imageries and diction lays some sarcasm which actually depicts Moor's real and honest thoughts.

3. As most people would recall, 1492 was an important year for Spain, for late in that year Christopher Columbus discovered a New World that was to enrich Spain for centuries to come. Lesser known, though no less important historically, it was also the year of the moor's last sigh. Moor's ancestor, Vasco da Gama explores the path to India for trading which became convenient for the foreigners to establish their rule. When Moor was in India he studied the disputes among the Indians against the politicians. In the mid of Rushdie's novel, he had mentioned about the strike that was held by the workers due to critical conditions which prevailed at that time period.

4. Salman Rushdie's novel *The Moor's Last Sigh* consists of twenty chapters separated into four sections; the selected passage (pages 285–286) serves as the introduction of section three named "Bombay Central", graphically illustrating Moor's cataclysmic plunge into a world of reflection in a sadistic milieu after having been arrested for the trafficking of narcotics. Through literary devices such as sharp structure, point of view, allusions, diction and explicit imagery, Rushdie embarks the reader on a transcendent yet unpalatable voyage of sincerity, leaving nothing to imagination.

This can be confusing in terms of causality—does the writing style convey something, hide something or stand in contrast to something?

This seems a different topic or focus. This introduction hints at some elements but there is a lack of precise and singular focus that results in a more haphazard than controlled approach. A general lack of unity prevails.

2. This does a good job of providing context.

This remains vague, relying on terms such as "sophistication" and "effectiveness" but without specific reference as to what.

This could prove a reasonable focus but needs more attention and clarification. I'm not sure how this all links to the context established above.

3. This is kind of a clever and fun "attention-grabber".

The rest of the introduction, unfortunately, fails to capitalize on the interesting start. What the "sigh" is is never mentioned and the concluding sentences seem a series of disparate statements. There is a lack of clear focus and, as a reader, I am still not aware of what is to come.

4. This seems to suggest that it is the title that illustrates this. How?

"Allusions, diction and explicit imagery" These remain very vague terms—even slightly more detail would help. For example, allusions to what? What kind of imagery?

Phrases like this final sentence are ultimately hollow. Some particular elements are mentioned but I'm not quite sure about the point other than the material is graphic and, presumably, unpleasant.

Background Realism

Realism is, in a very broad sense, a reference to any literature that professes allegiance to reproducing the actual world in fiction (known as **verisimilitude**). But here the reference to realism relates slightly more specifically to an artistic movement that occurred from the mid-19th century to the final decade of that century and can primarily be identified or defined by its opposition to romanticism which preceded it (for more on romanticism, see the background section on page 136).

Realism concerned itself with, as suggested by the name, the "real" world. Specifically, realism was concerned with the "here and now," specific actions and behaviours and the verifiable. Realism sought to identify the common, ordinary experiences of the common and ordinary people trying to deal with very real problems, issues and phenomena contemporary with the times. Whereas Romanticism sought to transcend the immediate to find the ideal, realists believed that the problems, issues and concerns of everyday humankind were such that they had an ethical responsibility to address such phenomena in an effort to discover a way of living and of conduct here in an all-too-earthly world. Realists believed that by exploring the actual, they would find governing laws and norms and, in a very democratic tradition, could possibly exact change for the better.

In the Western world, this was a time of rapid industrial development as well as scientific progress and such an aesthetic movement makes sense against this backdrop. Many writers, such as Charles Dickens in England or Mark Twain in the United States, found plenty with which to find fault. Romanticism could feel overly sentimental and even false or pretentious and realism as a movement was keen to deal with and treat the more authentic problems that were highly visible. Interestingly, many of the writers during the realist era—and even realist writers in a more contemporary era—relied on satire and humour as much, if not more than, rant, protest or tragedy. Regardless of approach, however, what the realists shared was an intention towards mimetic art, or a one-to-one correspondence between representation and the objects or ideas being represented.

Activity

Read the short passage from the beginning of Mark Twain's *The Adventures of Huckleberry Finn* on page 204 and consider the following questions.

- What kind of realistic setting does Twain create?
- How is the language used to add to the sense of realism?
- What other elements of realism mentioned above are already apparent in this passage?
- How might this text suggest an ethical response to real social issues?

Background   Modernism

Modernism was an artistic and aesthetic movement from the very end of the 19th century through much of the 20th century (its exact dates, of course, are not fixed and many attributes of modernism continue to influence literature but mid-20th century is a reasonable approximation). Modernism was a period of incredible productivity, both in quantity and in quality, and the era remains well-renowned for some of the greatest works of the century. Modernism was a true movement that had an impact and influence on all of the arts and philosophy and was generally considered more widespread and encompassing than movements before or since. Though still generally limited to the Western world, modernism was both a trans-continental as well as a trans-Atlantic movement that had far-reaching influence.

Modernism can be most simply characterized as a break away from established rules, conventions and traditions. Modernism sought a new way of perceiving humankind's position and influence in the universe as well as new experiments in style and form. Though all movements can really be characterized by their reaction to and change from previous movements, modernism went further with some profound changes in approach, philosophy, style, method and product. Perhaps the single most interesting change was with that of perception. In reconsidering humankind's position and influence in the universe, modernists turned inward. They became concerned with the inner self and perceptions, including the subconscious or even unconscious (the rise of Freud, Jung and other psychoanalysts certainly aided in this). Modernism shifted the focus or frame of reference to within the mind rather than on any external object or notion and articulated a worldview where knowledge and understanding were *created* through perception rather than simply *received* through perception. This **solipsism** was a large part of the modernist project.

Of course, as with any movement, there was as much—if not more—variety as sameness. But a notion certainly arose of the "genius" artist who produced the most elevated art forms even if they were experimental. Some of the more common attributes of the modernist endeavour include the following:

- Historical discontinuity—no longer did modernists see the world or society as a product of history as the notion of cause-and-effect was disrupted. A linear progression of human improvement and positive historical growth was certainly challenged by the world wars, the Holocaust and the use of atomic weapons.

- Individual over the social—largely the result of the above point, the world was no longer viewed as a social entity that had common meaning for all but rather a world that may be perceived and understood uniquely by individuals.

- Alienation, loss and despair—the idea that we live in a solipsistic environment creates a sense of isolation: the individual alone creates and understands a unique universe and must labour in isolation through life.

- Unconscious—the unconscious has the force and power of the conscious or social world.

As a period of tremendous experimentation, tens of smaller sub-movements developed along the way in everything from dance to art to architecture to criticism to philosophy to literature. Even just a small sample of sub-movements that had a direct impact on literature includes:

- surrealism
- formalism
- dadaism
- existentialism
- constructivism
- expressionism
- futurism
- imagist poetry
- stream of consciousness.

Finally, a sense of the vitality, variety, success and quality of the period can be gleaned from even a cursory glance at some of the famous writers of the time. Associated with modernism are writers as varied as these:

T S Eliot	Ezra Pound	Wallace Stevens
Ernest Hemingway	William Faulkner	W B Yeats

W H Auden	D H Lawrence	James Joyce
Gertrude Stein	Marianne Moore	Sylvia Plath
Andre Gide	Marcel Proust	Albert Camus
Jean-Paul Sartre	Rainer Maria Rilke	Thomas Mann
Samuel Beckett	Luigi Pirandello	Eugene Ionesco
Eugene O'Neill	Tennessee Williams	Arthur Rimbaud

And the list could go on and on…

Insight Does Theory Matter?

We are often asked by teachers and students alike if it is important or necessary to learn about literary theory and different critical approaches (such as Marxism or feminism, featured in this book, or others such deconstruction, which are not). The answer is a bit of "yes" and a bit of "no".

There is no set body of content that you must learn in this course, thus you will never be directly assessed on whether or not you are familiar with the basic tenets of different literary theories or criticisms, or on any ability to apply particular critical approaches to texts. In this way, the answer to the eponymous question is "absolutely not". But such a simple answer belies the true complication of the question.

The truth is that the question itself is fundamentally flawed. Such a question harks back to an issue already addressed; that is, the nature of this subject. Though you are asked to demonstrate knowledge and understanding of all the works in your study, there is no required knowledge or content across all students in all schools (your teachers will have great choice in selecting works that fit best with the context of the school, student interest, text availability and their own areas of expertise). The reason is that the study of English language and literature is, again, not about a common body of content but rather skills and a particular disciplined way of knowing. In order to be most successful, you must learn what it is to "do" the discipline of English with reading, thinking, analysis and conveying ideas through a variety of formats. Ours is a discipline of critical exploration, hypothesis and sensitivity to an array of approaches and perceptions and a part of all of this work has included literary theory and literary criticism for several decades now.

This is not a universally embraced position. There are some, even prominent, thinkers within the discipline and in other influential positions who publicly declaim the purpose, use and value of theory and even more who reject it for its level of abstraction and difficulty. We hope, though, you might glean through the few sections on literary theory or critical approaches that we have included in this book, that even a position rejecting theory is itself a theoretical—perhaps even political—position. And this is the glory of this subject: that it allows for and embraces such a wide variety of readings and interpretations. Perhaps most ironically, it is principally the work of literary theory that has helped establish this as a central tenet of the discipline.

Literary theory is complex. It rarely simplifies or reduces texts but anything that promises such in this discipline should be treated with healthy scepticism. Instead, theory can illuminate other subtle layers and ideas about knowledge and truths. Applying different theories can also bring intellectual stimulation and pleasure in addition to knowledge and truths. But, again, it is the additional subtlety and complexity that remains core to the discipline. While you are not expected to master material at this stage of your study, we believe it is appropriate for you to be exposed to theory and criticism and, by extension, to an authentic experience with what it means truly to practise the work of this interesting field.

We are willing to admit to some enthusiasm towards theory that will certainly not be shared by all. If so inclined, you can skip the sections on theory in this book and attempt to stay clear of it throughout your study in this course. The value, though, in exploring theory is the wider exposure to and further practice of all of the skills and values important to the discipline. Even if not directly measured, we believe such knowledge can only make you a better student of English overall.

Reception Diction and Syntax

Diction is the word choice employed or the vocabulary used by a writer. Syntax is the word order or the arrangement of words used by a writer. Together, the combination of diction and syntax is what helps create an author's unique style.

In most language works, diction and syntax are important elements. Together, these aspects help define the intended audience and something about the subject and have an impact on the effect on the reader. With literature, diction and syntax can be—depending on genre and intention—highly stylized and even artificial in style and arrangement. Poetry, for example, frequently employs an artificial (meaning carefully constructed rather than "not real") diction (sometimes referred to as **poetic diction**) and syntax, while realist prose fiction might aim for greater verisimilitude with everyday diction and syntax.

The selection and use of words typically falls into one of the four following categories.

- **Formal**—an elevated and serious use of diction and syntax that is grammatically accurate and very polished. With word choice in particular, this can be referred to as **high diction**.
- **Informal**—an accurate standard use of diction and syntax that is more relaxed than formal but still intentionally polite and accurate.
- **Colloquial**—a more "everyday" use of diction and syntax that is widely acceptable even if not formally accurate though may be unique to smaller groups or communities. With word choice in particular, this can be referred to as **low diction**.
- **Slang**—a new use of diction and syntax that is not accepted or understood as formal usage and largely understood by only an esoteric community or group.

These categories are not fixed, however, as today's slang will most likely soon become tomorrow's colloquial and, one day, informal (if not formal). Neither is formal language likely to remain stagnant as the English language remains living and changing. For more information about syntax, see the reception section on page 25.

> ### Activity
>
> Play with the following lines by changing the diction and/or syntax. Think of using antonyms, synonyms and homonyms as well as more formal and/or colloquial language.
>
> - "We are all in the gutter, but some of us are looking at the stars." (Oscar Wilde)
> - "A loafer always has the correct time." (Kin Hubbard)
> - "Let us be thankful for the fools. But for them the rest of us could not succeed." (Mark Twain)
> - "It is not the oath that makes us believe the man, but the man the oath." (Aeschylus)
> - "Words are, of course, the most powerful drug used by mankind." (Rudyard Kipling)

Extension

- Turn Anne Bradstreet's poem *The Author to Her Book* on page 199. Rewrite the poem with different diction and/or syntax to create a different voice while keeping the same topic. Try using different voices (for example one formal and one more slang-like) and different genres to feel the effects diction and syntax can make.

Reception — Allusion, Repetition, Metonymy and Synecdoche

Allusion

Allusion is an implicit reference, within a work, to another work of literature or art or to a person or event. Though implicit, the reference may be brief or casual. Allusion is primarily used as a kind of appeal to the reader to share some experience with the writer or to enrich the work by association and thereby give the work greater depth.

Biblical allusions are frequent in much literature written in English (especially works from English literature) that, through such reference, could convey grave moral or philosophical issues. In such fashion, allusion can be very useful in adding breadth to a work.

Allusion, however, must make assumptions on the part of the reading audience. The use of allusion clearly assumes an established literary tradition and/or shared social knowledge. The ability of a reading audience to recognize and understand allusions is what ultimately determines its effectiveness as a device. By extension, the use of allusions that are not recognizable by an audience may either alienate a reader or, certainly, lead to misunderstanding. T S Eliot, in his famous poem *The Waste Land*, intentionally uses complex and esoteric allusion to make the reading difficult and demonstrate his protest against the lack of classical learning and knowledge among readers of the time (particularly his American countrymen). Most writers, however, employ allusions more conservatively and in ways that deepen engagements of readers.

> **Activity**
>
> Do you think it is possible to read a work where you do not understand every allusion? Every time you read a piece of literature in translation, for example, it is likely that you are unfamiliar with some allusion being used (unless noted through a gloss or using a concordance). How much impact does this have on your overall understanding? What uses or value might there be in reading such works despite missing some allusions? In considering such questions, you may find a worthwhile topic for a **further oral activity** or a **written task** (to say nothing of a link to **theory of knowledge**).

> **Activity**
>
> Read through the following excerpt from Herman Melville's *Billy Budd, Sailor*. The paragraph contains some specific allusions, though it also somewhat defines them. How much to you think you understand as it is? How much do you believe you miss? Do a quick Google search on the reference to the "Rights-of-Man" and to the "Bellipotent" (another ship mentioned in the story) – would this knowledge, do you think, enhance your reading of the story? Would it be necessary? Would it matter at all?

> *Billy Budd, Sailor*
>
> The transfer from chest to bag was made. And, after seeing his man into the cutter and then following him down, the Lieutenant pushed off from the *Rights-of-Man*. That was the merchant-ship's name; tho' by her master and crew abbreviated in sailor fashion into *The Rights*. The hard-headed Dundee owner was a staunch admirer of Thomas Paine whose book in rejoinder to Burke's arraignment of the French Revolution had then been published for some time and had gone everywhere. In christening his vessel after the title of Paine's volume, the man of Dundee was something like his contemporary shipowner, Stephen Girard of Philadelphia, whose sympathies, alike with his native land and its liberal philosophers, he evinced by naming his ships after Voltaire, Diderot, and so forth.
>
> HERMAN MELVILLE

Repetition

Repetition is a rhetorical device reiterating a word or phrase, or a rewording of the same idea, to achieve emphasis. The key here is that it is intentional—a rhetorical device—rather than unintentional which can be frustrating to read. When usefully employed, repetition adds force to an idea and acts as an essential unifying element, especially in poetry (in poetry, a repeated verse is referred to as a **refrain**). As a kind of rhyme, repetition is especially effective with persuasion or passionate appeal (hence its frequent use in oral language). Repetition is generally effective through meeting one of the following intentions.

- It is used to arouse—as in arousing interest, curiosity or heightened emotion.

- It is used to satisfy—as in bringing relief or familiarity, especially through the use of the refrain (this is true in music as well).

- It is used to surprise—as in failing to bring the expected satisfaction mentioned above.

Finally, repetition can occur through any of the following.

Sounds	Particular syllables and words	Phrases
Stanzas	Metrical patterns	Ideas
Allusions	Shapes	Images

> **Activity**
>
> Read through the following excerpts and compare the use of repetition. What features does each employ to achieve repetition? What purpose or effect does each seem to strive towards with its use of repetition?

Metonymy and synecdoche

Two final literary features that you are likely to encounter are metonymy and synecdoche. Metonymy is a figure of speech that is the substitution of a term naming an object closely associated with a word for the word itself. For example, we often refer to "sweat" when we mean hard labour, "the crown" when referring to a king or monarchy, or "suits" when we mean businesspeople. Synecdoche is actually a kind of metaphor that, in mentioning a part of an object, an entity or an idea, comes to signify the whole (or vice versa: mentioning the whole signifies a part, but this is far less common). For example, it may be common to say that "Man U won again last night," where "Man U" actually refers to the whole title Manchester United Football Club (that is, actually refers to the entire club, its players, managers and more). Synecdoche is successful when the part referred to is an important part of the whole and often the part most directly associated with the whole. We might say "engine" and actually be referring to the whole car and this could make an effective use of synecdoche. To write of the "axel" however, would not. In the above example of Manchester United, you might refer simply to "United" and convey your meaning if the context is appropriate, but without a context this could easily be confused with Liverpool United, Sheffield United, etc. And simply mentioning "Man" would never effectively convey a specific club.

Together, metonymy and synecdoche are used far more often in our language than recognized by many students. While these features do not necessarily create one effect or serve one purpose, they remain interesting turns of language that can create intimacy or a sense of community, serve to enhance the poetic diction in works or operate as a form of allusion and enhance the depth of the work through association.

Activity

- Read through the excerpt from Lorrie Moore's *How to Become a Writer* on page 204. How many examples of metonymy and/or synecdoche can you locate and what effect does each use create?

- As a creative exercise, write your own metonymy or synecdoche, trying your hand with a variety of topics.

Production Body

The body of your work—most often thought of in terms of written essay but which could also apply to oral presentation, commentary or essay—is, as the name implies, where the bulk of your argument and analysis is developed. Body paragraphs, then, are sometimes referred to as the developmental paragraphs. The primary work of the body is to support your thesis clearly and logically, which means that the body focuses on support, explanation of support and arrangement of points in an effective manner.

The production of a strong body really begins with work done before even getting to the writing, or even pre-writing, process. To succeed in producing a strong body, you must do the following:

- With the analysis of text or texts, you must know the work. Nothing is more fundamental than this—without a thorough knowledge of the works you are analysing, you will find it difficult to develop points or effectively support them.

- Have something to say. This, we hope, seems obvious but if you haven't adequately decided upon points, producing a body will be an exercise in frustration. This also presumes that you have a viable thesis from which ideas will come.

- Feel strongly about the subject and your points. If you are not convinced about what you are saying, you are unlikely to be able to convince others in your work. Feel committed to your project, your thesis and the points you will make to support them.

- Have a strong introduction, at least in outline. Though you may make further adjustments to your introduction later, at least having a strong thesis statement is required in order to have a sense of your endpoint.

After you have a sense of the points you would like to make, the next step is organizing your points in the form of paragraphs (see the production section on page 209 for more information on writing paragraphs). Though there is no absolute prescribed way of organizing your body paragraphs, your points may move chronologically through a work or from biggest to smallest example or most general to most specific. Whatever your approach, you will want to make sure there is an apparent logic and not just an unorganized assortment of ideas.

The use of support may be the most crucial part of your body and ultimately determine its success. For literary essays or oral presentations (further oral activity), support is manifest as selected quotations from the text or texts you are analysing as well as explanation. Finding appropriate quotations is really a function of having excellent knowledge of the texts (mentioned above) but the explanation is a component some students struggle with that can be remedied. Many students simply cite a quotation and leave the citation to stand alone, or as evidence in and of itself. The assumption in such cases is that the quotation is self-evident and "speaks" your point without further work. However, no use of support or proof is as effective without explanation as it is with explanation, even when it seems straightforward or obvious.

On a very simplistic level, think of your body as a legal case to be argued. A lawyer in a courtroom arguing a case calls a witness to the stand to testify. Though on television clever lawyers catch out those in the wrong, in reality a lawyer both extracts testimony from a witness and then explains or interprets it for a judge or jury. Without explaining the testimony, a lawyer leaves open the possibility for misunderstanding and that a jury may "read" the testimony as support for the other side. As a writer, you are meant to do the same work: show the reader the testimony—in the form of a quotation or evidence—and then clearly interpret or explain the interpretation of that testimony and walk through how that further supports your main idea. If you are doing this with every paragraph, your body should develop as focused and convincing support for your thesis.

Sample student work

1. There are three main acts of deception in *Much Ado About Nothing*: the friends of Benedict and Beatrice luring them into believing the other is in love with them, Don John's evil plan to make Claudio doubt Hero's innocence, and Friar Francis' idea to make the public believe Hero has died. Although most characters in the play employ either deception or self-deception, their motives vary greatly. While Beatrice's and Benedict's friends use deception to give the two lovers the final push towards concomitance, Don John's plan is driven solely by his desire to do evil upon others so as to make up for his own unhappiness. The use of deception therefore functions as a simple way of characterization by emphasizing the difference between good and evil characters.

   Yet the theme of deception also allows for a deeper insight into the character's minds. In many of his plays Shakespeare's protagonists like Hamlet struggle with some sort of identity crisis. In *Much Ado About Nothing* some of the most distinct characters are Beatrice and Benedict. Both of them initially deceive themselves into thinking that they will never get married, nor fall in love. At the beginning of the play each of two deception scenes in which their friends trick them into thinking the other one is in love with them, both Beatrice and Benedict have a soliloquy in which they emphasize their initial attitude towards love. It is worth noting that their friends know exactly

Quite clear focus.

You need to get to some of these details. This is a strong general answer but needs support.

A nice notion and transition to dig deeper into the play.

How do we know they are deceiving themselves? Again, more specific support and explanation is required.

the right things to say in order to make them fall. Hence at times the deceivers are portrayed as intelligent. Beatrice and Benedict, on the other hand, come across as silly as shortly after they have been deceived, in another soliloquy they utter words of love for one another. Yet this strengthens their character because whereas in public they always tried to come across strong, after they have realized their self-perception their true nature comes to light. This also adds to the comedic atmosphere in the play because even the strongest characters are defeated by love.

On the other hand, some schemes of deception challenge the play's nature as a comedy. Although Don John claims of himself that he is a "plain dealing villain", his inner evil comes to light through his plan to deceive Claudio into thinking Hero has cheated on him. Although initially this is Boracchio's plan, it is Don Pedro who finds a way to employ it. It can be argued that if Don John was really a plain dealing villain, he would not have made use of such an intricate scheme to get revenge from his brother. Although plans are made at the end of the play to deal with Don John, the play finishes on a festive note and the audience never finds out what actually happened to him. Yet it is obvious that Don John has further alienated himself from the happy crowd due to his use of deception. Therefore as a contrast to Benedick and Beatrice's happy ending due to the use of deception, the character of Don John ends in vain. Although Don John's plan played an essential role in the story line, towards the end of the play when most characters again find happiness, it seems less significance. Due to the nature of the play, good defeats evil.

2. "What is it you express in your eyes?" is the question Whitman asks the oxen who either pull carts or rest in the shade. He then goes onto state that "it [is] more than all the print that [he] has read in [his] life". This is particularly powerful, as Whitman is essentially saying that one look says more than a thousand words. Whitman senses that the Oxen's gaze is so deep and full of meaning, and deciphering what it says, and understanding it, will give him much more knowledge that everything he has ever read in his whole life. This is ironic as he expects the readers to read his lengthy poems, but is, at the same time, telling them that they would find more meaning and knowledge out in nature.

In stanzas 5 and 6 Whitman discusses the other animals he comes across on his "day long ramble". Whitman says that he appreciates all the colors in nature as they are, and he recognizes them in himself. He goes on to say that everything is intentional in nature ("...consider the green and violet and the tufted crown intentional") and so he does not call anything in nature unworthy, he never compares one aspect of nature to another. This plays into the overarching theme of accepting and embracing everything.

The repeated use of 'and' in the last two stanzas of the poem not only give it a sense of coming to a close, but also make each line more significant. Using 'and' on multiple occasions creates

Again, this is good as an idea and focus but I think you could point to more specific moments.

Transitions are effective.

A good point. There is a clear and unified approach evident here but this would be strengthened with further support and explanation.

Good point.

You could tighten the focus on some of the particulars of imagery here and offer a little more explanation.

There is implied transition as you move through the poem.

the illusion of something big, rather than having everything as a simple list. In addition, it serves to create some repetition and rhythm to the poem.

The last two lines are particularly important, because they contain the full effect of what Whitman is trying to say: that nature is perfectly designed, and that it is awe-inspiring. "And the jay in the woods never studied the gamut, yet trills pretty well to me" suggests that nature is designed in a way to be beautiful, yet perfectly simple. And in nature, the jay does not need to be taught how to sing, but it simply knows. The last line of the poem, and perhaps the more powerful, "And the look of the bay mare shames the silliness out of me" is Whitman telling us that the sight of this beautiful animal just leaves him simply awestruck.

Background Marxism

Marxism is named after Karl Marx and represents a critical approach to literature that is closely associated to the economic theory developed by Marx and Friedrich Engels: communism (Marx and Engels consistently used the term "Marxism" over "communism"). Marxism viewed the world from a materialist perspective, meaning that the world could be understood as a set of natural of humanly constructed rules rather than through idealist or metaphysical influences. Because the world is based on such rules, therefore, it can also be changed. Looking for logical and observable "facts", Marxism found a world based on struggle for economic, social and political advantage, all based on control of economic resources. Marxism defines these resources as the **base** as it is from control of this base that all further power follows.

Marxism's connection to literature comes from its definition of a **superstructure** which is the culture that emerges from any base (including for example law, religion, art and ideas). If one, or a particular group, controls the base, it will then be in a position to control the superstructure or culture as culture is also not a metaphysical phenomenon but a material object that emerges from the same logic and facts (and conflict) as economic resources. What is interesting about the superstructure emerges from the concept of **hegemony**, which was developed after the time of Marx and Engels. Hegemony is the concept that the superstructure oppresses; not through violence or force but rather as being "innocently" packaged as the common, prevailing or cultural worldview. In this way, we willingly accept and embrace a culture as our own even if we are not a part of the **bourgeoisie** that truly controls the base that truly controls the superstructure. In other words, culture *feels like* an abstract or universal concept rather than a product of economic control but that is its greatest feature of control: we do not even suspect that it is not "real" and therefore willingly embrace the very culture that continues to forward the very base that enjoys control over the masses (or **proletariat**).

Marxism as a literary perspective, then, focuses on literature as an artefact of superstructure than can reveal the underlying base. The conflict for control of economic resources can be revealed through careful textual analysis. Literature must be a product of the economic, social and political circumstances in which it is produced and, therefore, clues about these circumstances can be uncovered. Marxist criticism seeks to do the following:

- It aims to uncover the covert, or underlying, content that reveals Marxist themes such as class conflict, hegemony, control over resources, historical and ideological conflict, and to understand distinctions from the overt content that reveals the superstructure.

- It seeks to consider the socio-economic conditions of the writer that, according to Marxism, could have a greater impact on the work than even that of which the writer may have been aware.

- It seeks to consider the social assumptions of the culture in which the work is consumed (for example why we continue to read Shakespeare, uphold him as one of—if not the—greatest writers in the English language and demand reading his works in so many schools today).

Marxism believes that this kind of criticism is a brand of class struggle and that this work can be productive in working towards a more egalitarian and classless society. Marxism, then, is not just a critical approach for aesthetic understanding but a determined political act that seeks to right an unequal world.

> **Activity**
>
> Read through the excerpt from George Orwell's *How the Poor Die* on page 199.
>
> - What kinds of cultural values (superstructure) are conveyed?
> - What kinds of conflict and struggle might be conveyed in the text?
> - What might be revealed by your culture through how you react to, consume or interpret the text?

Production Writing Paragraphs

Paragraphs are the basic units of thought that will make up your essays in formal composition but are also the basic building blocks in all of your analytical analyses, whether written or oral. As individual paragraphs are the basic units of thought, it is through their arrangement that you build the body of your work (see separate production sections on body (page 159), introduction (page 149) and conclusion (page 169) for more specific information on these aspects of production). But even within each of these individual units of thought, or paragraphs, there are several components with unique functions.

In some ways, you can think of a paragraph as an essay in miniature. As an essay contains a thesis statement (or something closely related to a thesis statement) and body paragraphs with main points that support and "prove" this thesis, an individual paragraph includes a topic sentence with other sentences supporting this topic sentence. A topic sentence simply identifies the topic or focus of the paragraph and the remaining sentences of a paragraph should be closely related to the topic sentence. Ensuring that all sentences in a paragraph relate to the topic sentence ensures that a paragraph attains **unity**.

The topic sentence serves as the engine that drives any paragraph. Though we are reticent to support a formula as *the* recipe for good writing or analysis of any sort, many people think of a topic sentence rather formulaically as the addition of a limited topic plus a specific impression. Thus, for a literary analysis, one might come up with the following topic sentence:

"The minor characters" [limited topic] + "are used to create tension in the works" [specific impression] = a viable topic sentence.

Once you have developed a viable topic sentence, a paragraph may be fleshed out with additional sentences that clarify and finally complete the unit of thought. Building on the example above, a student may come up with the following clarifying and completing sentences:

"The minor characters stand at odds with the protagonists, instead siding with the works' antagonists at every turn." [clarifies topic and topic sentence]

"For instance, when the Bad Guy accuses the Good Woman of abuse in work 1, the minor character says, 'yes, I have often witnessed you abusing poor Bad Guy.' As the minor character sides with the antagonist, this demonstrates the Good Woman's isolation in work 1 and it is this sense of being isolated and alone that heightens the tension in the text." [completes the topic]

A good paragraph is one that not only supports the larger work's thesis but can stand on its own as a unified unit of thought. As part of a larger body of work, however, it is important to include transitions. A transition may form the beginning of a paragraph and note the transition from the topic in the paragraph above it or it may form the end of a paragraph and telegraph a change in topic for the next paragraph. Transitions effectively link paragraphs, hence ideas, together into a unified whole. Commonly used transitions focus on one of these:

- numbering or showing a chronological or time-based progression
- comparing
- contrasting
- additional information or further evidence or support of a point
- the transition to conclusion.

Finally, organizing a paragraph may be as varied as organizing an essay. Often writers will organize a paragraph from most general to most specific information but much will depend on the use of transition and your purpose. You will want to change, rearrange and/or delete sentences that reduce the effectiveness or compromise the unity in order to develop the most effective structure. Beyond an organization that effectively develops a topic and links to other ideas in the body, you will want to use a variety of words (keeping your voice but also trying to avoid repetition) and a variety of sentence structures; through this you add colour.

Sample student work

1. Franzen touches on controversial topics such as the Iraq war and China's one-child policy, and interestingly places his characters on the less popular and largely criticized side of the argument. His characters—namely Walter and Joey—who are implicated in these

A very clear topic sentence.

controversial issues have been developed and have led the reader through their lives, and hence Franzen draws the reader to hear out the characters and sympathize with them when troubles arise due to their beliefs or values. For instance, Walter firmly views that overpopulation will occur should global population continue rising at the current rate, and since America spends the most amount of natural resources, he believes that a one-child-per-family policy should also be adopted in America. He becomes more extreme in his opinion, going so far as to describe the foreseeable overpopulation as "cancer[ous]". Eventually he is viciously attacked by national newspapers for his opinions, and his misfortune is further compounded by his secretary's death. Due to Franzen's portrayal of Walter as a diligent, family-oriented and self-sacrificing man prior to Walter's demise, readers are able to hear out Walter's reasoning for his views and sympathize with his troubles—a very uncommon occurrence in the real world.

An explanation of how this topic is seen in the text; a difficult point but clear.

A nice summation gives this paragraph a sense of clear organization and singular purpose. Perhaps some further detail would enhance, but this is solid and very understandable.

2. Natalia's conversation with Vera is one of the most interesting scenes of the play and is carefully crafted by Turgenev to reveal a lot about Natalia and her personal values and attitudes. One could argue that up until this point Natalia has not been aware of Vera's feelings for Beliaev. Though she has noticed the two together she has not considered there to be feelings between them:

Clear topic.

> NATALIA: Seriously I don't think it at all *convenable* for her to be wandering in the garden all by herself with a young man, really I don't.
>
> RAKITIN: I thought you said she was a child?
>
> NATALIA: What? Of course she's a child—but still it's not quite proper. I shall have to be cross with her. (p 35)

Natalia's phrase "What? Of course she's a child" is key in illustrating that she is not suspicious of romantic feelings. When Natalia calls Vera in to speak with her, directly after Natalia has admitted her sentiments towards Beliaev to Rakitin, she immediately tries to set Vera at ease, "You'll make believe I'm your elder sister—and we'll straighten out these things together—what do you say?" (p 56) Natalia is kind to Vera and happily brushes off the prospect of marrying Bolshintov when Vera is not enthusiastic. However, she seems to abuse the bond that has formed between the two of them when she tries to extract from Vera a confession as to who else she has feelings for. Natalia suggests an officer who Vera knows as well as Rakitin before proposing "the new tutor". It is at this point in the play that the audience and Natalia become fully aware of Vera's feelings and most importantly how Natalia feels about them. The stage directions that appear directly after Vera's line "I like him very much" read "(*She has blushed*; NATALIA *is watching her narrowly*)" (p 58) and are key in Turgenev's representation of what has happened.

Though this might be expanded, this does represent explanation of the support used above and is effective.

Perhaps explaining more clearly how would help, but this paragraph does reaffirm and take the topic further forward.

As with all literary and artistic movements, post-modernism must be seen in light of the modernism that preceded it (post-modernism is our most contemporary, fully formed aesthetic movement and, as of yet, there is no new formalized reaction to it). What is substantially different, however, is that the reaction of post-modernism to modernism is far different from earlier breaks. Modernism and post-modernism tend to be associated with common elements in fiction including the fragmentation of forms (**eclecticism**), the incorporation of randomness or elements of chance (**aleatory writing**) and parody and pastiche. What does seem to distinguish the two movements from one another, however, is the reaction to these elements as a part of literature, art or the universe.

Modernism struggled with these issues in a serious fashion, producing objects (across the arts) that we continue to view as works of sublime genius, beauty and ingenuity. These objects were often an expression of either lament or fighting against fragmentation, chance and isolation in an effort to truly know the self. Post-modernism, however, celebrates these components and wonders whether the modernist reactions to understand the self are even possible. In fact, post-modernists argue that the fragmentation of the contemporary world is such that even a sense of a unified self is a fiction. Modernism is often associated with **epistemological** thought (that asks the question of how one knows what one knows and looks for understanding of how individuals can be certain of their knowledge) while post-modernism is often associated with **ontological** thought (that asks the question of how one can ever know that one does truly exist as an individual in the first place or whether there can ever be understanding of the self, let alone what a self might truly know).

For the reasons above, post-modernism concerns itself with play over seriousness. Only in play and a kind of detached irony can one find any liberation from a system that has no "real" (authentic meaning or purpose) underneath. While the high art of modernism sought to make sense of a fragmented world, post-modernism takes pleasure in the opposite: gaudiness, excess, playfulness and celebrating popular culture as equal to "high art" in value. Post-modernism, then, is more a style of writing or other art rather than a critical approach. But there are elements in fiction that post-modernism does look to recognize and explore. The following are among the most popular.

- Evidence of post-modern themes, attitudes and concerns in earlier—primarily 20th century or modernist—works is explored. In fact, one component of post-modernism is the revisionist approach that recognizes aspects of post-modernism in earlier works, pointing to post-modernism as less a time period than a movement with roots in many eras.

- Post-modernism explores evidence of the disappearance of the "real" or authentic or blurred lines that effectively demarcate reality from artificiality—post-modernism looks for mixing of genres and blurred distinctions that we find in trying to discern, for instance, the reality of Disney or Las Vegas as distinct from "other" reality or the difference between war and video games as we watch news coverage of the first gulf war.

- Intertextuality, or the way that all text are connected through an "over-laying" of shared meanings, references, and forms is explored.

- Regarding irony and ironic detachment, post-modernism looks to the past but has no expectation of finding effect that clearly arises out of a cause.

- Post-modernism looks at narcissism or a reflective focus on the ends and processes of production as part of its content. This can be referred to as metafiction, which implies knowledge of itself.

- Distinctions between so-called "high art" and popular art, "low" art or kitsch are challenged—post-modernism may celebrate the postcard as much as the "finely-wrought novel" or *Buffy and the Vampire Slayer* in equal measure to a "serious" drama.

> **Activity**
>
> - Read through the excerpts from Lorrie Moore's *How to Become a Writer* on page 204 and Folman and Polonsky's *Waltz With Bashir* on page 207. Note all of the elements that may be considered evidence of post-modernism and how these may be different from elements of earlier modernism.

Reception   Ambiguity and Paradox

Ambiguity

Ambiguity is the notion that things may not be clearly what they might at first seem and that there can be multiple possible interpretations. Ambiguity comes from the fact that words can connote far more than they denote and can mean more than one thing. Post-structuralist thought demonstrated that no word can have one singular, absolute meaning known to all people and that ambiguity, rather than being an exception, is more likely the norm. In literature, however, ambiguity may be intentionally used on a larger and more obvious scale to demonstrate intentional ideas or to leave room for alternative reactions. Ambiguity is divided into seven types, as popularized by William Empson in 1930. The types are not limited to creating confusion or uncertainty and include the following:

- Details are effective in several ways simultaneously.

- Two or more alternative meanings are resolved as a singular meaning.

- Two unconnected meanings are suggested by a single word simultaneously.

- Alternative meanings are used to convey the uncertainty of the speaker or situation.

- A simile is used that refers to two apparently unconnected things or ideas but demonstrates the speaker coming to some greater understanding (this appears as fortunate coincidence but is a rhetorical trope).

- The readers are left to create meaning or an interpretation on their own in the face of contradiction.

- There is a contradiction so severe that it reveals confusion on the part of the author.

Paradox

Paradox is a statement that seems, at first glance, contradictory or even absurd but upon further consideration seems to reveal a kind of meaning or truth that ultimately reconciles the contradiction. Paradox usually occurs in the form of statement such as "I must be cruel to be kind" or "The man is child to the son". But paradox can occur on a grander scale such as with the whole sub-genre of theatre of the absurd that points out paradox in terms of our overall use of language, behaviour and even the state of humanity.

From *Two Kinds of Paradoxes*, originally printed in the *Illustrated London News*.

For there are two kinds of paradoxes. They are not so much the good and the bad, nor even the true and the false. Rather they are the fruitful and the barren; the paradoxes which produce life and the paradoxes that merely announce death. Nearly all modern paradoxes merely announce death. I see everywhere among the young men who have imitated Mr Shaw a strange tendency to utter epigrams which deny the possibility of further life and thought. A paradox may be a thing unusual, menacing, even ugly—like a rhinoceros. But, as a live rhinoceros ought to produce more rhinoceri, so a live paradox ought to produce more paradoxes. Nonsense ought to be suggestive; but nowadays it is abortive.

The new epigrams are not even fantastic finger-posts on the wild road: they are tablets, each set into a brick wall at the end of a blind alley. So far as they concern thought at all, they cry to men, "Think no more," as the voice said "Sleep no more" to Macbeth. These rhetoricians never speak except to move the closure. Even when they are really witty (as in the case of Mr Shaw), they commonly commit the one crime that cannot be forgiven among free men. They say the last word.

I will give such instances as happen to lie before me. I see on my table a book of aphorisms by a young Socialist writer, Mr Holbrook Jackson; it is called "Platitudes in the Making", and curiously illustrates this difference between the paradox that starts thought and the paradox that prevents thought. Of course, the writer has read too much Nietzsche and Shaw, and too little of less groping and more gripping thinkers. But he says many really good things of his own, and they illustrate perfectly what I mean here about the suggestive and the destructive nonsense.

Thus in one place he says, "Suffer fools gladly: they may be right." That strikes me as good; but here I mean specially that it strikes me as fruitful and free. You can do something with the idea, it opens an avenue. One can go searching among one's more solid acquaintances and relatives for the fires of a concealed infallibility. One may fancy one sees the star of immortal youth in the somewhat empty eye of Uncle George; one may faintly follow some deep rhythm of nature in the endless repetitions with which Miss Bootle tells a story; and in the grunts and gasps of the Major next door may hear, as it were, the cry of a strangled god. It can never narrow our minds, it can never arrest our life, to suppose that a particular fool is not such a fool as he looks. It must be all to the increase of charity, and charity is the imagination of the heart.

I turn the next page, and come on what I call the barren paradox. Under the head of "Advices", Mr. Jackson writes, "Don't think—do." This is exactly like saying "Don't eat— digest." All doing that is not mechanical or accidental involves thinking; only the modern world seems to have forgotten that there can be such a thing as decisive and dramatic thinking. Everything that comes from the will must pass through the mind, though it may pass quickly. The only sort of thing the strong man can "do" without thinking is something like falling over a doormat. This is not even making the mind jump; it is simply making it stop.
I take another couple of cases at random. "The object of life is life." That affects me as ultimately true; always presuming the author is liberal enough to include eternal life. But even if it is nonsense, it is thoughtful nonsense.

On another page I read, "Truth is one's own conception of things." That is thoughtless nonsense. A man would never have had any conception of things at all unless he had thought they were things and there was some truth about them. Here we have the black nonsense, like black magic, that shuts down the brain. "A lie is that which you do not believe." That is a lie; so perhaps Mr Jackson does not believe it.

G K CHESTERTON

Production Conclusion

Though the word "conclusion" can mean the end or last part of something, it is more often associated with the result of a process, a final decision reached after deliberation or what must follow logical premises. In other words, a conclusion is not often simply an ending but a final argument, deduction or interpretation based on material preceding it. For the most part of formal essays, commentaries and oral activities, you will want to conclude your work in this way. That is, you do not want simply to stop but to articulate your final word, main idea or thesis that brings together the whole of what you have argued before.

Writing a conclusion, though, does not involve so formulaic a process that there are easy steps to follow. You may have once learned that a good conclusion involves the restatement of your main points as well as a restatement of your thesis. In fact, though this can be a reasonable approach in concluding a speech (what your audience has heard followed by why it is important, possibly followed by what they should now do), it can read as tedious in written works. Instead, rather than specific steps to follow, there are some hints as to possible approaches to ensuring that your conclusion does more than just end a work but extends your thoughts and arguments further. Among the more common approaches are the following:

- Leave readers with a final thought that helps them see the importance of your work.

- Draw a final conclusion that demonstrates a clear and sophisticated understanding of your essay topic.

- Give readers something more to think about and that will keep your analysis "alive" after reading.

- Connect your argument or thesis to a larger idea in the world.

Sample student work

1. In conclusion, this poem is expansive because it goes from celebrating just the human body to nature itself. It is all embracing. Whitman, in this poem, is "sounding his barbaric yawp over the roofs of the word".

   This offers a concise summation of larger effect and purpose. This has a nice voice though is relatively limited in scope.

2. In conclusion, though neither play induces a crystal clear attitude in regards to the infidelity of characters in the audience, both plays provoke reflection on the actions of the characters. The plays seek to emulate people and realistic scenarios, though each playwright has done this in a way that reflects the ideals and values of the time periods, that is the modern society of Pinter and 1870s Russia of Turgenev. Audiences of both plays would be likely to feel both sympathy and anger towards the protagonists, and this mixture of emotion is achieved by the playwrights' creation of believable situations capable of inducing realistic responses.

   A very sound conclusion that manages to sum up previous work and extend with a final point of analysis. Good.

3. The overall effect of the poem is quite strong—the readers are being told, simply, of a day in Whitman's life, and what he observed, yet the readers can see how powerful nature is in Whitman's eyes. Poem 13 not only explores human, specifically male, beauty but

also talks of oxen and birds and colours in nature with such fluidity that the readers are forced to see that all nature is interconnected, and that everything in nature is a part of humans and vice-versa.

4. Overall, the poem is similar to a song. Dickinson uses various literary techniques to create variations in emotions and pace, similar to the variations in the structure of a song—changes in pitch, rhythm, and mood. Dickinson also ends the poem by describing the entire phenomenon as a work of God, as his artistic creation.

Concludes but refers to generalizations that do not encourage a reader to leave with a larger sense or "food for thought".

This is a rather matter-of-fact observation that makes two disparate points. More is needed to enhance the unity and really leave the reader with punch.

Production — Further Oral Activity

The further oral activity will make up a part of your formal assessment work that is submitted to the IB but the range and options for producing the further oral activity may vary substantially from school to school. Technically, during the course of your study you will need to complete at least two further oral activities, submitting your best work. Of the minimum two further oral activities, one must be based on material you study in part 1 of the course (language in cultural context) and one must be based on material you study in part 2 of the course (language and mass communication). Given, however, that oral presentations, discussion and creative analysis may form a substantial part of your class study, it is not inconceivable that you will actually produce more than the minimum two further oral activities and some of these may come from the literature parts of the course (parts 3 and 4). Though these may not be submitted formally, it is inevitably through the range of oral work that much of your learning will occur.

Regardless of the part of the course in which you are producing a further oral activity, it is important to keep in mind the following parameters:

- The further oral activity must discuss the relationship between language, meaning and context. Though this may seem limiting, in fact these three components (language, meaning and context) are so broad that they can accommodate a large variety of approach.

- The further oral activity must link the focus above to one of the works you are studying in class.

- At the conclusion of your further oral activity, you must write a reflective statement commenting on your overall performance and progress towards meeting your intended objectives (how well you feel you managed to perform and convey your intended ideas).

Beyond these parameters, the further oral activity can take a variety of forms. You can complete the further oral activity as an individual or as part of a group (each individual is assigned his or her own mark so you will want to ensure that you are involved and can distinguish your work—there is not simply one group mark). You can perform a familiar and straightforward oral presentation or experiment with an array of creative options and you can simply speak or incorporate a variety of other artefacts (from advertising image to website to film to prop) that you explain in your presentation.

Because of the variety of options available to you, a great deal of the work actually occurs in the brainstorming and planning stages. If you can come up with an interesting topic and then decide upon a format through which you will convey the topic, you will have completed much of the real work of the task and be well on your way towards success. However, this is easier said than done and the following considerations may assist you with your approach.

- Think through your learning in class. What is interesting about the works that you have studied? Between the works and class learning, what ideas do you have about meaning, context and language usage? What do you know about the works you have studied? What do you think is worth sharing?

- After you have an idea of topic, imagine the ways to convey the information. Do you have a topic that is well-suited for a creative presentation? Will your topic work well for a small group (will there be enough information and activity for multiple people to play an active role in production and performance)? Is your topic best accomplished through one approach over another?

  - Note: The further oral activity provides an excellent opportunity to pursue creative outlets. You must remember, however, that this is an oral activity and that you are to speak "live" in order to earn credit. It is not enough, then, to produce a video and simply show the video. Instead, you would produce a video and then speak to your class about what you have done, how you have done it and what larger intellectual ideas you have intended to convey as a result.

- At this point, it is imperative to discuss your ideas with your teacher. The teacher's primary role in supporting you with the further oral activity is to discuss topics and approach, ensuring that your work does address the aims of the course, is viable (is of appropriate scope and scale) and that you have support for understanding how to complete the assessment task. Your teacher, at this point, should be your biggest resource in helping to hone in on an appropriate topic and approach.

- The sheer variety of approach makes offering a formula for the process impossible. Your topic and how you ultimately decide to present material will determine how you go about preparing for the oral activity. However you do decide to prepare and present material, you must keep in mind that the intention of the assessment task is to present your own intellectual engagement and understanding of your topic, and of the works studied in class and to make a clear connection to context of some sort.

Sample student work

The following student samples are reflections on further oral activities. The standardized form will look different and one sample includes a presentation from part 3 of the course which could not be formally submitted to the IB. The two samples do represent a small drop, though, in the large bucket of possible approaches and provide an indication of how to approach the assessment task and how to reflect upon it.

1. Language and mass communication
   Activity: For my further oral activity, I created a display of photos from scenes around the city. I tried to capture photos

of "gritty" realism as well as some of the more positive aspects of the city. My collage of photos featured two versions of each picture: one taken on an SLR camera and one taken on my iPhone using the Hipstamatic app (the pictures were not always exactly identical if the subject moved because I had to shift from my camera to my phone). I shared my collage and led a class discussion on what the editing effect of Hipstamatic might be on how we view these scenes and whether the filter system seemed to impact how we reacted or responded to the subjects.

Link to work: I chose this activity based on the section we read from Roland Barthes *Camera Lucida* and the blogs around Damon Winter's award for photojournalism that he took on his iPhone. Specifically, Barthes' idea of the "punctum" and the very personal and painful reactions viewers can have to photos was something I liked and I thought about the criticism of Winter's photos during war. Some don't think the Hipstamatic effect was appropriate for a serious event like war and that it made it too easy to romanticize it because of its soft filter features. But I thought the photos conveyed something very personal and with a strong impact like Barthes' "punctum". Performance: I think I did a good job bringing up interesting ideas and people had a lot to say about the photos and whether they thought the Hipstamatic photos really seemed too unreal and too far away from the seriousness of the content. Sometimes I could have controlled the discussion more and sometimes it just got to what people liked but there were interesting ideas about whether one version could be more "real" than the other and if that was the role of photography or whether it should be a more personal medium that appeals to the "punctum". I think it was a good discussion and I am happy how I did. I did get my main points across.

2. Literature: texts and contexts
    Activity: I chose to present some of the poems from Ted Hughes' book *Birthday Letters*.

    Link to work: When we studied the poetry of Sylvia Plath, I was interested when we talked about her relationship with Ted Hughes and I thought it was an interesting story about how he published these poems near death as his first public response to the anger that people had against him for Plath's suicide. I thought that this represented a very different context. Even though the poems are different, they actually speak to some of Plath's poems and offer a different version of their time together and Plath's life and her poetry. I think it makes it different to read her poems now. I still like them but I think I have a different appreciation for some of her anger and her pain and also maybe that she was not always very well. My goal was to highlight how these poems showed how both of their poetry was so personal and based on the personal contexts and how these were very different. Performance: I think my discussion of the poems was good and I think the class understood that the poems were definitely responding to Plath. "The Bee God" and "Apprehensions" seemed to be the best part and I think I was successful explaining these poems as well as connecting them to the idea of different contexts between Plath and Hughes. I also think people had a different opinion from the popular feminist criticism against Hughes because they did show love and care. I think I achieved my goal and showed my knowledge of how context can be created.

Reception   The Novel

The novel is, for many students, the most basic and familiar of the genres of literature. In terms of formal study, however, the novel is so varied as to elude easy definition: we may *know* a novel (or think we know a novel) when we see it but it remains very difficult to define succinctly the elements and aspects common to most novels. As a result, it is popular to define the novel rather vaguely as an extended piece of prose fiction. Its length, then, is one of the more certain components that allow us to understand whether we are reading a long short story, novella or novel proper. As you might imagine, however, even what this precise length is remains contested and flexible.

Beyond length, the novel can best be understood as a work containing characters, action and incident that is broadly realistic and offers a story or narrative of life or experience. While these aspects may seem quite ordinary and universal in literature, there is a connection between the above and length. It is only in longer prose pieces that significant character development as a result of action and incident may occur. Further, it is only through this significant or sustained character and incident that a kind of life or experience can be revealed. Perhaps a concern with human beings involved in significant action will seem common to contemporary readers but, interestingly, the novel is a relatively recent genre in English. Though the novel in Europe can be traced back to Spain in the late-16th or early-17th century, it was not until the 18th century that the novel really developed in England and much of its greatest success has come in the 19th and 20th centuries.

While the above represents the best common definition of the novel, it may be most well-known for the diversity of subject matters, topics and themes. The novel has proved to be our most pliable and adaptable of genre forms, inspiring dozens of sub-genres such as the novel of manners, the sentimental novel, the novel of ideas, the detective novel, etc. The following list represents some of the more commonly studied forms of the novel and may inform your own study:

- Bildungsroman: a German term, refers to novels that treat the development from adolescence to maturity
- dystopic novel: a novel that imaginatively extends tendencies, beliefs and principles to extreme and most unpleasant conclusions
- epistolary novel: a novel written in the form of letters exchanged by its characters

- gothic novel: a novel that employs elements of horror, chivalry, magic and mystery that often depicts a fallen world or other decrepit state of affairs in order to make a larger statement
- historical novel: a novel set in an earlier historical period where the circumstances have an impact on and help drive the plot
- picaresque novel: a novel that involves the actions and experiences of a scoundrel-like character but also conveyed in distinct episodes (**episodic**)
- protest novel: a novel that focuses on drawing attention to social problems and critiquing the conditions that give rise to such problems.

This is but a taste of the variety of the standard types of novel you may encounter (and some novels include elements of many types) and the novel continues to evolve today. It is the place of the novel, though, to be so apt at absorbing such disparate purposes and intentions and this may be the best indication of the novel's likely continuing popularity as a literary art form.

Reception   The Short Story

The short story can trace its roots to several millennia BC and even back to the oral tradition. But the short story as we know it today really began to materialize uniquely in the 19th century where writers and critics started consciously to articulate the short story as a unique art form or literary genre. Much of this definition and practice in producing short stories was rooted in the United States that enjoyed a strong tradition with the genre from the late 19th century to the present.

The short story is, first and foremost, a relatively brief fictional narrative in prose. But beyond the mere length of the prose is the concentration on a unique or single effect which is often manifest via a single narrated event. The short story emphasizes the totality of an effect as its primary objective and this effect can be an epiphany or revelation that a reader encounters though the work. Many writers of the short story believe that the short story should aim at revealing the true nature of a character through a single event rather than showing a character and his or her evolution or change over time or across multiple experiences (as you are likely to find in the novel).

Most critics do distinguish the short story from other kinds of prose fiction by this emphasis on a single effect only. But such an emphasis can be said to be similar to "simpler" formats like the tale or the sketch. What the short story does offer beyond these other forms (that are recognized as precursors to the short story) are the following.

- It offers a definite formal development: though often only narrating a single event, there is a clear narrative trajectory evident in the short story.
- Careful construction is apparent: there is an obvious artistic or aesthetic intention with the short story that is consciously or deliberately constructed. Short stories include beginnings, middles and endings though in a more compact format.
- The short story offers unity: the above points would suggest that the construction of parts is intended towards a singular purpose without extraneous detail, detour or effect.

As with the novel, defining precisely what a short story is proves elusive and you will find as many differences among the volumes of short stories available as you will find similarities. However, particularly in the last century and a half, the short story has become a unique form of prose with some aspects that distinguish it from its longer cousins. An understanding of its qualities as a genre, then, can help with a larger understanding of purpose and effect.

A somewhat new and playful off-shoot of the short story is the short-short story. The short-short story tends to be fewer than one thousand words, or other versions developing on media such as Twitter. These forms try to keep some of the aspects of the short story alive but experiment with ever more truncated versions to push the boundaries on how few words one can employ and still achieve the impact of the short story as defined above.

Activity

Select a short story—or short-short story—of your own to read. Looking closely at the work, locate the singular event or dramatic moment and the effect that this event or moment appears to create.

- How is the tension of the drama or event clearly constructed?
- What elements traditionally associated with longer prose (for example plot, conflict and resolution) are conveyed?

| **Background** | **New Historicism and Post-Colonialism** |

New historicism

New historicism is a critical approach to literature that views literary works as a kind of historical artifact that can best be understood by reading in the light of other historical documents and that can, in turn, help enhance the understanding of those other historical documents. New historicism does not distinguish between works of literary art and other historical documents. Instead of seeing art as a transcendent form that conveys metaphysical truth, new historicists read literature as a more material object both influenced and limited by the social and historical forces in place at the time of production. By studying other contemporary historical documents that reveal the dominant social, political and legal norms of a time, new historicists believe you can better understand the reasons for production, reception, intentions and critical reactions of a work. Because the work of literature must be simply another material object produced within that age and worldview, the literature will reflect those historical norms better than any larger transcendent truth.

New historicism takes its "new" in reaction to an earlier historicism (from the 1930s and 1940s). New historicism, however, was heavily influenced by post-structuralism and Marxism that began to sow distrust in not only language as a truthful or objective object, but also history. Instead, the new historicists viewed history as a competition between competing **discourses** that sought to offer different versions of historical cause-and-effect and historical truth. New historicism, then, looks at literary and non-literary works to locate either competing views or evidence of how the prevailing status quo was continued through a combination of literary and non-literary works that worked in concert with one another. For example, new historicists may explore Elizabethan drama (in fact, this has been a popular topic for new historicists) to find evidence of the norms of the Elizabethan court and life during the Elizabethan times but may also explore records of coronations to find the attention to dramatic effect and hyperbole. Together, this record of texts could illustrate a socio-historical period that maintained power and authority through a common discursive practice that is evident in all written records, literary and otherwise. (Note: new historicism is primarily associated with criticism coming out of the United States. In Europe, a very similar critical approach is known as cultural materialism. In fact, there are some subtle distinctions between the two approaches but plenty that the two do share.)

Post-colonialism

Post-colonialism is a critical approach that focuses on an intersection of literature and cultural studies with an emphasis on the treatment of the societies that have been colonized by European powers in the past. In particular, post-colonialism focuses on one of the following:

- It focuses on the portrayal of colonized (or formerly colonized) countries or peoples and the association of "otherness" to everything non-European. Post-colonialism looks closely at the myths that Western literature constructs around non-Western cultures and the way that these relegate these non-Western worlds to the outside. Popular myths and representations might include the exotic or the mystical but just as often would include, for example, the evil, dark, uncivilized, ignorant. In both cases, these myths would continue to inform larger opinion of the "otherness" or "less than" quality of these societies.

- Post-colonialism focuses on the ignored or overlooked writers, literary traditions or stories of the nations and peoples of colonized (or formerly colonized) countries. Post-colonialism also looks closely at works produced in colonized nations for reinterpretations of what literature is or can be. These stories could be of a different form, style or intention and would have, like the people and nations, been ignored, marginalized or patronized as the product of the "other".

Post-colonialism uses these two foci in particular as part of its larger intention to reject universal claims of what literature or culture is and to, therefore, inject a new kind of empathy that will recognize meaning, value and beauty that transcends cultural and ethnic barriers.

Activity

Turn to the poem *Quashie to Buccra* by Claude McKay on page 201 and to the excerpt from Zadie Smith's *White Teeth* on page 203. Try to address the following questions from the perspective of a post-colonialist or a new historicist.

- What kinds of cultural differences are made obvious and how does each writer most obviously achieve this?

- Where you find difficulty with understanding (either due to language or to content), how does such difficulty enhance your awareness of difference or help bridge difference?

- How is "otherness" shown to be a source of power, inspiration, energy or change as opposed to something to be avoided?

- What do you know about the historical norms of the times of each work's production and how can you see those norms reflected in or challenged by the works?

- In what ways do the works challenge the notion of the traditional literary canon? In what ways do they not?

Reception   Non-Fiction

Non-fiction represents an enormously wide array of kinds of writing that is distinguished from fiction by its focus on the factual. For the most part, the factual in non-fiction refers to actual events and real people and is distinct from fiction that may use either actual people or actual events, but rarely both. The factual in non-fiction also needs to be distinguished from the accurate or "correct" (it is possible to read an actual account of inaccurate information or misguided work as you might find in a rant or works such as Adolf Hitler's *Mein Kampf*). Non-fiction, however, does somewhat more than only offer a snapshot of the factual: non-fiction distinguishes itself as not just a statement of reality but as a crafted portrait of the factual towards an intended effect.

Like fiction, non-fiction attempts to bring a story to life even if the story is an actual occurrence. Because of these parallel aims, there are several elements that non-fiction has in common with fiction including (but not limited to):

- mood, tone and/or atmosphere
- setting

- character
- theme.

Similarly, non-fiction approaches the portrayal of its story in ways not unlike those of fiction. As a result, we will often approach non-fiction works with the same kind of analytic eye that we do fictional works. Questions you should ask yourself with any study of non-fiction include the following:

- What style does the writer adopt and how does the writer convey such a style?
- What seems to be the larger purpose or effect of the work?
- What might be the relationship between the subject matter of the work and the form of the work?
- How does the work reveal context, either in production or reception?

As the above questions make clear, though non-fiction is a unique genre in English, our approach to non-fiction works will not be that different from our approach to works of fiction. Throughout the course, you should be developing transferable skills applicable to these and other genres. But you also want to be sensitive to avoid ignoring unique features that may appear in different works and may be the telltale clues distinguishing essay from editorial from blog. Finding this balance will be the real work of your classroom study. Much of determining these features will be in the close consideration of intended audience and purpose.

While any study of non-fiction works in the literature parts of the course will probably be limited to essay, letter, travel writing, biography or autobiography, the range of non-fiction also includes:

creative non-fiction	diary	documentary
blog/rant/tweet	guide/manual	history
journal	journalism	criticism
memoir	natural history	philosophy
photograph	scientific writing	travelogue

Activity

Turn to the excerpt from Andre Agassi's *Open* on page 202.

- What elements distinguish this work as non-fiction?
- What elements seem to cross over into fiction?
- Does this excerpt read as a good story? If so, what about the excerpt helps create this sense?

Reception   Archetype

An archetype is defined as a universally understood symbol, pattern or image or the original prototype on which all other copies, approximations or renditions are based. An archetype in literature refers to common images, patterns, details or characters that recur frequently or repeatedly and it shares much in common with the archetypes of myth or folklore. If, for example, we read of a young man travelling alone, we can recognize the archetype of the quest where this character will undergo challenges (perhaps suffering and setback) but will ultimately reach a new "place". That place may be a physical destination, a new understanding of the self or the larger world, or the achievement or attainment of a goal (whether known or not in advance).

The understanding of archetype in literature bears resemblance to structuralism but archetypes represent not just patterns in language but patterns in human psychology. Though archetypes have been studied or referred to since the time of early Greek philosophers, it was the work of Carl Jung that popularized and furthered their use in literature. Jung argued that archetypes represent what he called a "pre-logical" or "primordial image" of experience that has occurred to humankind repeatedly throughout our history. As a result, we are psychologically "programmed" to understand these images and experiences as part of our collective unconscious even if we have not had the experience personally. Since, for example, darkness has been a time of fear, uncertainty or the unknown from our earliest ancestors right through to the much more recent present, we have "learned" to associate darkness with these feelings or emotions as a part of our collective human psychology; we now associate images of darkness with these qualities when we encounter it in literature: in other words, as an archetype. This does not mean that writers cannot subvert or play with archetypes, however. Quite the contrary, it is precisely because we collectively share such archetypes that writers—and readers—can play with archetypes and argue extensions, subversions or other reinterpretations of an archetype. Whether one agrees or not with Jung that an archetype is largely illogical and a part of our locked unconscious, the very repetition of archetypal images is such that we collectively recognize them in literary works and this does play a role in our interpretation and understanding.

Archetypes can run from fundamental aspects of life to character traits to theme and the list below represents just a few of the possible archetypes you might encounter.

Activity

Turn to page 202 and read from the excerpt from Andre Agassi's *Open*. What archetypal images can you find being used, exploited or subverted in the work and for what larger effect? Now do the same with the excerpt from Folman and Polonsky's *Waltz With Bashir* on page 207. Does one seem more effective than the other? Why?

Extension

Watch any of your favourite television programmes or movies and identify all of the archetypal images you can. How does the programme or movie make use of archetype to help achieve its intended effect?

Life aspects:			
birth	adolescence or growing up	love	family
dying	death	sibling rivalry	parent–child conflict

Personality types:			
child	rebel	Don Juan	martyr
hero or antihero	damsel in distress	siren	mentor
social climber	traitor	snob	wise old man or woman
mother	self-made person	villain	trickster

Animal archetypes:			
lion	eagle	snake	tortoise

Thematic archetypes:		
innocence before the fall	quest	vengeance
overcoming odds	descent into hell	fertility and rebirth

Issue	The Life and Times of the Author

Much of your study of literature in the IB English A: language and literature course will include some consideration of context, where context is understood as anything beyond the specific words of a text that may be relevant to understanding that text or may affect interpretation of that text. As you might imagine, the number of elements that exist beyond the words of a text are near infinite and so context becomes not only an important consideration (unless, of course, you are a devout New Critic) but an interesting and stimulating consideration. Even further, the ability to imagine multiple contexts and approach texts through a variety of contextual considerations will lead to greater sensitivity and understanding of cultural contexts different from your own as well as an enhanced understanding and appreciation of your own culture. While this is a clearly stated objective of the course in its own right, this understanding will also yield significant ideas for topics to approach in essays, written tasks, comparative commentary, commentary analysis and further oral activities.

Probably the most commonly taught and studied context is that of the life and times of the author. Even in your own experience, it is likely that for every major literary work you have studied your teacher has begun with some biographical information of the writer and/or something of, for example, the writer's background, society, beliefs, desires and challenges (or perhaps asked you to research this information for yourself). Perhaps you learned of the writer's economic status, sexual orientation or even psychological health, marital status and social habits and—in the context of learning this information as part of your literary study—contextually understood that this information was somehow important, if not essential, to your understanding of the work.

Many students find this historical contextual information valuable and it can certainly lead to interesting and extended readings of works as well as more sensitive intercultural understanding. But it is important to recognize that though this is the most commonly taught and learned context, the life and times of the author is neither mandatory nor the only (or even most important) contextual approach (other approaches are discussed in the other sections on issues in literature in this part of the book). If, however, you come to this information on your own or through larger class discussion, do take advantage to expand your understanding in light of your new knowledge.

The range of possible contexts around the life and times of the author is vast but some of the more common broad categories you may choose to consider include the following (be aware that for each of these broad categories there are many sub-topics).

Of the author:

gender	nationality	ethnicity	socio-economic status
childhood	education	family life	marital status
sexual orientation	other jobs	status as a writer	friends or connections
range of experience	age	hobbies or interests	political views
religion	other experience	physical health	psychological health

Of the times:

historical era	political policies	social norms	economy
social roles	world events	technology	relationship to past
literary traditions	worldviews	religious norms	world leaders
artistic trends	language usage	educational norms	environment

Activity

Try the following exercise as an example of historical context and even how this can lead to multiple interpretations.

Emily Dickinson remains a very popular poet to study and you may already be familiar with some of the more popular contextual knowledge—her association with being a spinster and her reclusiveness (by the end of her lifetime, she rarely ventured outside of her parents' home though was still fond of distributing candy to the neighbourhood children, albeit by dropping a bucket full of sweets from her bedroom window upstairs). This contextual knowledge is helpful in drawing attention to Dickinson's focus on the role of the imagination as we make connections with how she lived a life of the imagination with no need even to leave her home to her work with imagination in poetry. Read the following poem and see if this understanding of Dickinson's single-minded attention to imagination helps shed light on the poem:

Two Butterflies Went Out at Noon

XVIII

Two butterflies went out at noon
And waltzed above a stream,
Then stepped straight through the firmament
And rested on a beam;

And then together bore away
Upon a shining sea,—
Though never yet, in any port,
Their coming mentioned be.

If spoken by the distant bird,
If met in ether sea
By frigate or by merchantman,
Report was not to me.

EMILY DICKINSON

Now consider the context of the times. Dickinson was writing during the build-up and then duration of the American Civil War, yet neither in this poem nor in any other poem by her that has been recovered is there any mention whatsoever of this significant event. One might assume that a war just beyond your doorstep would attract a writer's attention (and Dickinson followed news of the war closely, wrote letters to friends regarding the war and had a brother nearly conscripted but who paid a fee to avoid being drafted) but Dickinson's poems seem to omit the event.

- Does this contextual information change your reading of the poem? If so, how?

- How might this contextual information reinforce the earlier contextual information regarding Dickinson's personality?

Reception . Motif and Leitmotif

A motif is any simple element that serves as a basis for, or elementary building block of, an expanded or larger narrative. Unlike a symbol, however, a motif is recurrent and helps unify the larger work by helping to forward a dominant idea or a main theme. In many ways, a motif works like a **conceit** or extended metaphor with its repetition but it behaves as a direct symbol rather than a substitution of related ideas or objects. A motif may occur in the form of any of the following:

- a character
- a recurrent image
- a verbal pattern
- a symbolic concept (for example a Greek myth, the notion of good or evil or the concept of separation or purity).

A leitmotif is similar to a motif though is more associated with a recurrent theme (for example "good triumphs over evil" or "practice makes perfect") than a motif. A leitmotif may be better thought of as a "notion" than a theme (to avoid confusion with the overall theme of a work) that also helps unify a larger literary work. However, often the terms "motif" and "leitmotif" are used synonymously. Leitmotif, though, can sometimes also refer to the recurrent themes or motifs that a single author employs across much of the entire body of work, or *oeuvre* (for example "A common leitmotif in the poetry of Emily Dickinson is her use of nature and an emphasis on the power of the imagination.")

Both "motif" and "leitmotif" are terms that come from music and refer to repetition of musical phrases. What is an interesting connection between the musical terms and their application in literature is the way motifs and/or leitmotifs can anchor a work. In music, the repetition of a motif provides a point of repeated familiarity from which the listener can be further guided and very much the same can be said to be true in literature.

Activity

Read through the excerpt from Nathaniel Hawthorne's short story *Young Goodman Brown* below. Though somewhat obvious, the introduction clearly establishes the motif of purity and innocence on the part of Faith. Even just reading the introduction to this story should, though, suggest how motif (innocence and purity) is established and plant clues as to how this will be used to unify the work further and help propel larger themes that will eventually appear.

From *Young Goodman Brown*

Young Goodman Brown came forth at sunset into the street at Salem village; but put his head back, after crossing the threshold, to exchange a parting kiss with his young wife. And Faith, as the wife was aptly named, thrust her own pretty head into the street, letting the wind play with the pink ribbons of her cap while she called to Goodman Brown.

"Dearest heart," whispered she, softly and rather sadly, when her lips were close to his ear, "prithee put off your journey until sunrise and sleep in your own bed to-night. A lone woman is troubled with such dreams and such thoughts that she's afeared of herself sometimes. Pray tarry with me this night, dear husband, of all nights in the year."

The motif of young and pure love is evident via the pink ribbons, names and the exchange between the two. Faith, in particular, is associated with this.

Faith's purity is reaffirmed by her concern for her husband as well as the references to night and fear.

> "My love and my Faith," replied young Goodman Brown, "of all nights in the year, this one night must I tarry away from thee. My journey, as thou callest it, forth and back again, must needs be done 'twixt now and sunrise. What, my sweet, pretty wife, dost thou doubt me already, and we but three months married?"
>
> "Then God bless you!" said Faith, with the pink ribbons; "and may you find all well when you come back."
>
> "Amen!" cried Goodman Brown. "Say thy prayers, dear Faith, and go to bed at dusk, and no harm will come to thee."
>
> So they parted; and the young man pursued his way until, being about to turn the corner by the meeting-house, he looked back and saw the head of Faith still peeping after him with a melancholy air, in spite of her pink ribbons.
>
> "Poor little Faith!" thought he, for his heart smote him. "What a wretch am I to leave her on such an errand! She talks of dreams, too. Methought as she spoke there was trouble in her face, as if a dream had warned her what work is to be done to-night. But no, no; 'twould kill her to think it. Well, she's a blessed angel on earth; and after this one night I'll cling to her skirts and follow her to heaven."
>
> NATHANIEL HAWTHORNE

Again, Faith reveals innocence, purity, goodness and support.

Here, Goodman Brown further reinforces Faith's purity and goodness.

Faith's actions—still watching after her husband, wishing he wouldn't go—are accompanied not by petulance but by a sense of continuing concern.

Even the need to hide truth from her speaks to Faith's purity. Though we suspect Goodman Brown will not be able or willing to keep his promise ultimately, his desire to be different in future is also a reference to Faith's goodness and purity.

Reception   Intertextuality

Intertextuality refers to the interdependence of all literary texts on one another (or, for that matter, all texts of all kinds). All texts, intertextuality argues, comprise pre-existing texts; that is, any work is the product of all works that have come before it. Intertextuality is related to structuralism in arguing that we can only express ourselves through words and forms that are already available to us. No work, then, is constructed in isolation but is instead a mosaic of all other works absorbed and transformed towards a new end. The most avant-garde poem today owes its existence to all of the previous versions of language, poetry or text of any type that has given humankind both language and the capacity to rework the words and form.

What distinguishes intertextuality is its own inevitability. Where allusion or pastiche, for instance, may be intentional, intertextuality is simply unavoidable. We cannot produce a text that does not arise out of all of the possible permutations we have experienced, consciously or collectively. Even "inventing" a new word, for example, can only come through the play and reference to words, references and meanings you have known before. This is not to say that one cannot be intentional about intertextual reference (one can) but rather that one cannot avoid intertextual reference even when not intentional.

Intertextuality makes clear that even the work of the most original artists must draw upon the work of its predecessors. You might ask, then, that if this is the case, what does give apparently original work the sense of being new, fresh or even avant garde? A basic answer is that the power of a work resides in the way that it recontextualizes its constituent parts that have been borrowed (many critics prefer the term "cannibalized") from works that have come before. What is creative, then, is a creative reworking rather than a creative endeavour arising from nothing: genius resides in novel manipulation not in novel production.

Intertextuality may *feel* reasonable to you (how can we produce something with absolutely no prior experience or context? Such an act of creation is generally reserved for deities). However, it actually represents an interesting challenge to much of our thinking about authorship, authenticity and intellectual property. We study literature in the context of a world largely defined by the ideology of the individual. That is, we tend to grant tremendous authority to the notion of an individual author and the uniqueness of the author's thoughts and style. In fact, such a worldview has really only enjoyed widespread acceptance since the Renaissance, which shifted a focus to the individual and independent pursuit of knowledge. Notions such as authorship and even plagiarism are relatively recent concepts. Intertextuality, however, makes this idea problematic, arguing that, in its purest form, there is no original authorship and, therefore, there cannot exist plagiarism—both interesting ideas to consider in your study of literature.

Intertextuality is treated mostly as an issue of production in the paragraphs above but intertextuality has a bearing on reception as well. When we read texts, we employ all of our individual experiences with all the texts that we have read, viewed, heard or experienced before as well, it is argued, with the collective experiences that form part of our unconscious. Interestingly, in terms of reading, this makes every reading experience unique even as we all may borrow from the same intertextual body of knowledge. Because every reading is always a rereading that builds upon previous "readings" (in the broadest sense), there is always an element of new fashioning and of the reader's substantial role in producing meaning.

In many texts, as mentioned above, intertextuality is not only an inevitable function of language and literature in our world but an intentional component to make a point or suggest an effect. *The Simpsons*, for instance, constantly refers to other television shows in ways that convey meaning. This, again, is more than an allusion as the references become rather necessary to "show" a viewer (or remind them) how to view *The Simpsons* as a show. When used in this way, intertexuality makes use of a tool critics refer to as **anchorage** that both draws attention to a work's own intertextuality as well as reminding us that all work is produced in a particular context. Anchorage is particularly common in advertisement, spoof and much of popular culture.

While the historical context, or life and times of the author, is usually the first context to which you are exposed and the most commonly taught, the next most obvious context is clearly that of the story itself. Often, this context will be similar to that of the life and times of the author: if an author is writing about his or her world, culture and "things that the author knows", the story will be said to be contemporary to the writer. In such cases, knowing the context of the one will also be the context of the other. But authors will just as often write stories that are foreign, either in place, time or both. In these instances a very clear contextual consideration would be the story world rather than the author's real world.

In fiction, you might believe that the story world simply does not matter. Some might argue that this may be true in some fantasy or science fiction work but literary works are rarely, if ever, so artificial that context does not play some role. Even when an author constructs a highly unreal story world, there is rarely a total lack of **verisimilitude** that helps a reader navigate that world and understand the larger purpose or effect. In fact, even when authors choose to create a story world different from their own they will often do substantial research on that story world context to ensure some degree of accuracy (for instance, they may do the historical research into a world of the past or even research the science around possible worlds of the future).

The context of the story probably rarely, if ever, completely displaces the historical context (and, again, by historical we mean the life and times of the author) but instead adds another layer of interest and complexity in approaching a work. To have an author of one time and place writing of another time and place more likely contains elements of both contexts that work in curious relationship with one another. In 1997, for instance, the American writer Thomas Pynchon published the novel *Mason & Dixon*. The novel centres on the British surveyors Charles Mason and Jeremiah Dixon as they plot the Mason-Dixon line (dividing the north from the south) just before the American Civil War. Not only does the novel deal with issues of slavery, British colonialism, authentic historical characters, expansion and exploration, and surveying during the time period, it is even written in the syntax and diction contemporary to that world. But the novel also clearly incorporates contextual elements closely related to the late 20th century including

Activity

Michael Ondaatje, a Canadian writer of Sri Lankan descent, wrote the novel *The English Patient* in 1992 (which was remediated as a successful film in 1996). The novel unravels the disparate lives of several characters who live out the final days of the second world war together in an abandoned villa in the Italian countryside. The novel considers issues such as nationality, love, war and race which could be argued to be timeless and, thus, could be considered in any story world context.

Based on what you know of the second world war (do some very brief research if necessary), how do you think some of the following topics—considered from the context of 1945 and the end of the second world war—would provide particular resonance to the primary issues listed below?:

spying   distrust   love   foreignness   atomic bomb

survival   honesty   alienation   hope   revenge

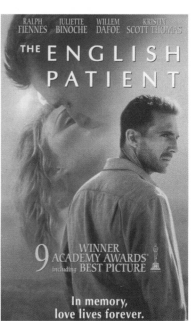

RALPH FIENNES   JULIETTE BINOCHE   WILLEM DAFOE   KRISTIN SCOTT THOMAS

THE ENGLISH PATIENT

9 WINNER ACADEMY AWARDS including BEST PICTURE

In memory, love lives forever.

conspiratorial plots, alien abduction, robots and a minor character who speaks suspiciously like the cartoon character Popeye the Sailor Man. To understand or consider only one of the contexts (that of the world of Mason and Dixon or that of the world of Thomas Pynchon) would be to miss out on much of the humour, genius and epic quality of the text.

Ultimately, whether a story intentionally plays with a multiplicity of contexts like *Mason & Dixon* or simply offers a story world different from that of the writer, the context of the story offers yet another contextual approach that you can consider in your study and in producing assessment tasks for the course.

Issue   Context of Reception

Still another part of your study of literature may involve the context of reception. Again, part of the aims and objectives of this course involve an understanding of a variety of contextual approaches and it is likely that a consideration of reception will prove fruitful in your study and in developing topics for many of your formal assessment tasks. Reception is really composed of two parts: the personal and the critical. In fact, the personal can be further divided into the individual reception and the larger social reception (by "critical" here we mean an approach based on a particular literary theory such as Marxism or feminism) but we will continue to use these two broad categories.

The context of reception starts, obviously, with the receiver. Even the decision to pick up a literary work and start reading has a context, either because it says something of your interests or your condition (perhaps you are "forced" to read due to a class assignment or your parents' haranguing). This might seem small, but this is actually quite an interesting contextual issue to explore.

- How do you make that initial decision to engage a literary work?
- What goes into the selection process when choosing a work?
    - How do teachers select the works that they teach?
    - How does the publishing industry publicize works?
    - How are book covers and **paratext** (text outside of the main body of work such as the copyright page and table of contents but also back covers, blurbs from critics or other writers, biographical information about the author or a list of other works written by them) significant or influential in this process?
- How are marketing, economics or awards influential?

There has been a recent rush of publications critical of large-scale retailers such as Wal-Mart for their outsized ability to make an impact on culture as a result of their market dominance. Because such retailers actually sell the majority of so many products, the argument goes, they can put pressure on suppliers to limit production to the kinds of products of which they approve. Though Wal-Mart is not primarily a book store, it is, in fact, one of the major retailers of books in the United States. Because so many books are sold through Wal-Mart (Wal-Mart is said to be the majority customer to many publishing houses in the country), publishers are more inclined to continue producing books they know Wal-Mart will find appealing. If Wal-Mart refuses to stock a book, sales of that book are almost guaranteed to face an uphill battle (see works such as Charles Fishman's *The Wal-Mart Effect* or Naomi Klein's *No Logo: Taking Aim at the Brand Bullies* to explore such topics further). In such a context, it is quite possible that some of your decisions to select a work are already compromised by issues of accessibility and exposure, by what is popularly available and popularly known already. If you are not a reader who actively seeks out new literary works, how do you come to decisions about text selection?

The context of personal reception, though, goes beyond just selecting a work. Once you have a literary work in hand (however that came about or against whatever odds), you now introduce all of your intertextual knowledge (see the reception section on page 233 for more on intertextuality), your personal experience and even, according to some theorists, your unconscious into your reading. As readers, we play a game with an implicit knowledge of our own personal contexts and how that fits into reading a literary work. We have established, some critics believe, a **horizon of expectations** that governs the way we approach texts. When we read a novel, for instance, we have learned that an action, for instance a failed romance, is fictional and can modulate our emotions to sympathize with the characters but with the recognition that this is not authentic (in this case, our horizon of expectations is to recognize the signs of a failed romance and understand a response). But what if we have just broken up with a partner and are feeling remorse, sadness or pain? It is possible that our personal context has an impact on our reading in unique and individual ways.

One of the skills with reading literature is balancing our personal contexts with our understanding of how literary works operate. Unpractised students frequently let their personal contexts override the story contexts in inappropriate ways. For instance, fans of science fiction might read the following short poem.

Portals

What are those of the known, but to ascend and enter the Unknown?
And what are those of life, but for Death?

WALT WHITMAN

If their love of science fiction is such that they see the title "Portals" and connect this to their favourite episode of *Star Trek* and, specifically, an episode where the captain transports through a portal to the planet of Xelbok, they are in trouble. In this case, they have allowed their personal context to dominate the story context and no longer read the poem as a poem (they have forgotten the horizon of expectations).

Personal context is never a bad approach but it does need to be balanced with an understanding of literature as literature. In the earlier example of someone with a recently ended relationship, it seems perfectly reasonable that this element of a novel resonates deeply with the reader. So long as there is some balance or recognition of story context as well, this can prove an insightful focus that draws this reader's attention to particular aspects and effects. It may be that on a later read, when the emotions of this relationship have cooled, this same reader barely registers the failed romance and instead is drawn to the protagonist's pursuit of money. In both of the readings, the personal context of the reader becomes a fascinating element that affects deeply the understanding and interpretation of the work and, thus, an understanding of the context of the reader aids in appreciating the multiplicity of interpretations available to readers.

In addition to the personal experiences, attitudes and interests that a reader brings to his or her reading, a reader may also choose to approach a text through the perspective of a particular critical lens. A reader can, either before reading the text at all or after an initial impression of the attitudes, features or other elements of the text, decide to "decode" a work based on any of the following approaches:

- Marxism—looking at how conflict or competition over control of resources may be revealed in a work

- feminism—looking at the representation of women and attitudes about constructed gender roles

- New Criticism—looking only at the formal literary features of a work with no concern for information beyond (such as information about the author or other contextual information)

- structuralism—looking for simple structures and patterns that occur repeatedly within and across works that help us understand and interpret works

- deconstruction—looking at the inherent ambiguity in language and the way that a text can speak against itself ("say" something different from what it might likely intend) as a result

- New historicism—looking at the way texts reveal historical norms, mores and worldviews that both govern literature and of which literature is a part

- psychoanalytic criticism—looking at the way an author's subconscious or unconscious desires are revealed through "slips" in the work

- post-colonial criticism—looking at the way the texts create, represent or comment on the "other", usually a figure from a colonized country or marginalized community.

(Many of these critical approaches are treated in more detail in other sections of this book.)

What makes the context of reception so interesting is the way it is always changing. A single reader's personal reception changes with each reading, reflected in changing appreciations of a work (it is quite possible to dislike on a second reading a book that you once loved or, thankfully more often the case with texts you might re-approach after high school, love a book towards which you once felt ambivalence if not something stronger). A single reader can also approach a single text through different critical lenses and develop vastly different readings, all mature and insightful in their own right. If nothing else, the context of reception certainly demonstrates the way different readers can approach works.

Activity

Look at the excerpts from: Andre Agassi's *Open* on page 202, Folman and Polonsky's *Waltz With Bashir* on page 207, Zadie Smith's *White Teeth* on page 203, and Edna St Vincent Millay's poem *Recuerdo* on page 206. Then consider the following questions.

- Do you feel that the works can be organized by their appeal to gender? That is, do you believe some works would appeal to women over men and vice versa? Why or why not?

- Which work appeals most immediately to you and why? Try to be specific, finding elements of your personal reception context that are aroused by the work. By extension, what kind of community do you think might have a difficult time engaging with this work and why? Again, try to be specific—recognizing both how you approach works and the different ways others approach works is a key aim in this course.

- Take the same work you have identified above (as that which appeals to you most strongly) and briefly try to outline two or three different formal critical approaches from the list above (or others of which you are aware).

The graphic novel, or graphic narrative as some prefer to call it, is a narrative that combines words and images (generally hand drawn). The graphic novel is distinguished from comics as tending to be of longer duration while comics are recognized as shorter, serial productions. Though the graphic novel has a long tradition in Japan (*manga*) and parts of Europe, it has only much more recently been embraced as a mainstream literary medium on a large scale (in terms of both production and reception). In 2004, however, *The New York Times Magazine* identified the graphic novel as an important literary art form that offers an accessible format with mass appeal in the way that used to define the novel. Such popular pronouncement certainly heralded the legitimacy of the graphic novel into the literary world.

While the presence of images is certainly unique to the graphic novel, the medium actually uses image in interesting relationships with text. The following are among some of the aspects that are truly unique to the graphic novel:

- Frames—the graphic novel breaks the page into distinct frames. Several frames can make up a panel.

- Gutters—the frames of a graphic novel are clearly divided with gaps between. These gaps—which may or may not include white (dead or empty) space—are not hidden but openly exposed as opposed to other media that use frames (such as film).

- Fragmented—through the above elements, the graphic novel mimics the processes of memory, recollection and story-telling where we piece together disparate elements and attempt to provide a whole narrative but where gaps always remain.

- Collapsed time and space—the frames of a graphic novel can convey multiple time periods on a single page simultaneously. One frame or panel may be in the present while that to the left is in the future and that below is in the past. In no other medium can the reader shift between viewing a part or viewing the whole page and, thus, between isolated time in space or multiple times across space.

Some critics argue that the graphic novel enjoys some singular advantages as a literary medium. These critics see both the process of producing a graphic novel and of reading a graphic novel as similar to the way we view and construct narratives of ourselves and our worlds. The graphic novel essentially "materializes" our thinking processes where we represent and interpret the world in framed visual images combined with language (either verbal or written). Further, the use of gaps in the graphic novel encourages the reader to "project" causality, which critics believe also mirrors our processes in "real" life. The graphic novel, then, may be a unique form of fiction that most accurately, even if in a highly stylized way, reflects the way we know both ourselves and our larger worlds.

One final unique quality that the graphic novel offers is the ability of the readers to exert some choice and control of where they place emphasis and focus. In film, for instance, the medium is also composed of frames but the film maker will decide on which frames to pause (through a panning perspective, slow motion movement or other visual features), which to rush and which will occur in the story's "normal" time. Without pausing frame by frame, viewers can only read the text as presented to them. But the graphic novel offers the reader choice: they can focus on the frame or panel of choice and linger as long as desired (though this may be possible with literary texts without images, the lack of visual representation gives this a fundamentally different effect and impact). Perspective and emphasis are shared with the writer rather than dominated by one party.

Activity

Turn to the excerpt from Folman and Polonsky's *Waltz With Bashir* on page 207 and consider the following questions.

- What effect do the panning frames seem to convey in this piece?
- What projections (of causality) do you, as the reader, add to the gutters?
- What impact and purpose does the mix of time periods convey in the work?
- In this particular excerpt, what gives the visual drawings their force? What ideas are conveyed visually that are not conveyed by text?
- How do the text and visuals work in harmony to create effect?
- How does the page seem to speak to the way we experience memory or represent our experiences?

Issue | Context of Production

In other chapters of the book, we have discussed historical context (the life and times of the author), the story world context and the different possible contexts of reception. One final significant context for considering literary works is that of its production. Literary production can be the physical means of production to publishing decisions to marketing (also discussed in the issue section on context of reception) to formatting and dissemination to access and availability. As part of the discipline of English, the context of production can be an approach that involves either personal analysis or detailed computational analysis of years of historical records though, for the purposes of this course, it will more likely be the former.

Some of the more common aspects of literary production that would be worth exploring include the following:

- **Social realities**—which could run from literacy rates or education to issues of state censorship. For example, in the former Soviet Union, the literature produced—in an official capacity—was limited to that promoting the ideals of Soviet Communism only. Similarly, a society where education and literacy are available only to its elite members will probably only continue to produce limited works that speak to the same values and worldview. In more open societies with widespread literacy, literary works can be a strong source of critical reflection and debate.

- **Circulation**—whether this means cheap and available works for the masses, libraries or the popularity of a literary form that allows for its transmission by word-of-mouth, circulation is an interesting aspect of literary production. Circulation can be affected by issues of marketing or the power of retailing (see the issue section on context of reception for more information on this topic) but also by technology as witnessed by circulation possibilities (or limitations) arising from e-books, amazon.com and wireless readers.

- **Technology**—which could be the advent of the printing press or the changes in technology mentioned above that will aid and affect literary production. Popular studies of the production of Shakespeare's work focus on technology as the written texts, whether folio or quarto, are both recorded after the original creation.

- **Literary culture and media**—a broad category that refers to how literature may be talked about, reviews and reviewing mechanisms, the effect of awards on production and some aspects of physical production. This category certainly overlaps with elements of reception and how work is received popularly but does affect production issues. A work may be reasonably successful but, taking an example from the United States, if it is nominated for a prize or mentioned in *O* magazine (a production of Oprah Winfrey), it is guaranteed greater exposure and sales which will guarantee greater numbers of production (which will, in the cycle of events, guarantee greater exposure and sales which will guarantee, and so on…). Also, in strong literary cultures, literary works may be published in newspapers or general periodicals (rather than only specialized literary journals) which may result in **serialization** (the production of longer works in short installments) or even works tailored to fit or appeal to these other mediums.

- **Intertextuality**—the production of works may be greatly affected by other works. New works may be produced to follow trends that are popular or successful or intentionally work against these to offer critique or alternatives. For example, though detective fiction has long been popular, some credit the success of television programmes such as *C.S.I.* for a new interest not just in forensic science but other gritty detective work. Perhaps it is no coincidence that Steig Larsson's *Millennium Series* (including *The Girl with the Dragon Tattoo*), published after his death, has enjoyed such concurrent popular acclaim.

Issues of context are important to consider in this course but equally important is the understanding that there are many different kinds of context to explore (whether as part of your study or as a topic for an assessment task such as the written task or further oral activity). In the end, an author, a work, a reader, the process of writing, the condition of production, appropriation, understanding, interpretation and communication are all mutually interconnected and relational. Understanding any one component should be tempered by an awareness of the others and should also remind us of the truly complex process involved in reading literary works, let alone developing a personal and intellectual interpretation or them.

Issue — Knowledge and Truth

It is possible that at some point in your lifetime of studying English, you have received a text and wondered—perhaps even aloud and in concert with your classmates—why you must read this. In response, you may have heard your teacher (or even your parent if you carried the concern or complaint home) say one or more of the following:

- "Because I said."
- "Because literature teaches us things about our experience and humanity that are unavailable through other media and necessary to truly reach for our 'higher selves.'"
- "Because literature teaches us how to look at things with a logical criticism, to question assumptions and the way the world is said to 'work.'"
- "Because literature teaches us how to be better communicators."

- "Because literature helps us understand our heritage as a culture and as part of larger humankind."
- "Because it is great fun."

The existence of English as a discipline has hinged on questions of the nature and value of literary study. For most people, value is measured against the ability to have an impact on or affect so-called "reality". Though this may be true for all academic disciplines to some degree, the question relating to literature is anchored in a kind of paradox: how does something that is intentionally fictitious speak to the conditions of the "real"? In other words, what possible knowledge or truth could an artificial story have to offer?

Though knowledge and truth may not be central thematic concerns in every literary work you encounter, issues involving knowledge and truth (as context or as theme) are probably bubbling very close to the surface in almost every text. There is no singular approach the works take, but you will find that the following foci are widely represented.

- **Mimetic** works focus on the mimetic level and merely intend to paint a picture of reality and present the world exactly as it appears. This is more commonly associated with works of non-fiction or documentary film. There are arguments about the true possibility of such an approach. Is it, in other words, ever possible simply to present material without comment (whether conscious or otherwise)? Regardless of questions, mimetic texts try to show a world for what it is, revealing a kind of unadulterated knowledge or truth.

- **Dogmatic** works focus on human behaviour and relationships, or how one should behave properly in a society. These works tend to be associated with ancient Greek drama or fables more than others but this is a misnomer: whether Machiavelli's *The Prince* or the works of Thoreau, dogmatic works come in different forms with different beliefs across different times.

- **Aesthetic** works try to affect readers viscerally and aesthetically only. Much poetry can be argued to be aesthetic (such as the work of some language poets) in this sense, meaning that such works try to resist our attempts to piece together an obvious narrative or purpose. In other words, the knowledge or truth of these works is that there does not need to be a larger knowledge or truth but the value may reside in simply a visceral, aesthetic *experience* that need not be reduced to a meaning.

- **Humanity** or **higher humanity** works address what it means to be human. Most would argue that this represents the widest approach to knowledge and truth and may appear in many "forms".

  - Propositional theory of literary truth—this theory (mostly popular in the UK and commonwealth countries) asserts that literature contains or contends general thematic statements about the world and/or our human condition. The reader, then, effectively accomplishes interpretation by either agreeing or disagreeing with a text's assertions. In either case, the reader comes away with a fuller appreciation of these statements about the world and/or our human condition and one's own position in relationship to them.

  - One theory is that literature contains inherent truths and it teaches us to recognize these through reason that is tempered by affections of pleasure and sympathy—skills uniquely learned and achieved through reading literature—including:

- what it is to interpret
- making sense of the self
- increasing self-understanding
- increasing awareness of our own understanding
- increasing awareness of our encounters with the world
- connecting strands of life that seem otherwise disconnected.

  ❑ Metaphysical works address a "greater human truth" or some knowledge about ourselves and/or our world that surpasses "knowing" in a more traditional sense. These works suggest that literature and its value or knowledge is beyond classification, abstraction or transfer but still reveals what can only be illuminated through literature.

- **Cultural** works contain and convey a cultural heritage and illustrate ideas, ideals and values of a society. These works may seek to reveal "universal truths" about humankind (and are linked to the above point) or more "local" truths that reveal unique cultures and unique worldviews.

- **Artistic** works focus on the value of themselves and seek to highlight what the medium intends to show or how the medium is uniquely constructed and/or valuable. This is a kind of metaknowledge or truth but you are likely to run across much poetry, for instance, that on some level may be communicating about the question "what is poetry?" This is slightly different from aesthetic above in this list in that there is an intellectual argument about the role and purpose of literature inherent.

- **Post-modern** works seek to question the possibility of knowledge and truth ever being a knowable theme and these works may actually subvert all efforts to locate meaning. Of course, there is some irony inherent as the "meaning" or knowledge or truth resides in this very lack and instead offers a prescription for play or for physical, spiritual or emotional effect in the face of such uncertainty.

Reception Fantasy and Science Fiction

Fantasy fiction is a very broad category of fiction that designates any work that consciously breaks free from reality. To break away from reality may involve places non-existent in the real world (not by name or precise destination but rather as an "unreal" world such as a fairyland), people or characters that are unreal or other physical and scientific principles either not yet recognized or in contrast to principles that make up our current understanding. Popularly, fantasy is associated with medieval and pre-medieval-like worlds though often with a healthy dose of anachronistic technologies or knowledge. The mixing of contemporary or even future with aspects of the distant past frequently appear in fantasy works. Though the setting, characters and/or governing principles, norms or laws are substantially different in fantasy literature from our own reality, fantasy fiction may often offer serious comment on the real world. Though fantasy has been associated with more fanciful imagination and escapist pursuit in the past, there are plenty who argue for its legitimate place in the larger canon of respectable literature. As evidenced by its popularity, fantasy is certainly a sub-genre of fiction that cannot be ignored. Its influence is felt beyond traditional literary texts (it is most associated with prose fiction) and components of fantasy may be found from television programmes to graphic novels to video games, music and role-playing games.

Science fiction literature is technically a component of the fantasy sub-genre. However, science fiction is treated uniquely as it tends to be built specifically upon scientific and technological facts and theories which are extended to fictional (fantastical) ends. Current understandings are stretched or extended to imaginative heights, applying variants of these understandings to new worlds, planets, dimensions in time and space and alternative scientific realities. While science fiction is most popularly associated with space ships and alien beings, many science fiction works treat issues as wide ranging as:

- technological change
- scientific breakthroughs or experiments
- social change
- climate change
- ecological change
- resource depletion
- social, sexual and moral norms
- the place of earth and humankind in the universe.

While science fiction, and all fantasy for that matter, may comment on the real world and real issues, it should stretch the imagination with the suspension of disbelief.

Works as disparate as Shakespeare's *The Tempest*, Don DeLillo's *White Noise*, Jonathan Swift's *Gulliver's Travels*, Voltaire's *Candide*, Mary Shelley's *Frankenstein* and many works by Edgar Allen Poe could technically be classed as fantasy and science fiction. Most readers today tend to apply slightly more limiting constraints on what is or is not fantasy and science fiction but the following represents some of the more popular story types.

- "Hard" science fiction deals with stories anchored in authentic experimental science and its accurate portrayal and usage.
- "Soft" science fiction deals with stories anchored in the social sciences.
- Cyberpunk deals with stories anchored in information technology.
- Alternate history imagines alternative results to significant historical events and the resulting alternative realities.
- Dystopic or apocalyptic works are concerned with the end of "civilized" society or the end of the world as we know it.

As already stated, both fantasy and science fiction are enjoying new attention as literary sub-genres with value and purpose beyond pulp entertainment. Their influence can be detected across popular culture (whether through movies, television programmes, increases in publishing statistics, internationally recognized conferences or influence throughout digital gaming). This influence shows no sign of waning.

TOM GAULD

It is quite possible that at least one of the literary works in your study from part 1 or part 2 of the course will be a dramatic work. Works of drama are fundamentally different from the other genres you may study not only in how the texts appear physically (being filled mostly with dialogue in addition to other kinds of writing you will not find in other genres, such as stage directions) but in how you must approach them. In brief, the primary distinction is that drama is meant to be performed rather than "simply" read. While we are sure this is not a new idea to you, it is much more difficult to remember or internalize as you are studying a dramatic work. Many students will go about reading a dramatic work as though it is a novel or short story and thus forget this most primary element of drama.

In other works, we have referred to drama as an "indirect" literature. We mean this in contrast to prose that can provide a complete world for the reader with fully fleshed-out characters, events and background. Drama, though, is filled with empty spaces that need to be completed, or filled in, by the reader or director. Drama demands that a reader considers both the text and an interpretation of the work to move towards a production or performance and, with drama, the ultimate performance can take many formats. Many readers of prose fiction believe that they visualize the stories they read as performances. But these performances are scripted by the detail already provided by the story. Drama, on the other hand, demands that you do this same feat but without all of the detail. Instead, you must fill in this detail based with how you see the play developing and/or on how you would ultimately like to see the work presented (both of these approaches represent interpretation but slightly different kinds of interpretation). Drama, then, provides the raw ingredients (dialogue, stage directions, act and scene breaks, set or prop suggestions) but you must ultimately put them together and produce the final recipe. To read the words of a play as you would a poem or a piece of prose is to miss out on much of what most distinguishes drama as a unique genre.

The following are some of the major elements of drama.

- Dialogue—this is the primary vehicle through which we learn about characters in a play. Dialogue in drama conveys information through its content and style. The content can certainly convey ideas, themes or aspects of character and it should be remembered that dialogue in drama is always more complex than dialogue in real life: in drama, the conversations are meant to be overheard and, thus, they reveal not just conversations between two or more characters but also conversations between characters and the audience. Often, these conversations can be quite different from one another. Style implies the use of speech (for example accent, pace, diction) that can reveal further elements about the character or generally illustrate the character.

- Soliloquies, monologues and asides—all are other forms of speech with specific intention.

  - Soliloquy is a long speech where a character speaks to himself, herself or to an absent character. Soliloquies dramatically replicate a character's private thoughts and feelings as they are staged as occurring in no one's presence (except, of course, the audience's).

- Monologue is similar to a soliloquy but it is spoken to another character. Both monologues and soliloquies tend to convey a lot of information to an audience quickly.

- An aside is a quick side speech in the presence of other characters that is intended to be hidden from those other characters. It is rather like speaking "under one's breath", making a comment out loud without really wanting others around you to hear it. Asides are meant to be heard by the audience but a dramatic aside is overtly directed at the audience while an aside is directed as though to no one.

- All three—soliloquies, monologues and asides—reveal information to the audience that other characters may not know. This leads to **dramatic irony** where the audience is aware of tension and conflict with knowledge of characters that even the characters themselves do not possess.

- Stage directions—these provide context for a play with direction in terms of props, costumes, lighting, movement and set. These can support a play's theme quite significantly but stage directions can also be easily flouted or modified to change the impact and effect of the play substantially.

- Plot and action—plot in plays occurs primarily through conflict, opposition and difference. "What happens" in drama is less a series of exciting events that unfold over time but rather a series of crises that need to be resolved (for good or ill). It is the various resolutions in a play that allow the work to move forward, which is quite different from other genres. This is not to say that there are no exciting moments of action or no play with time but the real momentum of a dramatic work seems to come via tension between characters or characters and the audience (in some avant-garde works, the tension between a play and society can spark much of the action and plot).

- Space—space occurs as any or all of the following.

  - The setting—whether a play takes place indoors or out, in bright light or in the dark, on a ship, in a jail or in a school forms a significant element of the overall work. Setting, of course, can be changed throughout the play.

  - Movements—how the characters engage with one another physically, for example whether they are near one another or not, carries much information in a play.

  - The fourth wall—this is an imaginary divide between the audience and the stage or play that can be shifting, solid or non-existent and can convey much about the play. Do characters employ dramatic aside or only aside? Does the play attempt to ignore an audience and convey an idea or engage the audience to convey something different?

Together, these elements feed into any performance or need to be considered to move a drama from the page to the stage. But what is most unique about these elements is how open they are to a variety of readings and interpretations than can significantly affect the larger effect. Tom Stoppard, in the author's note to the acting edition of his play *Rosencrantz & Guildenstern Are Dead* once wrote the following "advice" for future directors:

> Author's note to *Rosencrantz & Guildenstern Are Dead*
>
> …whatever else it [the play] is, is a comedy. My intention was comic, and if the play had not turned out funny I would have considered that I had failed. Quite a lot of solemn and scholarly stuff has been written about it, which is fine and flattering, but it is worth bearing in mind that among the productions staged all over the world, two were comparative failures, and both of these took the play very seriously indeed.
>
> TOM STOPPARD

Though this represents an extreme example of differing interpretations, it does indicate how open and malleable drama is to different perspectives. But it is worth noting that, despite such opportunity for interpretation, drama as a genre does include some stock types that you may come across in your study, including the following.

- **Comedy and tragedy** based on a happy ending or an unhappy ending (for more on these types, see the reception section on page 255).
- **Farce** is comedy involving extreme stock characters, misunderstanding and slapstick humour. This can be known as *Commedia dell' Arte*.
- **Epic theatre** is a form that highlights its unreality by rejecting naturalism or emotional engagement by the audience.
- **Morality plays** offer an allegory, usually affiliated with a religious theme.
- **Problem plays** are overt social critiques that tackle a contemporary problem.
- **Noh** drama is a Japanese dramatic form that involves slow movements and highly stylized masks.
- **Ancient Greek theatre** provides the roots for the Western dramatic tradition and features a chorus, masks and an aim of promoting a unified cultural identify and behaviours.

Activity

Read the excerpt from Caryl Churchill's play *Top Girls* on page 205 and consider the following.

- In this short excerpt, very little activity occurs yet there is action and plot. Look at the conflicts, tensions and oppositions that are suggested between Joyce, Marlene and Angie and how these conflicts suggest much of the plot to come.

- Based on the short excerpt and the language used, how would you characterize each character?

- If you were to stage this play, what kind of set would you design (what do you imagine here)? What costumes or props would you suggest to include?

Issue	Social Critique, Power and Power Struggles

In his essay entitled *Why I Write*, George Orwell listed the following as his last and most significant reason for pursuing the life of a writer:

> From *Why I Write*
>
> *(iv) Political purpose* —Using the word 'political' in the widest possible sense. Desire to push the world in a certain direction, to alter other people's idea of the kind of society that they should strive after. Once again, no book is genuinely free from political bias. The opinion that art should have nothing to do with politics is itself a political attitude.
>
> GEORGE ORWELL

Orwell makes two points in this part of his essay: that he writes in order to affect and alter people's ideas and attitudes and that no book is ever free from political purpose. If we extrapolate slightly, we could contend that all works comment on society and social mores in some fashion.

Orwell's creative works, for example *Animal Farm* and *1984*, offer overt social critiques of society (or potential society) and he is certainly not the only writer in English to engage in such strong sentiment about what "kind of society people should strive after" (and, by extension as well as arguably more popular, what kind of society we should avoid). Especially in novel form (also referred to as the **social protest novel**), social critique can be said to be one of the most common thematic elements to be found in literature, particularly in the last two hundred years. Many believe that literature occupies a unique place in the culture where it reflects the social world and social realities around it but also manages to inhabit a privileged space slightly outside these same social realities allowing it to reflect critically on them. Because of this and coupled with the possibility that no work can truly be free of political impetus, as Orwell suggests, themes of social critique are especially rampant.

Very frequently, themes of social critique or protest are manifested as struggles over power. Obviously, themes of power may exist on smaller scales than we would typically associate with society (perhaps power conflicts between an adult and a child or a husband and a wife) but even these may allegorically represent larger critiques of social reality. Some of the more likely themes around power and power struggle include:

- good versus evil
- gender conflict
- economic conflict
- social status (wealth versus poverty or authority versus subservience))
- control (social, economic, the self or psychic)
- military or political might
- colonization/national conflict
- justice and rights
- literacy or education.

> **Activity**
>
> Turn to the poem *Quashie to Buccra* by Claude McKay on page 201. This poem represents a complex range of possible social critiques and power struggles through combinations of its form, use of language and themes. Closely analyse the work trying to find ways to comment on each of the three aspects.

Reception Set and Staging

The set and staging of drama is already mentioned briefly as an element in the reception section on the stage (not the page) but it is enough of a unique literary element to deserve additional attention here. The set of a dramatic work is the visual and physical embodiment of the setting (that is, the time and place where the dramatic narrative takes place). It is the visual or physical element that makes the set so interesting and different, however. While setting is important to most if not all literary works, in drama the set is so visible and so much a part of performance that it can dominate a performance and is hard to overlook. Just as in some other fictional works, the set can function as a unique character but it also functions significantly in creating the mood and in establishing context (historical and social).

Staging is the final enactment of setting, combining the set with, for example, lighting, movement, sound, costumes, stage directions, props and scenery. Taken together, these elements work with the acting to produce the actual performance of the play. As also mentioned in the earlier section, the staging is never a static or fixed component of drama (the way setting may be in prose, for instance). Instead, it is in the staging where the reader and director have the most freedom of interpretation and is where the play is most fully realized (this can be true of television, film and video productions as well that add further levels of staging, for example with cameras, angles or perspectives). One may accept some of the staging suggestions of the playwright or modify extensively based on either needs (for example the size of a stage or whether it is to be indoors or outdoors) or desires (for instance to stage a work realistically or in some non-realistic fashion).

Activity

Look closely at the following images of two different set and staging designs for Shakespeare's *Titus Andronicus* and consider the following questions.

- Do the two versions seem to speak to different time periods or contexts? For what purpose would a director be compelled to choose such different set designs?

- What atmosphere, tone or mood is created in each of the versions and through what elements?

- How might the different physical spaces be used to make an impact on the staging and the effect?

- Pick any element of each of the sets. How do they contribute to context, meaning or impact?

Texts

Grief

I tell you, hopeless grief is passionless;
That only men incredulous of despair,
Half-taught in anguish, through the midnight air
Beat upward to God's throne in loud access
Of shrieking and reproach. Full desertness,
In souls as countries, lieth silent-bare
Under the blanching, vertical eye-glare

Of the absolute heavens. Deep-hearted man, express
Grief for thy dead in silence like to death—
Most like a monumental statue set
In everlasting watch and moveless woe
Till itself crumble to the dust beneath.
Touch it; the marble eyelids are not wet:
If it could weep, it could arise and go.

ELIZABETH BARRATT BROWNING

The Author to Her Book

Thou ill-informed offspring of my feeble brain,
Who after birth did'st by my side remain,
Till snatched from thence by friends, less wise than true,
Who thee abroad exposed to public view;
Made thee in rags, halting, to the press to trudge,
Where errors were not lessened, all may judge.
At thy return my blushing was not small,
My rambling brat (in print) should mother call;
I cast thee by as one unfit for light,
Thy visage was so irksome in my sight;
Yet being mine own, at length affection would
Thy blemishes amend, if so I could:
I washed thy face, but more defects I saw,

And rubbing off a spot, still made a flaw.
I stretched thy joints to make thee even feet,
Yet still thou run'st more hobbling than is meet;
In better dress to trim thee was my mind,
But nought save homespun cloth in the house I find.
In this array, 'mongst vulgar may'st thou roam;
And take thy way where yet thou are not known.
If for they Father asked, say thou had'st none;
And for thy Mother, she alas is poor,
Which caused her thus to send thee out of door.

ANNE BRADSTREET

How the Poor Die

A thing we perhaps underrate in England is the advantage we enjoy in having large numbers of well-trained and rigidly-disciplined nurses. No doubt English nurses are dumb enough, they may tell fortunes with tea-leaves, wear Union Jack badges and keep photographs of the Queen on their mantelpieces, but at least they don't let you lie unwashed and constipated on an unmade bed, out of sheer laziness. The nurses at the Hôpital X still had a tinge of Mrs Gamp about them, and later, in the military hospitals of Republican Spain, I was to see nurses almost too ignorant to take a temperature. You wouldn't, either, see in England such dirt as existed in the Hôpital X. Later on, when I was well enough to wash myself in the bathroom, I found that there was kept there a huge packing case into which the scraps of food and dirty dressings from the ward were flung, and the wainscodings were infested by crickets. When I had got back my clothes and grown strong on my legs I fled from the Hôpital X, before my time was up and without waiting for a medical discharge. It was not the only hospital I have fled from, but its gloom and bareness, its sickly smell and, above all, something in its mental atmosphere stand out in my memory as exceptional. I had been taken there because it was the hospital belonging to my arrondissement, and I did not learn till after I was in it that it bore a bad reputation. A year or two later the celebrated swindler, Madame Hanaud, who was ill while on remand, was taken to the Hôpital X, and after a few days of it she managed to elude her guards, took a taxi and drove back to the prison, explaining that she was more comfortable there. I have no doubt that the Hôpital X was quite untypical of French hospitals even at that date. But the patients, nearly all of them working men, were surprisingly resigned. Some of them seemed to find the conditions almost comfortable, for at least two were destitute malingerers who found this a good way of getting through the winter. The nurses connived because the malingerers made themselves useful by doing odd jobs. But the attitude of the majority was: of course this is a lousy place, but what else do you expect? It did not seem strange to them that you should be woken at five and then wait three hours before starting the day on watery soup, or that people should die with no one at their bedside, or even that your chance of getting medical attention should depend on catching the doctor's eye as he went past. According to their traditions that was what hospitals were like. If you are seriously ill and if you are too poor to be treated in your own home, then you must go into hospital, and once there you must put up with harshness and discomfort, just as you would in the army. But on top of this I was interested to find a lingering belief in the old stories that have now almost faded from memory in England—stories, for instance, about doctors cutting you open out of sheer curiosity or thinking it funny to start operating before you were properly 'under'. There were dark tales about a little operating-room said to be situated just beyond the bathroom. Dreadful screams were said to issue from this room. I saw nothing to confirm these stories and no doubt they were all nonsense, though I did see two students kill a sixteen-year-old boy, or nearly kill him (he appeared to be dying when I left the hospital, but he may have recovered later) by a mischievous experiment which they probably could not have tried on a paying patient. Well within living memory it used to be believed in London that in some of the big hospitals patients were killed off to get dissection subjects. I didn't hear this tale repeated at the Hôpital X, but I should think some of the men there would have found it credible. For it was a hospital in which not the methods, perhaps, but something of the atmosphere of the nineteenth century had managed to survive, and therein lay its peculiar interest.

GEORGE ORWELL

From *Preservation*

Sandy's husband had been on the sofa ever since he'd been terminated three months ago. That day, three months ago, he'd come home looking pale and scared and with all of his work things in a box. "Happy Valentine's Day", he said to Sandy and put a heart-shaped box of candy and a bottle of Jim Beam on the kitchen table. He took off his cap and laid that on the table, too. "I got canned today. Hey, what do you think's going to happen to us now?"

Sandy and her husband sat at the table and drank whiskey and ate the chocolates. They talked about what he might be able to do instead of putting roofs on new houses. But they couldn't think of anything. "Something will turn up," Sandy said. She wanted to be encouraging. But she was scared, too. Finally, he said he'd sleep on it. And he did. He made his bed on the sofa that night, and that's where he'd slept every night since it had happened.

The day after his termination there were unemployment benefits to see about. He went downtown to the state office to fill out papers and look for another job. But there were no jobs in his line of work, or in any other line of work. His face began to sweat as he tried to describe to Sandy the milling crowd of men and women down there. That evening he got back on the sofa. He began spending all of his time there, as if, she thought, it was the thing he was supposed to do now that he no longer had any work.

Once in a while he had to go talk to somebody about a job possibility, and every two weeks he had to go sign something to collect his unemployment compensation. But the rest of the time he stayed on the sofa. It's like he *lives* there, Sandy thought. He *lives* in the living room. Now and then he looked through magazines she brought home from the grocery store; and every so often she came in to find him looking at this big book she'd got as a bonus for joining a book club—something called *Mysteries of the Past*. He held the book in front of him with both hands, his head inclined over the pages, as if he were being drawn in by what he was reading. But after a while she noticed that he didn't seem to be making any progress in it; he still seemed to be at about the same place—somewhere around chapter two, she guessed. Sandy picked it up once and opened it to his place. There she read about a man who had been discovered after spending two thousand years in a peat bog in the Netherlands. A photograph appeared on one page. The man's brow was furrowed, but there was a serene expression to his face. He wore a leather cap and lay on his side. The man's hands and feet had shriveled, but otherwise he didn't look so awful. She read in the book a little further, then put it back where she'd gotten it. Her husband kept it within easy reach on the coffee table that stood in front of the sofa.

RAYMOND CARVER

From *Tess of the d'Urbervilles*

The village of Marlott lay amid the north-eastern undulations of the beautiful Vale of Blakemore or Blackmoor aforesaid, and engirdled and secluded region, for the most part untrodden as yet by tourist or landscape-painter, though within a four hours' journey from London.

It is a vale whose acquaintance is best made by viewing it from the summits of the hills that surround it—except perhaps during the droughts of summer. An unguided ramble into its recesses in bad weather is apt to engender dissatisfaction with its narrow, tortuous, and miry ways.

This fertile and sheltered tract of country, in which the fields are never brown and the springs never dry, is bounded on the south by the bold chalk ridge that embraces the prominences of Hambledon Hill, Bulbarrow, Nettlecombe-Tout, Dogbury, High Stoy, and Bubb Down. The traveller from the coast, who, after plodding northward for a score of miles over calcareous downs and corn-lands, suddenly reaches the verge of one of these escarpments, is surprised and delighted to behold, extended like a map beneath him, a country differing absolutely from that which he has passed through. Behind him the hills are open, the sun blazes down upon fields so large as to give an unenclosed character to the landscape, the lanes are white, the hedges low and plashed, the atmosphere colourless. Here, in the valley, the world seems to be constructed upon a smaller and more delicate scale; the fields are mere paddocks, so reduced that from this height their hedgerows appear a network of dark green threads overspreading the paler green of the grass. The atmosphere beneath is languorous, and is so tinged with azure that what artists call the middle distance partakes also of that hue, while the horizon beyond is of the deepest ultramarine. Arable lands are few and limited; with but slight exceptions the prospect is a broad rich mass of grass and trees, mantling minor hills and dales within the major. Such is the Vale of Blackmoor.

The district is of historic, no less than of topographical interest. The Vale was known in former times as the Forest of White Hart, from a curious legend of King Henry III's reign, in which the killing by a certain Thomas de la Lynd of a beautiful white hart which the king had run down and spared, was made the occasion of a heavy fine. In those days, and till comparatively recent times, the country was densely wooded. Even now, traces of its earlier condition are to be found in the old oak copses and irregular belts of timber that yet survive upon its slopes, and the hollow-trunked trees that shade so many of its pastures.

The forests have departed, but some old customs of their shades remain. Many, however, linger only in a metamorphosed or disguised form. The May-Day dance, for instance, was to be discerned on the afternoon under notice, in the guise of the club revel, or "club-walking", as it was there called.

THOMAS HARDY

Quashie to Buccra

You tas'e petater an' you say it sweet,
But you no know how hard we wuk fe it;
You want a basketful fe quattiewut,
'Cause you no know how 'tiff de bush fe cut.

De cowitch under which we hab fe 'toop,
De shamar lyin' t'ick like pumpkin soup,
Is killin' somet'ing for a naygur man;
Much less de cutlass workin' in we han'.

De sun hot like when fire ketch a town;
Shade-tree look temptin', yet we caan' lie down,
Aldough we wouldn' eben ef we could,
Causen we job must finish soon an' good.

De bush cut done, de bank dem we deh dig,
But dem caan' 'tan' sake o' we naybor pig;
For so we moul' it up he root it do'n,
An' we caan' 'peak sake o' we naybor tongue.

Aldough de vine is little, it can bear;
It wantin' not'in' but a little care:
You see petater tear up groun', you run,
You laughin' sir, you must be t'ink a fun.

De fiel' pretty? It couldn't less 'an dat,
We wuk de bes', an' den de lan' is fat;
We dig de row dem eben in a line,
An' keep it clean—den so it mus' look fine.

You tas'e petater an' you say it sweet,
But you no know how hard we wuk fe it;
Yet still de hardship always melt away
Wheneber it come roun' to reapin' day.

CLAUDE McKAY

From *Wuthering Heights*

"If I were in heaven, Nelly, I should be extremely miserable."

"Because you are not fit to go there," I answered. "All sinners would be miserable in heaven."

"But it is not for that. I dreamt once that I was there."

"I tell you I won't harken to your dreams, Miss Catherine! I'll go to bed," I interrupted again.

She laughed, and held me down; for I made a motion to leave my chair.

"This is nothing," cried she: "I was only going to say that heaven did not seem to be my home; and I broke my heart with weeping to come back to earth;..."

EMILY BRONTE

From *Open*

THEN, CATASTROPHE STRIKES. The night before the final, I'm taking a shower and I feel the hairpiece Philly bought me suddenly disintegrate in my hands. I must have used the wrong kind of conditioner. The weave is coming undone—the damned thing is falling apart.

In a state of abject panic I summon Philly to my hotel room.

Fucking disaster, I tell him. My hairpiece—look!

He examines it.

We'll let it dry, then clip it in place, he says.

With what?

Bobby pins.

He runs all over Paris looking for bobby pins. He can't find any. He phones me and says, What the hell kind of city is this? No bobby pins?

In the hotel lobby he bumps into Chris Evert and asks her for bobby pins. She doesn't have any. She asks why he needs them. He doesn't answer. At last he finds a friend of our sister Rita, who has a bag full of bobby pins. He helps me reconfigure the hairpiece and set it in place, and keeps it there with no fewer than twenty bobby pins.

Will it hold? I ask.

Yeah, yeah. Just don't move around a lot.

We both laugh darkly.

Of course I could play without my hairpiece. But after months and months of derision, criticism, mockery, I'm too self-conscious. *Image Is Everything?* What would they say if they knew I've been wearing a hairpiece all this time? Win or lose, they wouldn't talk about my game. They would talk only about my hair. Instead of a few kids at the Bollettieri Academy laughing at me, or twelve thousand Germans at Davis Cup, the whole world would be laughing. I can close my eyes and almost hear it. And I know I can't take it.

WARMING UP BEFORE THE MATCH, I pray. Not for a win, but for my hairpiece to stay on. Under normal circumstances, playing in my first final of a slam, I'd be tense. But my tenuous hairpiece has me catatonic. Whether or not it's slipping, I imagine that it's slipping. With every lunge, every leap, I picture it landing on the clay, like a hawk my father shot from the sky. I can hear a gasp going up from the crowd. I can picture millions of people suddenly leaning closer to their TVs, turning to each other and in dozens of languages and dialects saying some version of: Did Andre Agassi's *hair* just fall off?

My game plan for Gomez reflects my jangled nerves, my timidity. Knowing he doesn't have young legs, knowing he'll fold in a fifth set, I plan to stretch out the match, orchestrate long rallies, grind him down. As the match begins, however, it's clear that Gomez also knows his age, and thus he's trying to speed everything up. He's playing quick, risky tennis. He wins the first set in a hurry. He loses the second set, but also in a hurry. Now I know that the longest we'll be out here is three hours, rather than four, which means conditioning won't play a role. This is now a shot-making match, the kind Gomez can win. With two sets completed, and not much time off the clock, I'm facing a guy who's going to be fresh throughout, even if we go five.

Of course my game plan was fatally flawed from the start. Pathetic, really. It couldn't work, no matter how long the match, because you can't win the final of a slam by playing not to lose, or waiting for your opponent to lose. My attempt to orchestrate long rallies merely emboldens Gomez. He's a veteran who knows this might be his last shot at a slam. The only way to beat him is to take away his belief and his desire, by being aggressive. When he sees me playing conservative, orchestrating instead of dominating, it gives him heart.

ANDRE AGASSI

From *White Teeth*

Then, when their bumps become too large and cinema seats no longer accommodate them, the women begin to meet up for lunch in Kilburn Park, often with the Niece-of-Shame, the three of them squeezed on to a generous bench where Alsana presses a thermos of P. G. Tips into Clara's hand, without milk, with lemon. Unwraps several layers of cling-film to reveal today's peculiar delight: savoury dough-like balls, crumbly Indian sweets shot through with the colours of the kaleidoscope, thin pastry with spiced beef inside, salad with onion; saying to Clara, "Eat up! Stuff yourself silly! It's in there, wallowing around in your belly, waiting for the menu. Woman, don't torture it! You want to starve the bump?" For, despite appearances, there are six people on that bench (three living, three coming); one girl for Clara, two boys for Alsana.

Alsana says, "Nobody's complaining, let's get that straight. Children are a blessing, the more the merrier. But I tell you, when I turned my head and saw that fancy ultra-business thingummybob …"

"Ultrasound," corrects Clara, through a mouthful of rice.

"Yes, I almost had the heart attack to finish me off! Two! Feeding one is enough!"

Clara laughs and says she can imagine Samad's face when he saw it.

"No, dearie." Alsana is reproving, tucking her large feet underneath the folds of her sari. "He didn't see anything. He wasn't there. I am not letting him see things like that.

A woman has to have the private things—a husband needn't be involved in body-business, in a lady's… *parts.*"

Niece-of-Shame, who is sitting between them, sucks her teeth.

"Bloody hell, Alsi, he must've been involved in your parts sometime, or is this the immaculate bloody conception?"

"So rude," says Alsana to Clara in a snooty, English way. "Too old to be so rude and too young to know any better."

And then Clara and Alsana, with the accidental mirroring that happens when two people are sharing the same experience, both lay their hands on their bulges.

Neena, to redeem herself: "Yeah… well… How are you doing on names? Any ideas?"

Alsana is decisive. "Meena and Malana, if they are girls. If boys: Magid and Millar. Ems are good. Ems are strong. Mahatma, Muhammad, that funny Mr Morecambe, from Morecambe and Wise—letter you can trust."

But Clara is more cautious, because naming seems to her a fearful responsibility, a god-like task for a mere mortal. "If it's a girl, I tink I like *Irie.* It patois. Means everyting *OK, cool, peaceful,* you know?"

Alsana is horrified before the sentence is finished: "'OK'"? This is a name for a child, You might as well call her *'Wouldsirlikeanypoppadomwiththat?'* or *'Niceweatherwearehaving'*."

ZADIE SMITH

From *How to Become a Writer*

First, try to be something, anything, else. A movie star/astronaut.

A movie star/missionary. A movie star/kindergarten teacher. President of the World. Fail miserably. It is best if you fail at an early age—say, fourteen. Early, critical disillusionment is necessary so that at fifteen you can write long haiku sequences about thwarted desire. It is a pond, a cherry blossom, a wind brushing against sparrow wing leaving for mountain. Count the syllables. Show it to your mom. She is tough and practical. She has a son in Vietnam and a husband who may be having an affair. She believes in wearing brown because it hides spots. She'll look briefly at your writing, then back up at you with a face blank as a donut. She'll say: "How about emptying the dishwasher?" Look away. Shove the forks in the fork drawer. Accidentally break one of the freebie gas station glasses. This is the required pain and suffering. This is only for starters.

In your high school English class look only at Mr. Killian's face. Decide faces are important. Write a villanelle about pores. Struggle. Write a sonnet. Count the syllables: nine, ten, eleven, thirteen. Decide to experiment with fiction. Here you don't have to count syllables. Write a short story about an elderly man and woman who accidentally shoot each other in the head, the result of an inexplicable malfunction of a shotgun which appears mysteriously in their living room one night. Give it to Mr. Killian as your final project. When you get it back, he has written on it: "Some of your images are quite nice, but you have no sense of plot." When you are home, in the privacy of your own room, faintly scrawl in pencil beneath his black-inked comments:

"Plots are for dead people, pore-face."

As a child psychology major, you have some electives. You've always liked birds. Sign up for something called "The Ornithological Field Trip." It meets Tuesdays and Thursdays at two. When you arrive at Room 134 on the first day of class, everyone is sitting around a seminar table talking about metaphors. You've heard of these. After a short, excruciating while, raise your hand and say diffidently, "Excuse me, isn't this Birdwatching One-oh-one?" The class stops and turns to look at you. They seem to all have one face—giant and blank as a vandalized clock. Someone with a beard booms out, "No, this is Creative Writing." Say: "Oh—right," as if perhaps you knew all along. Look down at your schedule. Wonder how the hell you ended up here. The computer, apparently, has made an error. You start to get up to leave and then don't. The lines at the registrar this week are huge. Perhaps you should stick with this mistake. Perhaps your creative writing isn't all that bad. Perhaps it is fate.

Take all the babysitting jobs you can get. You are great with kids. They love you. You tell them stories about old people who die idiot deaths. You sing them songs like "Blue Bells of Scotland", which is their favorite. And when they are in their pajamas and have finally stopped pinching each other, when they are fast asleep, you read every sex manual in the house, and wonder how on earth anyone could ever do those things with someone they truly loved. Fall asleep in a chair reading Mr. McMurphy's *Playboy*. When the McMurphys come home, they will tap you on the shoulder, look at the magazine in your lap, and grin. You will want to die. They will ask you if Tracey took her medicine all right. Explain, yes, she did, that you promised her a story if she would take it like a big girl and that seemed to work out just fine. "Oh, marvelous," they will exclaim.

Try to smile proudly.

Apply to college as a child psychology major.

LORRIE MOORE

From *The Adventures of Huckleberry Finn*

Now the way that the book winds up is this: Tom and me found the money that the robbers hid in the cave, and made us rich. We got six thousand dollars apiece—all gold. It was an awful sight of money when it was piled up. Well, Judge Thatcher he took it and put it out at interest, and it fetched us a dollar a day apiece all the year round—more than a body could tell what to do with. The Widow Douglas she took me for her son, and allowed she would sivilize me; but it was rough living in the house all the time, considering how dismal regular and decent the widow was in all her ways; and so when I couldn't stand it no longer I lit out. I got into my rags and my sugar-hogshead again, and was free and satisfied. But Tom Sawyer he hunted me up and said he was going to start a band of robbers, and I might join if I would go back to the widow and be respectable. So I went back.

The widow she cried over me, and called me a poor lost lamb, and she called me a lot of other names, too, but she never meant to harm by it.

MARK TWAIN

The Dream

O God, in the dream the terrible horse began
To paw at the air, and make for me with his blows,
Fear kept for thirty-five years poured through his mane,
And retribution equally old, or nearly, breathed through his nose.

Coward complete, I lay and wept on the ground
When some strong creature appeared, and leapt for the rein.
Another woman, as I lay half in a swound
Leapt in the air, and clutched at the leather and chain.

Give him, she said, something of yours as a charm.
Throw him, she said, some poor thing you alone claim.
No, no, I cried, he hates me; he is out for harm,
And whether I yield or not, it is all the same.

But, like a lion in a legend, when I flung the glove
Pulled from my sweating, my cold right hand;
The terrible beast, that no one may understand,
Came to my side, and put down his head in love.

LOUISE BOGAN

From *Top Girls*

ANGIE: "Driving across the states for a new job in L.A. It's a long way but the car goes very fast. It's very hot. Wish you were here. Love from Aunty Marlene."

JOYCE: Did you make a lot of money?

MARLENE: I spent a lot.

ANGIE: I want to go to America. Will you take me?

JOYCE: She's not going to America, she's been to America, stupid.

ANGIE: She might go again, stupid. It's not something you do once. People who go keep going all the time, back and forth on jets. They go on Concorde and Laker and get jet lag. Will you take me?

MARLENE: I'm not planning a trip.

ANGIE: Will you let me know?

JOYCE: Angie, / you're getting silly.

ANGIE: I want to be American.

JOYCE: It's time you were in bed.

ANGIE: No it's not. / I don't have to go to bed at all tonight.

JOYCE: School in the morning.

ANGIE: I'll wake up.

JOYCE: Come on now, you know how you get.

ANGIE: How do I get? / I don't get anyhow.

JOYCE: Angie. Are you staying the night?

MARLENE: Yes, if that's all right. / I'll see you in the morning.

ANGIE: You can have my bed. I'll sleep on the sofa.

JOYCE: You will not, you'll sleep in your bed. / Think I can't

ANGIE: Mum.

JOYCE: see through that? I can just see you going to sleep /with us talking.

ANGIE: I would, I would go to sleep, I'd love that.

ANGIE: It's a secret.

JOYCE: I'm going to get cross, Angie.

ANGIE: I want to show her something.

JOYCE: Then bed.

JOYCE: Then I expect it's in your room so off you go. Give us a shout when you're ready for bed and your aunty'll be up and see you.

ANGIE: Will you?

MARLENE: Yes of course.
ANGIE *goes*.
Silence.
It's cold tonight.

JOYCE: Will you be all right on the sofa? You can / have my bed.

MARLENE: The sofa's fine.

JOYCE: Yes the forecast said rain tonight but it's held off.

MARLENE: I was going to walk down to the estuary but I've left it a bit late. Is it just the same?

JOYCE: They cut down the hedges a few years back. Is that since you were here?

MARLENE: But it's not changed down the end, all the mud? And the reeds? We used to pick them when they were bigger than us. Are there still lapwings?

JOYCE: You get strangers walking there on a Sunday. I expect they're looking at the mud and the lapwings, yes.

MARLENE: You could have left.

JOYCE: Who says I wanted to leave?

MARLENE: Stop getting at me then, you're really boring.

JOYCE: How could I have left?

MARLENE: Did you want to?

JOYCE: I said how, / how could I?

MARLENE: If you'd wanted to you'd have done it.

CARYL CHURCHILL

Recuerdo

We were very tired, we were very merry—
We had gone back and forth all night on the ferry.
It was bare and bright, and smelled like a stable—
But we looked into a fire, we leaned across a table,
We lay on a hill-top underneath the moon;
And the whistles kept blowing, and the dawn came soon.

We were very tired, we were very merry—
We had gone back and forth all night on the ferry;
And you ate an apple, and I ate a pear,
From a dozen of each we had bought somewhere;

And the sky went wan, and the wind came cold,
And the sun rose dripping, a bucketful of gold.

We were very tired, we were very merry,
We had gone back and forth all night on the ferry.
We hailed, "Good morrow, mother!" to a shawl-covered head,
And bought a morning paper, which neither of us read;
And she wept, "God bless you!" for the apples and pears,
And we gave her all our money but our subway fares.

EDNA ST VINCENT MILLAY

From *Titus Andronicus*

Act III, Scene 1

Rome. A street.

[Enter Judges, Senators and Tribunes, with MARTIUS] [p]and QUINTUS,

bound, passing on to the place of [p]execution; TITUS going before, pleading]

Titus Andronicus. Hear me, grave fathers! noble tribunes, stay!
For pity of mine age, whose youth was spent
In dangerous wars, whilst you securely slept;
For all my blood in Rome's great quarrel shed;
For all the frosty nights that I have watch'd;   1130
And for these bitter tears, which now you see
Filling the aged wrinkles in my cheeks;
Be pitiful to my condemned sons,
Whose souls are not corrupted as 'tis thought.
For two and twenty sons I never wept,   1135

Because they died in honour's lofty bed.
[Lieth down; the Judges, &c., pass by him, and Exeunt]
For these, these, tribunes, in the dust I write
My heart's deep languor and my soul's sad tears:
Let my tears stanch the earth's dry appetite;   1140
My sons' sweet blood will make it shame and blush.
O earth, I will befriend thee more with rain,
That shall distil from these two ancient urns,
Than youthful April shall with all his showers:
In summer's drought I'll drop upon thee still;   1145
In winter with warm tears I'll melt the snow
And keep eternal spring-time on thy face,
So thou refuse to drink my dear sons' blood.
[Enter LUCIUS, with his sword drawn]
O reverend tribunes! O gentle, aged men!   1150
Unbind my sons, reverse the doom of death;
And let me say, that never wept before,
My tears are now prevailing orators.

WILLIAM SHAKESPEARE

From *Waltz with Bashir*

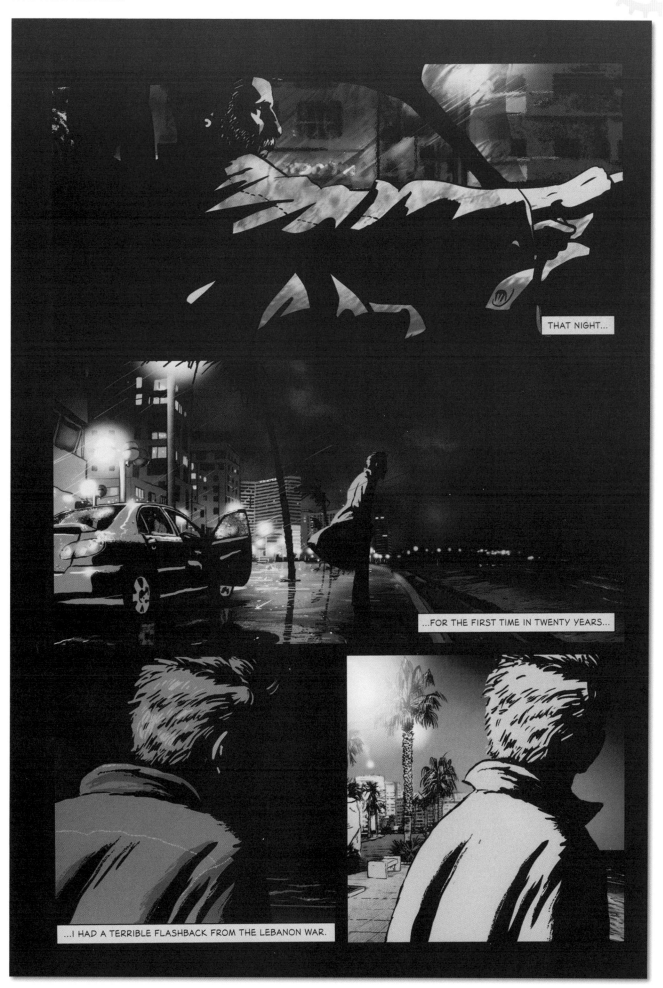

Index